PRIMO
Rewriting the Holocaust

Lucie Benchouiha

PRIMO LEVI
Rewriting the Holocaust

t

Copyright © 2006 Lucie Benchouiha and Troubador Publishing Ltd

Apart from any fair dealing for the purposes of research or private study, or criticism or review, as permitted under the Copyright, Designs and Patents Act 1988, this publication may only be reproduced, stored or transmitted, in any form or by any means, with the prior permission in writing of the publishers, or in the case of reprographic reproduction in accordance with the terms of licences issued by the Copyright Licensing Agency. Enquiries concerning reproduction outside those terms should be sent to the publishers.

Published by
Troubador Publishing Ltd
9 De Montfort Mews
Leicester LE1 7FW, UK
Tel: (+44) 116 255 9311
Email: books@troubador.co.uk
Web: www.troubador.co.uk

Series Editor
Professor George Ferzoco
University of Leicester, UK

ISBN 1-905237-23-5

Typesetting: Troubador Publishing Ltd, Leicester, UK

Contents

Acknowledgements   vii
Abbreviations   viii

Introduction   1

1   *Se questo è un uomo*: 'Il mondo alla rovescia'   5

2   *La tregua*: 'I segni dell'offesa'   22

3   *Storie naturali* and *Vizio di forma*:
'I mostri generati dal sonno della ragione'   38

4   *Il sistema periodico*:
'L'uomo salvato dal suo mestiere'   62

5   *La chiave a stella*: 'Arbeit macht frei'   81

6   *Lilít e altri racconti*, *L'altrui mestiere*,
Racconti e saggi: 'Una certa curiosità per i vortici'   92

7   *Se non ora, quando?*: La dignità dell'uomo   106

8   *Ad ora incerta* and *Altre poesie*:
'Dopo Auschwitz non si può piú fare poesie
se non su Auschwitz'   120

9   *I sommersi e i salvati*: 'Alla ricerca
permanente di una giustificazione'   132

Conclusion   144

Bibliography   147

Acknowledgements

I am grateful to the editors of *Italian Studies* for their permission to republish a revised version of an article originally published in 2001, "L'uomo salvato dal suo mestiere': Aspects of *Se questo è un uomo* Revisited in Primo Levi's *Il sistema periodico*', which constitutes Chapter 4 here. Sections of Chapter 3 are also reprinted here with the permission of the editors of *Modern Language Review*, from an article entitled 'The Perversion of a Fairy Tale: Primo Levi's 'La bella addormentata nel frigo" (April 2005).

I would like to thank all colleagues past and present at the Universities of Bristol and Exeter, in particular Mark Davie and Paul Diffley for their academic and personal support, accompanied by a constant willingness to read early drafts of these chapters. Special thanks also go to George Ferzoco and Jeremy Thompson at Troubador, for their interest in, as well as their encouragement and help with this project from the start.

Above all, the least articulable but most profound thanks to all my family and friends, but especially to my husband and children who have been wonderfully supportive throughout the entire research and writing process. This book is dedicated to my daughters, without whom it would have been written much sooner.

Lucie Benchouiha
November 2005

Abbreviations

All page references for Levi's works are taken from the 1997 two-volume collection of Levi's works, *Opere*, vols. I-II, edited by Marco Belpoliti and published by Einaudi. The titles of Levi's works, as well as chapter titles, are referred to in Italian. For clarity, references are given by an abbreviation of the title of the individual text (SQ = *Se questo è un uomo*; LT = *La tregua*; SN = *Storie naturali*; VF = *Vizio di forma*; SP = *Il sistema periodico*; CS = *La chiave a stella*; L = *Lilít e altri racconti*; AM = *L'altrui mestiere*; SNOQ = *Se non ora, quando?*; OI = *Ad ora incerta*; AP = *Altre poesie*; RR = *La ricerca delle radici*; RS = *Racconti e saggi*; SS = *I sommersi e i salvati*) followed by the volume number, then the page number.

Whilst acknowledging the problematics of the term Holocaust, I use it in this work since it remains, in spite of its implications, the most widely-used English-language term and it is not within the ambit of this volume to attempt to redefine the various contested terminologies. I have also employed the German word *Lager*, Levi's preferred term for the concentration camps, and a word in common usage in Italian.

All translations into English are my own unless otherwise stated.

Introduction

Primo Levi's writing career began almost immediately after his return to Italy from the concentration camp of Auschwitz, with the composition of *Se questo è un uomo*, his testimony to the experience of the *Lager*. His writing spans four decades as well as embracing a wide range of literary genres including testimony, autobiography, essays, articles, poetry, a personal anthology, and fictional short stories in addition to full-length novels. Whilst there has often been the suspicion amongst critics and readers alike that aspects of Levi's experience in the concentration camp are not limited to the texts which deal explicitly with this subject[1] and that echoes and traces of *Se questo è un uomo* appear throughout Levi's subsequent writings, these echoes have yet to be comprehensively identified or analysed. This volume enters upon such a task, following not the historical echoes of the Holocaust itself but more precisely the resonances of Levi's concentration camp experience as originally portrayed within *Se questo è un uomo*, tracing the ways in which Levi's first text is revisited, reworked and rewritten in various forms and guises throughout his literary output.

Such a study of Levi's work necessarily involves an intertextual approach. Yet clearly this is not a Kristevan intertextuality, but rather an analysis of intertextual relations within the body of work of one particular author. It is, to adopt the terms applied by Ricardou and Dällenbach, not an 'intertextualité générale (rapports intertextuels entre textes d'auteurs différents)' but rather an 'intertextualité restreinte (rapports intertextuels entre textes du même auteur)'.[2] This volume also examines, in parallel with the *intertextualité restreinte* of Levi's work, later defined by Dällenbach as autarkic intertextuality or *autotextualité*, the intertextual connections functioning across the apparent barriers of genre, between *Se questo è un uomo* as a work of testimony and Levi's later works of fiction, poetry and essays. The nearest relevant approach is that of Ann Jefferson whose consideration of autobiography as intertext in the works of Barthes, Sarraute and Robbe-Grillet and whose formulation of critical terms are particularly valid for this study. In describing the relations between texts within the body of work of a given author, Jefferson writes that:

> These relations are not actively intertextual in that they don't entail explicit or implied comment on one text by another, nor any transformation through rewriting of one text by another, but it is

nevertheless an intertextual relationship that is enormously powerful for readers. [...] Since we are dealing here with texts that are 'from the same stable', I coin the term sister-text to describe the relation between novel and novel – and novel and autobiography when the latter is regarded as a continuation of the former.[3]

Jefferson's definition and exploration of sister-textual intertextuality within the corpus of any one author is particularly useful for the analysis here of Levi's works, yet Jefferson's theories can also function, and are in fact applied here in the opposite direction to that of her own research, that is where the autobiographical work precedes the fiction and yet the latter is still considered, for the purposes of this study, as an extension of many aspects of the former. The fact that the sister-textual intertextuality outlined above does not produce any alteration through the rewriting of one text by another is also significant, for the texts subsequent to *Se questo è un uomo* are not examined here in the light of how they might influence or affect our reading of this first testimony. The rewriting of the focus of this study is the progressive rewriting in different contexts of issues and themes which originate in the concentration camp testimony, rather than any revision or amendment through the rewriting of *Se questo è un uomo* itself. What is examined here is a thematic hypertextuality rather than a strictly textual hypertextuality, falling somewhere inbetween Jefferson's theories and those of Gérard Genette. Genette's definition of hypertextuality embraces 'toute relation unissant un texte B (que j'appellerai *hypertexte*) à un texte antérieur A (que j'appellerai, bien sûr, *hypotexte*) sur lequel il se greffe d'une manière qui n'est pas celle du commentaire'.[4] In Levi's case, both the sister-textual and the hypertextual intertextuality considered here are really an issue of his-story repeating itself to varying degrees throughout the body of Levi's literary work, the ways in which Levi's later works explore and revisit the issues originally raised in *Se questo è un uomo*, rewriting aspects of this first text in a variety of different ways and from diverse angles.

The first chapter will examine *Se questo è un uomo* in the light of the aspects of this text to be considered in subsequent chapters, and is divided into broad sub-sections accordingly: multiple testimony and Levi's use of a collective narrative voice; emotional detachment, and an examination of Levi's alleged authorial distancing; and the dehumanisation of man consisting of the loss of human dignity, understanding, language, thought and memory, man's humiliation through enslavement, and perceptions of time and atemporality. Texts subsequent to *Se questo è un uomo* will be dealt with chronologically as much as possible,[5] with chapter divisions corresponding to the individual texts, the better to enable and facilitate the observation over time of alterations and developments in the particular echoes of *Se questo è un uomo* under examination. Chapter two, dedicated to *La tregua*, explores the text's connections with *Se questo è un uomo* in terms of both subject matter and style of narration, examining the pervasive influence of the concentration camp experience on the structure, language and use of metaphor in *La tregua*. It considers Levi's depiction of character, his authorial stance and narrative voice, the instances of emotion against authorial detachment, as well as the role of language within the text, before concluding that surprisingly little has altered here from Levi's first testimony to the world of the concentration camp. The third chapter, which deals with *Storie naturali* and *Vizio di forma*, analyses the contrasts between Levi's short story writing and his non-fiction, evaluating the consequences of this alteration of genre on his subject matter. It explores the role of science and the mis-use of scientific and technological innovations in these collections, alongside the characters' loss of human traits, identity and dignity in favour of the bestial, and the recurrence of issues such as slavery, abuse, imprisonment, degradation and timelessness. Chapter four, *Il sistema periodico*, discusses the representation of chemistry and the effects of Levi's distortion of Mendeleev's Periodic Table. It studies the structure and division of this text into the pre- and post-Auschwitz in parallel with stylistic issues like narrative voice and the re-establishment and reassertion of dignity through the use of emotion, as well as considering Levi's quest for understanding as a consequence of the aftermath of the concentration camps and how the act of writing *Il sistema periodico* reacts against the very experiences depicted within *Se questo è un uomo*. The fifth chapter, *La chiave a stella*, connects Levi's portrayal of work and the work ethic in this text as a direct continuation of and response to the slave labour of the concentration camps, in addition to outlining the testimonial narrative structure of the work and the role of language and metaphor here. Chapter six, which deals with *Lilít e altri racconti*, *L'altrui mestiere*, and *Racconti e saggi*, examines the variations of the Auschwitz stories in the first section of *Lilít e altri racconti* and the new testimony they provide. It analyses the thematic echoes of *Se questo è un uomo* in the fictional tales in these collections, Levi's role as observer in his articles, and the continuing quest for comprehension of the world around him. The seventh chapter, *Se non ora, quando?* expands on the comparisons and contrasts between the fictional wartime experiences in this text and the opposing experiences outlined in Levi's previous testimony. It studies the characters' perceptions of time and timelessness and the humanising and dehumanising potential of language, placing particular focus on questions of dignity in the text, suggesting that here Levi rewrites the concept of dignity precisely on the basis of and as a reaction against his concentration camp experience. Chapter eight looks at the collections of Levi's poetry, *Ad ora incerta* and the posthumously published *Altre poesie*. It traces the enduring recurrence of Holocaust themes throughout his poems as well as the instances in which a borrowing of phrasing from the testimonial writing occurs. It details the unique intertextual relationship that exists between Levi's poetry and his narrative through an analysis of the occasions of self-quotation and self-reference, proving that Levi's poetry provides some of the strongest examples of cases in which Levi rewrites his Holocaust experiences. Chapter nine examines *I sommersi e i salvati*, and whilst the thematic echoes of the concentration camps are evident on every page, this chapter draws attention to this text's role as metatext to all of Levi's writings and interviews about the Holocaust. It assesses this work's connections with the eponymous chapter of *Se questo è un uomo*, alterations in Levi's approach to writing of the camps, the persistence of a multiple narrative voice, and the perpetuation of Levi's quest for understanding and comprehension of his experiences in the context of the wider picture as it appears here.

In spite of Levi's own comment, with regard to all of his works, that 'Io credo che c'entri in fondo abbastanza poco il fatto del Lager rivisitato'[6] (I believe that, all things considered, the issue of the *Lager* revisited has relatively little to do with it), echoes of the Holocaust exist throughout his writing, often more profoundly than expected and in unlikely and unexpected places. This study will identify precisely where the traces of Levi's original depiction of his concentration camp experience have taken root and flourished, and will establish to what extent the *Lager* is both revisited and rewritten through the course of Levi's entire literary output. It will investigate the role of *Se questo è un uomo* as the fundamental basis for many aspects of Levi's later texts, questioning whether issues that arise in these subsequent works serve as a kind of appendix to parallel aspects of *Se questo è un uomo*, and clarifying whether in fact Levi's later works can ever be wholly comprehended without prior reference to, or knowledge of, *Se questo è un uomo*. This work will conclude by establishing whether each text subsequent to the Holocaust testimony is, in any or many respects, a rewriting of the sister-text, a rewriting of *Se questo è un uomo*.

Notes

1. Those writings which deal undisguisedly with the concentration camps are Levi's first work of testimony, *Se questo è un uomo*; the 'Cerio' and 'Vanadio' chapters of *Il sistema periodico*; the 'Passato prossimo' section from the collection of short stories entitled *Lilít e altri racconti*; a number of Levi's articles, and *I sommersi e i salvati*.
2. Lucien Dällenbach, 'Intertexte et autotexte', *Poétique*, 27, 1976, pp. 282-96, p. 282.
3. Ann Jefferson, 'Autobiography as Intertext: Barthes, Sarraute, Robbe-Grillet' in Michael Worton, and Judith Still, eds., *Intertextuality: Theories and Practices*, 1990, pp. 108-129, p. 110-111.
4. Gérard Genette, *Palimpsestes: La littérature au second degré*, 1982, p. 11-12.
5. There is, however, an unavoidable overlap in the composition of many of Levi's short stories, hence my decision to deal with *Lilít e altri racconti*, *L'altrui mestiere* and *Racconti e saggi* in the same chapter.
6. Levi's words to Giuseppe Grassano in an interview dated 17 November 1979, later published by Grassano as *Primo Levi*, 1981, p. 10.

I
Se questo é un uomo: 'Il mondo alla rovescia'

Levi readily admitted that it was his experience of deportation which led him to become a writer: 'se non avessi vissuto la stagione di Auschwitz, probabilmente non avrei mai scritto nulla. [...] È stata l'esperienza del Lager a costringermi a scrivere' (if I hadn't lived the time in Auschwitz, I would probably never have written anything [...] It was the experience of the *Lager* which compelled me to write) (Appendix to *SQ*, I, p. 200). First published in 1947 by De Silva, *Se questo è un uomo* initially suffered a similar fate as that of other early Italian Holocaust testimonies and was not widely read or recognised until its republication by Einaudi in 1958.[1] The act of bearing witness to his experiences at Auschwitz, and of providing a form of documentation to the events suffered there was of tremendous importance to Levi. As he writes in the preface to *Se questo è un uomo*:

> Il bisogno di raccontare agli "altri", di fare gli "altri" partecipi, aveva assunto fra noi, prima della liberazione e dopo, il carattere di un impulso immediato e violento, tanto da rivaleggiare con gli altri bisogni elementari: il libro è stato scritto per soddisfare a questo bisogno; in primo luogo quindi a scopo di liberazione interiore. (*SQ*, I, pp. 5–6)

> (The need to tell our story to the "others", to render the "others" participants, had assumed among us, before and after liberation, the character of an immediate and violent impulse, so much so that it competed with our other elementary needs; the book was written to satisfy this need: first and foremost, therefore, for the purpose of internal liberation.)

The desire to attain internal liberation through a written testimony and through recounting his experiences to others, served as a catalyst for the composition of *Se questo è un uomo*; testifying was akin to a basic, fundamental need, the *bisogno elementare* to 'sopravvivere, *per* raccontare, *per* portare testimonianza' (to survive, *in order to* tell our story, *in order to* bear witness) (*SQ*, I, p. 35, my italics) and also a duty to those who did not survive to tell of their own experiences: 'raccontare dobbiamo, è un dovere verso i compagni che non sono tornati' (we must tell our story, it is a duty towards those who did not return).[2] The therapeutic value Levi found in bearing witness cannot be overstated. As he commented in 1975:

> Io penso che se mi sono "salvato" – e dico salvato nel senso vasto della parola- è perché ho scritto *Se questo è un uomo*. Cioè senza saperlo, in modo piú intuitivo che calcolato, mi sono liberato scrivendo delle cose che mi pesavano dentro. E infatti, a mano a mano che scrivevo, mi sentivo sempre piú leggero. Chiaro che non può essere una regola generale. A me è andata così perché sono un uomo che ha bisogno di raccontare, che prova piacere nel farlo, e questo piacere è liberatorio.[3]

(I think that if I have been "saved" – and I say saved in a wide sense of the word – it is because I wrote *Se questo è un uomo*. That is to say that without knowing it, in a more intuitive than calculated way, I liberated myself by writing about the things weighing inside me. And indeed as I was writing, I felt continually lighter. Clearly this cannot be a general rule. It was like that for me because I am a man who has a need to tell his story, who gets pleasure out of doing so, and this pleasure is liberating)

Se questo è un uomo, born of a primordial need to testify and to gain some sense of release from his memories, began Levi's literary career. Alongside the themes of deportation and imprisonment, hunger, slave labour, selections for the gas chamber, and the conditions of the camp, common to the majority of Holocaust memoirs, there are a number of factors unique to Levi's testimony. These particular elements of *Se questo è un uomo*, consisting of the aspects outlined here, will form the focus of this chapter, as well as that of some of the later chapters: these are the primary components of *Se questo è un uomo* which establish, and will confirm its position as hypotext for Levi's later works. The aspects of *Se questo è un uomo* examined here are some of the clearest hypotextual elements of the relationship between Levi's works, and an analysis of these key aspects of *Se questo è un uomo* also contributes towards the study of the body of the recurring themes throughout Levi's subsequent writing.

Multiple testimony

Se questo è un uomo is more than a purely autobiographical recording of Levi's experiences in the Buna Monowitz satellite camp of Auschwitz as it consistently fails to place Levi himself in the centre of the text, or to focus on the experiences of Levi's life as distinct from those of the other prisoners. Instead, what renders *Se questo è un uomo* particularly unusual and unique among Holocaust testimonies is that Levi has composed what is in many instances a multiple testimony, as though written collectively on behalf of all the prisoners. Rarely employing the first-person singular of a tense, perhaps more appropriate for a testimony to his own experiences, Levi for the most part opts for the first-person plural, the *noi* or *we* form of verbs, only implicitly involving himself as a part of this collectivity: 'andiamo in su e in giú', 'parliamo', 'lo preghiamo di chiedergli che cosa aspettiamo', 'stiamo zitti, quantunque ci vergogniamo un poco di stare zitti' (we go up and down; we talk; we beg him to ask him what we are waiting for; we are silent, although a bit ashamed of being silent) (*SQ*, I, p. 18). The instances in which the *io* or *I* of autobiography proper is observed are limited to Levi's description of episodes and occurrences strictly his own: his detention, prior to deportation, in Fossoli; his admission into the camp hospital, or Ka-Be; the episode of the chemistry exam; his work in the camp laboratory, plus the relating of particular conversations and Levi's personal reflections. For the recounting of experiences common to most deportees, *Se questo è un uomo* functions as a multiple testimony, with one author speaking for a mass of mostly unnamed others.[4] The emphasis of *Se questo è un uomo* lies not on Levi's own experiences but on a balance between the individual and the collective, with primary focus more often placed on the latter.

Emotional detachment

As with a number of cases of Holocaust literary testimony, it is not uncommon for there to exist a degree of authorial self-effacement, usually as a narrative technique to grant credibility to otherwise incredible events, and achieved in Levi's case through minimal usage of the first-person singular. As Young comments:

> (T)he Holocaust writer faces an especially painful quandary: on the one hand, the survivor-scribe would write both himself and his experiences into existence after the fact, giving them both expression and textual actuality; but on the other hand, in order to make his testimony seem true, he would simultaneously efface himself from his text.[5]

Any individual effacement or authorial distancing on Levi's part with regard to *Se questo è un uomo* has generally been connected to the influence of his full-time career as chemist, assumed to grant an observational or scientific stance to his writing, resulting in a subsequent emotional detachment from the events narrated. If the emotional elements of *Se questo è un uomo* have yet to be noted, it is probably due at least in part to the fact that Levi's own comments about the text often reinforced others' assumptions in this respect. Levi outlines his own emotional state during imprisonment as precisely one of detachment, 'Da molti mesi non conoscevo piú il dolore, la gioia, il timore, se non in quel modo staccato e lontano che è caratteristico del Lager' (For many months I hadn't known pain, joy, fear, if not in that detached and distant way which is characteristic of the *Lager*) (*SQ*, I, p. 148), and an observational and more remote approach to testifying is often more than alluded to: in Levi's statement of his intentions to 'fornire documenti per uno studio pacato di alcuni aspetti dell'animo umano' (provide documentation for a peaceful study of some aspects of the human mind) (*SQ*, I, p. 5), and by drawing attention to an anthropological approach in his examination of the 'comportamento dell'animale-uomo di fronte alla lotta per la vita' (the behaviour of the human animal facing a battle for life) (*SQ*, I, p. 83). In the appendix to *Se questo è un uomo*, written in 1976, Levi writes:

> Nello scrivere questo libro, ho assunto deliberatamente il linguaggio pacato e sobrio del testimone, non quello lamentevole della vittima né quello irato del vendicatore: pensavo che la mia parola sarebbe stata tanto piú credibile ed utile quanto piú apparisse obiettiva e quanto meno suonasse appassionata; solo cosí il testimone in giudizio adempie alla sua funzione, che è quella di preparare il terreno al giudice. I giudici siete voi. (Appendix to *SQ*, I, p. 175)

> (In writing this book I have deliberately assumed the peaceful and sober language of the witness, not the lamenting language of the victim or the irate voice of someone seeking revenge; I thought my words would be all the more credible and useful the more objective they appeared and the less impassioned they sounded: only in this way does the witness on trial fulfill his role, which is that of preparing the ground for the judge. You are my judges.)

However, in spite of Levi's declared efforts to write as an unemotional witness with the 'linguaggio pacato e sobrio del testimone', and his reference in the preface to *Se questo è un uomo* as 'uno studio pacato' (a peaceful study) (*SQ*, I, p. 5), there are instances of a direct expression of hatred and anger as well as cases of explicit condemnation. Levi's reaction to Alex whose act of wiping his hand on Levi's shoulder forms the basis of Levi's judgement of him, 'alla stregua di questo suo atto io oggi lo giudico, lui e Pannwitz e gli innumerevoli che furono come lui, grandi e piccoli, in Auschwitz e ovunque' (on the basis of this action of his I judge him today, him and Pannwitz and the innumerable others like him, big and small, in Auschwitz and everywhere)

(SQ, I, p. 104); the Greek doctor who throws a book onto Levi's bunk as he is leaving the camp, of whom Levi writes that 'ancora oggi lo odio per questa sua frase' (I still hate him today for this sentence of his) (SQ, I, p. 151), and Levi's angry response to Kuhn, who thanks God for saving him from the selections:

> Non sa Kuhn che la prossima volta sarà la sua volta? Non capisce Kuhn che è accaduto oggi un abominio che nessuna preghiera propiziatoria, nessun perdono, nessuna espiazione dei colpevoli, nulla insomma che sia in potere dell'uomo di fare, potrà risanare mai piú? Se io fossi Dio, sputerei a terra la preghiera di Kuhn. (SQ, I, p. 126).
>
> (Does Kuhn not know that next time it will be his turn? Does Kuhn not understand that what happened today is an abomination which no propitiatory prayer, no pardon, no expiation by the guilty, nothing which is within man's power to do, could ever remedy again?)

Specific mention is made throughout the text of the emotional state of both himself and his fellow prisoners, even if these are by no means frequent,[6] and there is enough evidence of Levi's emotional connection with the events he narrates to indicate that he is by no means writing as an emotionally-detached observer of the events of the concentration camp.

The Dehumanization of Man

The dehumanization and degradation of man in the *Lager* is portrayed and brought about through a number of key issues in *Se questo è un uomo*, each of which functioned in combination to break the spirit and destroy the humanity of the concentration camp prisoners. It is precisely through his depiction of the degradation of man that Levi reveals what he holds to be uniquely and essentially human. His portrayal of the prisoners' loss of dignity, understanding, language, positive work, free will, thought, memory, and perceptions of time demonstrates the necessity of these factors in the retention and protection of the essence of humanity.

a. The loss of human dignity

The prisoners' dehumanisation, referred to by Levi as 'la demolizione di un uomo' (the demolition of a man) (SQ, I, p. 20), was brought about by the amalgamation of a number of factors in the horrendous conditions of life in the camp. Devoid of many human characteristics, existing in a state in which 'condizione umana piú misera non c'è, e non è pensabile' (there is no human condition more wretched, it is unthinkable) (SQ, I, p. 20), and 'ridotto a sofferenza e bisogno, dimentico di dignità e discernimento' (reduced to suffering and need, oblivious to dignity and discernment) (*SQ*, I, p. 21), the deportees were compelled to adopt bestial behaviour at the expense of their humanity precisely in order to survive. As Levi concludes in the 'I sommersi e i salvati' chapter of *Se questo è un uomo*, 'di fronte al bisogno e al disagio fisico assillanti, molte consuetudini e molti istinti sociali sono ridotti al silenzio' (faced with tormenting need and physical discomfort, many customs and social instincts are reduced to silence) (*SQ*, I, p. 83). The transformation and degradation of the deportees into a bestial state is by no means a theme unique to Levi's testimony,[7] although the bestialization of the camp prisoners is particularly dominant in Levi's work. Cohen writes that 'In the concentration camp man was beaten back to his most animal basis. His only concern was with that which would help to keep him alive. This was a regression to the primitive phase of the drive to self-preservation',[8] and it is this very regression to man's most animal basis which occupies much of *Se questo è un uomo*.

The objectification of the prisoners is one of the first elements of the inhumane treatment they encounter in the camp, and constitutes one of the first steps of their dehumanisation. Upon arrival, the deportees are immediately referred to as 'pezzi' (pieces) (*SQ*, I, p. 10), denying their humanity, whilst the obliteration of identity through the removal of personal names, and their replacement with a tattooed number, indelibly marks them as subhuman masses, like beasts destined for the slaughterhouse. Although suffering identically desperate living conditions and deprivations, their situation was not a unifying factor. The intensity of their battle for survival minimised companionship and solidarity amongst the prisoners: 'qui la lotta per sopravvivere è senza remissione, perché ognuno è disperatamente ferocemente solo' (here the battle to survive is without remission, because everyone is desperately ferociously alone) (*SQ*, I, p. 84). Animal-like, they treated one another with the utmost suspicion, and soon learnt that 'intorno, tutto ci è nemico [...] Tutti ci sono nemici o rivali' (around us, everything is hostile [...] Everyone is either an enemy or a rival) (*SQ*, I, p. 36). Physically and emotionally deprived of all of their possible human needs, 'i personaggi di queste pagine non sono uomini. La loro umanità è sepolta, o essi stessi l'hanno sepolta, sotto l'offesa subita o inflitta altrui' (the personages in these pages are not men. Their humanity is buried, or they themselves have buried it, under an offence suffered or inflicted on someone else) (*SQ*, I, p. 118).

The further metamorphosis of the prisoners is often demonstrated in this text by Levi's abundant use of animal similes and metaphors, applied to both himself and the other deportees ('tremare come bestie' [p. 114]; 'il torpore opaco delle bestie domate con le percosse' [p. 114–5]; 'come tre bestie selvagge che si addentrino in una grande città' [p. 135]; 'gli occhi come le bestie impaurite' [p. 150]) (tremble like beasts; the opaque torpor of beasts suppressed with blows; like three wild beasts entering a big city; eyes like those of frightened beasts). The *Lager* itself is described as 'una gran macchina per ridurci a bestie' (a great machine to reduce us to beasts) (*SQ*, I, p. 35), whilst the men are no more than 'bestie stanche' (tired beasts) (*SQ*, I, p. 38), or 'vermi vuoti di anima' (soulless worms) (*SQ*, I, p. 64). The loss of humanity is also reflected in the prisoners' use of language since 'questo nostro mangiare in piedi, furiosamente, scottandoci la bocca e la gola, senza il tempo di respirare, è "fressen", il mangiare delle bestie, e non certo "essen", il mangiare degli uomini, seduti davanti a un tavolo, religiosamente' (this way of eating on our feet, furiously, burning our mouths and throats, without time to breathe, is "fressen", the animals' way of eating, and certainly not "essen", the human way of eating, seated at a table, religiously) (*SQ*, I, p. 71). Life in the concentration camp de-evolves to its most elementary forms, requiring the prisoners to learn this new way of eating, as well as a different manner of washing, walking, sleeping, dressing and behaving. Every human or dignified aspect of their former lives has been effaced and life's most basic lessons have to be relearned in a degrading and debasing fashion, according to the rules, prohibitions and rites of the camp. The essence of the prisoners' humanity is destroyed by the concentration camp system, as Levi demonstrates how this suffering affected the prisoners' very notions of dignity and humanity: 'Possono venire i russi: non troveranno che noi domati, noi spenti, degni ormai della morte inerme che ci attende. Distruggere l'uomo è difficile, quasi quanto crearlo: non è stato agevole, non è stato breve, ma ci siete riusciti, tedeschi.' (The Russians can come: they will only find us, broken in, lifeless, by now worthy of the unarmed death which awaits us. To destroy a man is difficult, almost as difficult as creating one: it has not been easy, it has not been quick, but you Germans have managed it) (*SQ*, I, p. 146) In *Se questo è un uomo*, where the laws of existence have to be relearnt and common notions of both humanity and human dignity are turned on their heads, Levi portrays a world turned upside down, a world he describes as 'il mondo alla rovescia'[9] (the world overturned), a world reversed, which in turn undoes the social and cultural evolution as well as the pride, self-regard and dignity of those it imprisons.

b. Understanding
Understanding is one of the central themes of both *Se questo è un uomo* and the rest of Levi's writing. Levi's urge both to analyse and to understand the world around him, stemming from the pervasive influence of his scientific background ('io sono un chimico, voglio capire il mondo intorno a me')[10] (I am a chemist, I want to understand the world around me) and revealed through his belief that 'nessuna umana esperienza sia vuota di senso e indegna di analisi' (no human experience is without meaning and unworthy of analysis) (*SQ*, I, p. 83), persists throughout *Se questo è un uomo*. One of the

central tensions in the text is the author's battle to make sense of his surroundings, to understand why the camp exists and to comprehend its rules whilst everything around him within the *Lager* system conspires to make such a comprehension impossible. Initiation into the concentration camp *mondo alla rovescia* requires not just a new way of living, but an understanding of the new rules, yet these laws are never explained and initiation takes place without explication as nobody is willing to hear or answer the prisoners' questions. On his first day Levi grabs an icicle in an attempt to quench his thirst only to have it instantly snatched from him by a guard whose response outlines one of the rules of the camp: 'Hier ist kein Warum' – (qui non c'è perché)' (here there is no why) (*SQ*, I, p. 23). It is a theme of the concentration camps repeated often during the course of Levi's text as the prisoners have to learn that 'in Lager non si fanno domande' (you don't ask questions in the *Lager*) (*SQ*, I, p. 149); 'la nostra saggezza era il "non cercar di capire", non rappresentarsi il futuro, non tormentarsi sul come e sul quando tutto sarebbe finito: non porre e non porsi domande' (our wisdom lay in "not trying to understand", not imagining the future, not tormenting ourselves as to how and when it would all be over: not asking others or ourselves any questions) (*SQ*, I, p. 112); a lesson quickly absorbed by Levi, who states early on in the text that 'da molto tempo ho smesso di cercare di capire' (I gave up trying to understand a long time ago) (*SQ*, I, p. 42).

c. Language

The failure to understand the languages in common usage within the camp further hampered the prisoners' ability to make sense of their surroundings. A vital component of both the dehumanisation and the incomprehension of the prisoners was their abrupt loss of the ability to communicate upon entry into the camp. Brutally plunged into an environment containing 'migliaia di individui diversi per età, condizione, origine, lingua, cultura e costumi' (thousands of individuals differing in age, condition, origin, language, culture and customs) (*SQ*, I, p. 83), most of the prisoners were unable to comprehend the *Lagerjargon* of the concentration camp world, and many were incapable of communicating with one another in any language other than their own. A lack of effective communication amongst the prisoners themselves, combined with their inability to comprehend their surroundings, resulted in a greater sense of isolation amongst the prisoners, increasing the divisions between the men as it added to their sense of hopelessness, despair and alienation. In Levi's words, spoken in an interview in 1984:

> C'era una differenza enorme tra chi parlava il tedesco o il polacco e chi non lo parlava. Questo è stato per molti italiani un fattore di morte, l'esperienza di diventare improvvisamente sordomuti: scaraventati in

un mondo alieno, persino il mezzo piú normale di comunicare veniva a cessare, quello di farsi capire e di capire l'ambiente.[11]

(There was an enormous difference between those who spoke German or Polish and those who didn't. This was, for many Italians, an element of death, the experience of becoming suddenly deaf and dumb: flung into an alien world, even the most normal means of communication, that of making oneself understood and understanding your environment, came to a halt.)

The multilingual nature of the camp is in part recreated in *Se questo è un uomo* by the fragments of many languages which are inserted into the text: bread is 'pane-Brot-Broit-chleb-pain-lechem-kenyér' (*SQ*, I, p. 33) and bricks are 'mattoni, Ziegel, briques, tegula, cegli, kamenny, bricks, téglak' (*SQ*, I, p. 68). This multilingual environment is experienced by Levi as 'una perpetua Babele' (a perpetual Babel) and the personal consequences of the inability to comprehend the languages spoken by the other prisoners are clearly outlined:

Capisco che mi si impone il silenzio, ma questa parola è per me nuova, e poiché non ne conosco il senso e le implicazioni, la mia inquietudine cresce. La confusione delle lingue è una componente fondamentale del modo di vivere quaggiú; si è circondati da una perpetua Babele, in cui tutti urlano ordini e minacce in lingue mai prima udite, e guai a chi non afferra a volo. (*SQ*, I, p. 32)

(I understand that they are ordering me to be silent, but this word is new to me, and since I do not know its meaning or implications, my apprehension grows. The confusion of languages is a fundamental component of the way of living down here; one is surrounded by a perpetual Babel, in which everyone shouts orders and threats in languages never heard before, and woe betide whoever doesn't grasp the meaning immediately.)

Linguistic incomprehension is a difficulty encountered immediately by Levi whose failure to identify the language spoken by the four men who shave the heads of the newly-arrived prisoners is experienced as alienating: 'I quattro parlano una lingua che non sembra di questo mondo' (the four of them are speaking in a language which doesn't seem of this world) (*SQ*, I, p. 17), and whose frustration at his powerlessness to communicate with Schlome is instantly apparent: 'vorrei domandargli molte cose, ma il mio frasario tedesco è limitatissimo' (I would like to ask him many things, but my German is extremely limited) (*SQ*, I, p. 24). In parallel with the prisoners' powerlessness to communicate runs the inadequacy of any language to express the realities of the concentration camp experience.[12] In *Se questo è un uomo*, the shortcomings of language are one of the prisoners' first realisations: 'Allora per la prima volta ci siamo accorti che la nostra lingua manca di parole per esprimere questa offesa, la demolizione di un uomo' (Then for the first time we realised that our language lacks the words to express this offence, the demolition of a man) (*SQ*, I, p. 20); added to by the failure of language to encapsulate and convey the truth of the concentration camp experience to readers: 'Noi diciamo "fame", diciamo "stanchezza", "paura", e "dolore", diciamo "inverno", e sono altre cose. Sono parole libere, create e usate da uomini liberi che vivevano, godendo e soffrendo, nelle loro case. Se i Lager fossero durati piú a lungo, un nuovo aspro linguaggio sarebbe nato' (We say "hunger", we say "tiredness", "fear", and "pain", we say "winter", and they are other things. They are free words, created and used by free men who lived, enjoying and suffering, in their homes) (*SQ*, I, p. 119). Both the lack of language and, consequentially, of the proper comprehension of their environment served to further dehumanise and debase the deportees, reducing the possibility of any potential unity amongst them and further detaching them from the outside world.

d. Degrading work.

This feeling of disconnection from the rest of the world was greatly intensified by means of the prisoners' work. Concentration camp labour involved what Sofsky refers to as Sisyphean tasks, devoid of any productive aim and which thereby destroy the purposeful structure of human work.[13] The result of this fruitless labour, designed precisely to exploit and debase, was utter alienation on the part of the deportees, severing them from any lingering dignity or notion of their own humanity. The harsh and often pointless tasks assigned to the prisoners meant that their work necessarily adopted an inhuman and degrading form, and the delegation of the most demeaning tasks to the intellectual prisoners in a system in which 'i professori lavorano di pala, gli assassini sono caposquadra'[14] (the professors work with shovels, the assassins are foreman), was designed to achieve the utmost humiliation. Levi's own experience highlights the pointlessness of the work assigned to him as chemist:

> noi siamo i chimici, e perciò lavoriamo ai sacchi di fenilbeta. Abbiamo sgomberato il magazzino dopo le prime incursioni, nel colmo dell'estate: la fenilbeta ci si incollava sotto gli abiti alle membra sudate e ci rodeva come una lebbra; la pelle si staccava dai nostri visi in grosse squame bruciate. Poi le incursioni si sono interrotte, e noi abbiamo riportato i sacchi nel magazzino. Poi il magazzino è stato colpito, e noi abbiamo ricoverato i sacchi nella cantina del Reparto Stirolo. Ora il magazzino è stato riparato, e bisogna accatastarvi i sacchi ancora una volta. (*SQ*, I, p. 132)

(we are the chemists and therefore we work at the phenylbeta sacks. We cleared out the warehouse after the first air raids, in the height of summer; the phenylbeta glued our clothes to our sweating limbs and gnawed us like leprosy: the skin came off our faces in large burnt patches. Then the air raids were interrupted and we carried the sacks back to the warehouse. Then the warehouse was hit and we took the sacks into the cellar of the styrene department. Now the warehouse has been repaired and once again we need to pile up the sacks in there.)

Sofsky's analysis of concentration camp labour concludes that the 'work did not secure life; it ravaged it. [...] (L)abour was principally a means of torture and abuse'[15] and that the result of this drudgery was the prisoner 'depersonalized by humiliation and misery, stripped of humanity, transformed into an animal-like bundle of reactions, and ultimately killed.'[16] The portrayal of camp labour in *Se questo è un uomo* does not depart from this: Levi depicts the torture of this 'lavorare senza speranza' (working without hope) (*SQ*, I, p. 64); the total exhaustion and severe physical suffering that were a consequence of the labour itself ('è impossibile andare oltre, il carico mi grava ormai interamente sul braccio; non posso sopportare piú a lungo il dolore e la fatica' [it's impossible to go any further, the load is now weighing entirely on my arm; I cannot stand the pain and exhaustion any longer] [*SQ*, I, p. 38]; 'dopo mezz'ora sarò morto di fatica' [after half an hour I'll be dead with exhaustion] [*SQ*, I, p. 60]; 'per me è una tortura, il carico mi storpia l'osso della spalla, dopo il primo viaggio sono sordo e quasi cieco per lo sforzo, e commetterei qualunque bassezza per sottrarmi al secondo' [for me it is a torture, the load is crippling my shoulderbone, after the first journey I am deaf and almost blind from the effort and I would resort to anything to get out of the second journey] [*SQ*, I, p. 61]; 'Dopo una cinquantina di passi sono al limite di quanto si suole chiamare la normale sopportazione: le ginocchia si piegano, la spalla duole come stretta in una morsa, l'equilibrio è in pericolo' [After about fifty paces I am at the limit of what is usually called normal endurance: my knees are buckling, my shoulder hurts like it's caught in a vice, my balance is endangered] [*SQ*, I, p. 61]); its effect on the prisoners ('io resto impalato, cogli occhi vuoti, la bocca aperta e le braccia penzoloni, immerso nella estasi effimera e negativa della cessazione del dolore' [I just stand there, with my eyes empty, my mouth open and my arms swinging, immersed in the ephemeral and negative ecstasy of the cessation of pain] [*SQ*, I, p. 62]; 'cercherò di nascondermi con la certezza di essere immediatamente rintracciato, deriso e percosso; ma tutto è meglio di questo lavoro' [I will try to hide, with the certainty of being immediately tracked down, derided and beaten; but anything is better than this work] [*SQ*, I, p. 61]), and the prisoners' treatment at the hands of the *Kapos*, for whom they are indeed stripped of humanity and animal-like, beaten 'come fanno i carrettieri coi cavalli' (as cart drivers do with their horses) (*SQ*, I, p. 61). The labour of the concentration camps operated as a vital component in the degradation of the prisoners from men into beasts.

e. Thought and memory

Accompanying the deportees' debasement through their living and working conditions is their loss of free will ('ogni nostra azione è, a tempo e luogo, sensibilmente l'unica possibile' [every one of our actions is, given the time and place, the only one possible] [*SQ*, I, p. 94]), felt all the more acutely when the imprisonment is not a punishment for a crime committed and is for an indefinite period of time. Alongside the loss of the capacity to eat, sleep, work and live like men, comes the loss of man's innate ability to think and remember.

The loss of the prisoners' power of thought is common to many Holocaust memoirs.[17] In *Se questo è un uomo* the inability to think which results from the combination of severe deprivation and hard labour ('La lotta contro la fame, il freddo e il lavoro lascia poco margine per il pensiero' [The battle against hunger, cold and work leaves little margin for thought] [*SQ*, I, p. 121]) is noted primarily during physical activity ('Non c'è piú volontà [...]; non pensano e non vogliono, camminano' [There is no more will [...]; they don't think and they don't want, they walk] [*SQ*, I, p. 45]; 'Finché si cammina non c'è tempo di pensare' [For as long as we are walking there is no time to think] [*SQ*, I, p. 98]) but has further-reaching ramifications with regard to memory as the inability to think results in the prisoners being detached from and unable to remember the past: 'Quando si lavora, si soffre e non si ha tempo di pensare: le nostre case sono meno di un ricordo' (When we work, we are suffering and we don't have time to think: our homes are less than a memory) (*SQ*, I, p. 49). The difficulty of recalling the details of life before deportation recurs throughout the text: this past is virtually inaccessible, 'conservavamo i ricordi della nostra vita anteriore, ma velati e lontani' (we conserved the memories of our previous lives, but veiled and distant) (*SQ*, I, p. 112) and appears to belong to another lifetime altogether as attempting to recollect details relating to Levi's former life 'è come se cercassi di ricordare gli avvenimenti di una incarnazione anteriore' (it is as if I were trying to remember the events of a previous incarnation) (*SQ*, I, p. 103). The expunction of memory is most clearly emphasised in the chapter entitled 'Il canto di Ulisse' in which Levi attempts to recite and convey the meaning of Dante's *Divina commedia* to another prisoner, Jean. After the first six lines Levi's mind goes blank, leaving 'il nulla. Un buco nella memoria' (nothing. A hole in my memory) (*SQ*, I, p. 108). In spite of Levi's efforts, the gap in his memory remains: 'Mi sforzo di ricostruire per mezzo delle rime, chiudo gli occhi, mi mordo le dita: ma non serve, il resto è silenzio' (I force myself to reconstruct it through the rhymes, I close my eyes, I bite my fingers: but it doesn't work, the rest is silence) (*SQ*, I, p. 110) and Levi is unable to bridge the divide in his memory between the *Lager* and his pre-concentration camp life. Yet there are also occasions which indicate that the lack of opportunity to remember can often be a blessing. Working in the camp laboratory grants Levi the time to reflect on what his life has become and to remember his previous way of being in the world, and it is accompanied by an unanticipated and painful emotion, 'la pena del ricordarsi, il vecchio feroce struggimento di sentirsi uomo, […] mi assalta come un cane all'istante in cui la coscienza esce dal buio' (the agony of remembering, the old, ferocious longing to feel like a man […] attacks me like a dog the instant in which my consciousness comes out of the darkness) (*SQ*, I, p. 138). Thinking and remembering for Levi revolve around this *feroce struggimento di sentirsi uomo*. Levi's desperation to remember the end of Dante's canto, 'darei la zuppa di oggi per saper saldare "non ne avevo alcuna" col finale' (I would give today's soup to know how to link the "non ne avevo alcuna" to the last lines) (*SQ*, I, p. 110) proves that the recitation of this poem is about far more than recalling the lines themselves, that Levi is searching for far more than a sequence of verses. The very act of remembering here is tantamount to staying alive and remaining human: thought and memory may be agonising but their loss is debasing, whilst their reaquisition results in the reaffirmation of Levi's existence as a man.

f. Time

Recollecting the details of their former lives is further problematised by the issue of time, particularly by the prisoners' concept of a schism in time, which Langer refers to as the Holocaust's assault on 'the very notion of temporal sequence'.[18] With no physical means of measuring the passage of time,[19] the prisoners experience a sense of atemporality as if their existence were continuing outside the normal passage of time. Sofsky's analysis of concentration camp time, of how 'Terror shuffles time's order, shifting the present to center stage, extinguishing past and future. […] Terror reduces the field of human consciousness to the passing moment […] the absolute primacy of the present, the here and now'[20] corresponds with Levi's comments of the prisoners' perceptions of camp time: 'uno dei fenomeni piú regolari, piú costanti del Lager è quello di perdere la nozione del passato e del futuro. Il passato sparisce e il futuro anche, ci si occupa del presente […]; si vive nel presente'[21] (one of the most regular and constant phenomena of the *Lager* is that of losing all notion of the past and the future. The past disappears along with the future, you attend to the present […]; you live in the present). This concept of an eternal present is displayed in *Se questo è un uomo* through the depiction of time frozen. The *Lager* appears as a place where 'il tempo passa goccia a goccia' (time passes drop by drop) (*SQ*, I, p. 16), where time is 'il nostro tempo sterile e stagnante a cui eravamo ormai incapaci di immaginare una fine. […] [P]er noi, ore, giorni e mesi si riversavano torpidi dal futuro nel passato, sempre troppo lenti, materia vile e superflua di cui cercavamo di disfarci al piú presto' (our sterile and stagnant time to which we were by now incapable of imagining an end. [...] For us, hours, days and months flowed, sluggish, from the future to the past, always too slow, a worthless and superfluous substance of which we tried to rid ourselves as soon as possible) (*SQ*, I, p. 113) and where one soon learns to 'dare un colpo di spugna al passato e al futuro' (put the past and the future out of your mind) (*SQ*, I, p. 30). Not only do the prisoners lose their memories of their pre-deportation pasts, but even their very recent pasts quickly fade into oblivion: 'anche oggi, anche questo oggi che stamattina pareva invincibile ed eterno, l'abbiamo perforato attraverso tutti i suoi minuti; adesso giace conchiuso ed è subito dimenticato, già non è piú un giorno, non ha lasciato traccia nella memoria di nessuno' (we have pierced through all the minutes even today, even this very day which this morning seemed invincible and eternal; now it is over and is immediately forgotten, already it is no longer a day, it has left no trace in anyone's memory) (*SQ*, I, p. 129). The future in *Se questo è un uomo* is inconceivable and impossible, 'chi potrebbe seriamente pensare a domani?' (who could seriously think about tomorrow?) (*SQ*, I, p. 129), referred to as 'il futuro lontano' (the distant future) (*SQ*, I, p. 25) or 'il futuro remoto' (the remote future) (*SQ*, I, p. 30), which 'stava davanti grigio e inarticolato, come una barriera invincibile' (stood in front, grey and inarticulate, like an invincible barrier) (*SQ*, I, p. 113).

The narration of *Se questo è un uomo* reflects the dominance of the present in the prisoners' minds, along with the obliteration of both past and future, through Levi's prevailing use of the present tense throughout this work. The first-person plural present is the principal narrating tense here, used for outlining daily events in the camp ('tutti lavoriamo', 'tutte le mattine usciamo', 'tutte le sere, inquadrati, rientriamo' [*SQ*, I, p. 29]) (we all work; every morning we go out; every evening, in cadres, we return), with the first-person singular present naturally reserved for Levi's own experiences ('io mi sento come Edipo davanti alla Sfinge. Le mie idee sono chiare, e mi rendo conto anche in questo momento che la posta in gioco è grossa; eppure provo un folle impulso a scomparire, a sottrarmi alla prova' [I feel like Oedipus in front of the Sphinx. My ideas are clear and I am aware even at this moment that the position at stake is huge; yet I feel a mad impulse to disappear, to escape from the challenge] [*SQ*, I, p. 101]). The frequent appearance of the words *oggi*, *adesso* and *ora* indicate a second level to the historical present tense at work here as they can correspond both to the historical present of the *Lager*, as well as to the present of the time of writing. There are reflections by the author at the time of writing ('oggi, questo vero oggi in cui io sto seduto a un tavolo e scrivo, io stesso non sono convinto che queste cose sono realmente accadute' [today, this very today in which I sit at a table and write, I myself am not convinced that these things truly happened] [*SQ*, I, p. 99]), and the interruptions of a narrative voice which can, with hindsight, explain events to the reader which must have been indecipherable or unknown to Levi at the time ('Quello che accadde degli altri, delle donne, dei bambini, dei vecchi, noi non potemmo stabilire allora né dopo: la notte li inghiottí, puramente e semplicemente. Oggi però sappiamo che in quella scelta rapida e sommaria, di ognuno di noi era stato giudicato se potesse o no lavorare utilmente per il Reich' [What happened to the others, to the women, the children, the elderly, we could not establish either then or afterwards: the night swallowed them up, pure and simple. Today, however, we know that in that rapid and brief choice, every one of us had been judged as to whether or not he could usefully work for the Reich.] [*SQ*, I, p. 14]), both of which function alongside the historical *now* of 'Adesso è il secondo atto' (Now begins the second act) (*SQ*, I, p. 17) and 'Oramai siamo stanchi di stupirci' (By now we are tired of being amazed) (*SQ*, I, p. 19). The past tense, on the other hand, is mainly employed prior to the deportees' arrival at the camp, and is mostly limited to the first chapter of the text where it is particularly used in Levi's account of his voyage to Auschwitz ('il treno viaggiava lentamente', 'passammo il Brennero', 'soffrivamo per la sete e il freddo', and 'vedemmo sfilare le alte rupi pallide della val d'Adige' [the train travelled slowly; we passed the Brenner; we were suffering from thirst and cold; we saw the tall pale cliffs of the Adige valley slip away] [*SQ*, I, p. 12]). The overwhelmingly *present* testimony of *Se questo è un uomo* therefore operates to dehistoricise the events of the concentration camp: both the *now* of writing and that of the prisoners' experiences within the camp remain current and present to Levi. Levi's continuous usage of the present tense gives the impression that the events he is describing are not past events at all, but are still very much present, thereby highlighting the persistent continuity, in Levi's mind, of the Holocaust experience.

These are the principle elements of *Se questo è un uomo* which constitute its status as hypotext and as a referential core for Levi's later writings: its workings as a multiple, collective testimony; its author's emotional connection with the events narrated; its portrayal of the dehumanisation of man through mankind's loss of dignity, understanding, language, thought and memory, man's humiliation through enslavement, and the experience of atemporality. Subsequent chapters will ascertain the degree to which Levi's later works revisit some or all of these issues since the recurrence and rewriting of these points in various contexts throughout the body of Levi's later works will form a rewriting of *Se questo è un uomo* and, consequently, a rewriting of the Holocaust.

Notes

1. For a complete bibliography of Italian Holocaust writings up to 1973 see Vincenzo

Pappalettera, *Tu passerai per il camino*, rev. edn., 1997, and, more up-to-date, Anna Bravo and Daniele Jalla, *La memorialistica della deportazione in Italia*, 1990.
2. Primo Levi, 'Cosí fu Auschwitz' (9 February 1975), in *Pagine sparse*, *Opere I*, pp. 1190-3, p. 1190.
3. This is part of a response given to an anonymous reader at the 'Incontro con Primo Levi', Cuneo, 1975, who asked him: 'Ma com'è possibile, a uno scampato da Auschwitz, ridiventare un uomo normale? Vivere come tutti, scherzare, amare, incontrare gli amici?' Transcribed in Poli and Calcagno, 1992, p. 194-5.
4. Thus, to provide but one example according to my own figures, in the chapter dealing with the prisoners' arrival at the camp, 'Sul fondo', the first-person plural is used one hundred and eleven times, compared to the first-person singular which occurs only forty-five times; the pronoun *ci* appears fifty-one times against the twenty-five instances of *mi*, and the possessive variations of *il nostro* recur fifty times compared to the fourteen instances of the author's *il mio*.
5. James E. Young, *Writing and Rewriting the Holocaust: Narrative and the Consequences of Interpretation*, 1988, p. 10.
6. In the entirety of the text there are nineteen references made to the collective emotions of Levi along with the other prisoners, a few examples of which are 'non provammo dolore [...] soltanto uno stupore profondo' (p. 11), 'non avevamo piú paura' (p. 13), 'siamo contenti' (p. 100), and 'ci sentiamo sprofondare di vergogna e di imbarazzo' (p. 138). There are twenty instances in which Levi specifies his own, individual emotional state as distinct from that of any others', including, for example, 'mi sento pieno di una tristezza serena' (p. 25), 'mi sento minacciato, insidiato' (p. 32), 'un pensiero mi colma di gioia' (p. 51), and 'mi sentivo prossimo a piangere' (p. 162). (All calculations are my own)
7. To provide just one further example, Wiesel writes of how 'within a few seconds we had ceased to be men' (Elie Wiesel, *Night*, 1958, p. 48).
8. Elie, A. Cohen, *Human Behaviour in the Concentration Camps*, 1954, p. 134.
9. Levi's phrase to describe the concentration camps in his preface to Anna Bravo and Daniele Jalla, eds., *La vita offesa: Storia e memoria dei Lager nazisti nei racconti di duecento sopravvissuti*, 1988, p. 8, also in *Pagine sparse*, II, 1347-50.
10. Levi's words to Giorgio Calcagno, 'PL: capire non è perdonare' in Belpoliti, ed., 1997a, pp. 142-6, p. 144.
11. Spoken to Marco Vigevani, 'Le parole, il ricordo, la speranza', *Bollettino della Comunità Israelitica di Milano*, xl, May 1984, also published in Belpoliti, 1997a, pp. 213-22, p. 215.
12. For other writers who have struggled with this issue, see the chapter entitled 'In the Beginning Was the Silence' of Lawrence L. Langer, *The Holocaust and the Literary Imagination*, 1975, pp. 1-30.
13. Wolfgang Sofsky, *The Order of Terror: The Concentration Camp*, 1997, pp. 190-1.
14. Levi's words published as 'L'ha ispirato un'insegna', *Il Giorno*, 12 October 1966.
15. Sofsky, 1997, p. 168.
16. Sofsky, 1997, p. 172.

17. Perhaps the most poignant example is in Elie Wiesel, *Night*, 1958, where he writes: 'We were incapable of thinking of anything at all' (p. 47).
18. Lawrence L. Langer, *The Holocaust and the Literary Imagination*, 1975, p. 251.
19. Sofsky notes that the hands never moved on the one clock on the station platform at Auschwitz and that 'no prisoner, aside from a few of those belonging to the Prominents, was allowed to wear a watch' (Sofsky, 1997, p. 77).
20. Sofsky, 1997, p. 88.
21. Levi's words spoken in an interview with Beniamino Placido, broadcast on 27 October 1983, and transcribed in part in Poli and Calcagno, 1992, p.185-6.

2
La tregua: 'I segni dell'offesa'

Sixteen years separate the first publication of *Se questo è un uomo* (1947) from that of *La tregua* (1963). *La tregua* is a key text for this study since it is the first of Levi's works to demonstrate that the after-effects of the concentration camps remain pervasively in his writing over the course of time, in a work whose very starting point is an apparent breaking away from the previous setting and the preceding text. A number of thematic continuities between the two works (hunger, the search for food, deprivation) remain necessarily constant, although they are often less intense in the second text; it would be only natural to expect that after such a long period of time there would be at least some alterations in Levi's approach to narrating the events of almost two decades earlier. Yet even a cursory analysis of *La tregua* indicates that surprisingly little has changed in the duration of these sixteen years. Minor modifications exist in Levi's subject matter and in the style of narration, but many of the predominant themes of the two texts remain unchanged. Of primary significance for the purposes of this inquiry are, in any case, precisely the persisting elements of *Se questo è un uomo*: those aspects, echoes and evocations of the earlier text which reveal its influence on both this work and its author; factors which, even if altered from Levi's first work, now differ in ways which can be interpreted as highlighting a connection with Levi's portrayal of his experience of the Holocaust.

Although functioning almost as a sequel to *Se questo è un uomo*, as an appendix to and an extension of the narration of Levi's experiences, from the outset *La tregua* departs from the concentration camp itself, commencing with the liberation of the camp and with Levi's physical departure from it. Levi makes little specific reference here to the events and experiences of the concentration camp: this is not a work about the *Lager*, but about its immediate aftermath, addressing not the Holocaust itself but the consequences of the Holocaust. With *La tregua* Levi is not so much rewriting the Holocaust as extending it; demonstrating how the effects of the *Lager* did not stop with liberation, but rather continued, with consequences both for this survivor's life and, perhaps more significantly, for his writing. It is this pervasive influence of the concentration camp experience on the structure, style and composition of *La tregua* which will be of particular interest here, rather than the more limited approach of exclusively examining common themes.

Levi was concerned with emphasising the differences between *Se questo è un uomo* and *La tregua*. In the *Prefazione all'edizione scolastica di La tregua* he states that 'credo si distingua agevolmente che esso [*La tregua*] è stato scritto da un uomo diverso: non solo piú vecchio [...] ma piú pacato e tranquillo, piú attento alla tessitura della frase, piú consapevole'[1] (I think it is easily discerned that this [*La tregua*] is written by a different man, one who is not only older [...] but more peaceful and tranquil, more attentive to sentence structure, more aware) and in interviews he often cites a shift in his inspiration for writing, with the motivation behind *La tregua* altered from the first work's desperate urge to bear witness to a desire to enjoy himself in the act of storytelling and to entertain his readers.[2] It is unlikely, however, that *La tregua* was composed purely for the enjoyment of either its readers or its writer: as Vincenti states, '*La tregua* nasceva come indifferibile epilogo di *Se questo è un uomo*, vale a dire dalla necessità [...] di portare a compimento l'opera di testimonianza intrapresa'[3] (*La tregua* was born as an urgent epilogue to *Se questo è un uomo*, that is to say from the necessity [...] to bring the work of testimony undertaken to completion). *La tregua* does continue the testimonial function of *Se questo è un uomo* in a number of ways, bringing the first work to a more protracted conclusion through the resumption of Levi's tale which progresses here from the precise point that *Se questo è un uomo* ends. *La tregua* is an historical extension of the former text, often accompanied by dates ('il 15 ottobre, trentunesimo giorno di viaggio' [15th October, thirty-first day travelling] [*LT*, I, p. 392]), and it does, in effect, retain *Se questo è un uomo*'s testimonial function in its act of bearing witness here to the immediate aftermath of the Holocaust and to the residual effects of the concentration camps and the Second World War.[4]

Whilst one of the testimonial aspects of *Se questo è un uomo* was apparent through Levi's use of multiple testimony and first-person plural narration, in *La tregua* this element has almost entirely disappeared. Experiences are related here, for the most part, in the first person singular, with any first-person plural narrative (for example, 'Partimmo da', 'Viaggiammo per' [We left from; we travelled through] [*LT*, I, p. 310-1]) usually used in reference to the journey itself. Although in this text Levi does describe his memories of Auschwitz as 'cose mie ma di tutti' (my things, but everyone's) (*LT*, I, p. 244), the events, post-Auschwitz, of *La tregua* focus more on Levi's individual, rather than collective, experiences. Whereas *Se questo è un uomo* transmitted the human focal point of the deportees' shared experiences through the plural narrative voice, in *La tregua* the episodes and events Levi recounts are more exclusively his own, as *La tregua* is primarily the personal history of Levi's experiences during his journey home. However, *La tregua* is not wholly Levi's story: there are no fewer than sixty-four named people whose life stories come into play in *La tregua*,⁵ with certain chapters, such as 'I sognatori', devoted almost exclusively to the narration of stories, events and behavioural patterns belonging to people other than Levi himself. This human focus of *La tregua* has not altered greatly from that of *Se questo è un uomo*. Although Levi believed that 'nel primo libro avevo badato alle *cose*; il secondo l'ho scritto nella consapevolezza di essere capace di trasmettere esperienze'⁶ (in the first book I had paid attention to the *things*; I wrote the second aware of being able to convey experiences), this was never entirely the case, for whilst in *Se questo è un uomo* the *cose*, or events, are indeed of great importance, they are only secondary next to the effect of these same events on the men upon whom they are inflicted. The human angle rather than any purely factual/historical aspect of *Se questo è un uomo* is vital and an analogous human focus continues to be at the forefront of Levi's second text. In *La tregua* also, the ex-deportees' perceptions of their experiences continue to be of prime significance; the act of transmitting human experiences is still more crucial than the mere recording of events. Consistent with this is the attention Levi pays to the people he encounters on this journey home and on their stories; the events and episodes of the journey itself persist in being subordinate to the experiences of those participating and involved in them.

Similarly altered from the plural narration of Levi's first work are the narrative temporal modes of *La tregua* and their implied significance, for it is in the selection and application of tenses that we can glimpse the real aftermath and legacy of the concentration camp. The temporal structure of *La tregua* is, unlike that of *Se questo è un uomo*, formed for the most part in the past tense and yet there is a schism in this past precisely because, in Levi's own words, 'la cesura di Auschwitz [...] spaccava in due la catena dei miei ricordi' (the caesura of Auschwitz [...] split the chain of my memories in two) (*LT*, I, p. 375). Auschwitz was the dividing factor in the time-line of Levi's memories: everything was either pre-Auschwitz, Auschwitz itself, or post-Auschwitz, and this is evident in the temporal structure of the text itself. There are four main symbolic, rather than literal, tenses in *La tregua*, each with its own implied significance: the ancient past, the near past, the present, and the future. The implicit ancient past in the text is rare and relates to pre-concentration camp time. It is normally shown through the use of the pluperfect tense, to symbolise what the ex-prisoners *had* been in the period of time *before* deportation. This ancient past is occasionally used in descriptions of the people Levi meets (for example Levi's description of Henek, who '*era stato* catturato, e deportato ad Auschwitz' [*had been* captured, and deported to Auschwitz] [*LT*, I, p. 217, my italics]) but is more conspicuous in its absence. There is remarkably little reference to the distant past of lives before deportation, and this is all the more poignant since it is surely to these previous existences that the deportees are returning. If the ancient past symbolises the ex-prisoners' lives before deportation, then the logical, resultant extension of this is that the implied *passato prossimo* or near past tense represents the period of time spent in the concentration camps. Levi's reference, therefore, to 'quelle mie cosí recenti esperienze, di Auschwitz vicina' (those so recent experiences of mine, of Auschwitz nearby) (*LT*, I, p. 245), his comment that 'era ancora troppo recente in noi la memoria [...] di Auschwitz' (it was still too recent in our minds the memory [...] of Auschwitz) (*LT*, I, p. 338), and his description of the events of Auschwitz as 'cose di ieri' (things of yesterday) (*LT*, I, p. 302) all accentuate the very nearness of this concentration camp 'past'.[7] It is this near-past tense which highlights the background of the *tregua*, the *Lager*, which casts a shadow over the ex-prisoners now. It is precisely this near-past tense which, although it is past, somehow does not give a sense of being over and completed. This particular past appears fragile and temporary, as though it were liable to return at any moment, an impression enhanced by the frequent recurrence of the words and derivatives of 'precario' (precarious) and 'provvisorio' (provisory) ('provvisoriamente' [p. 234], 'precariamente' [pp. 296 and 337], 'precaria' [pp. 207, 215 and 324], 'precario' [p. 265], 'precari' [p. 392], 'provvisorio' [p. 275], 'provvisori' [p. 378], and 'provvisorie' [p. 385]). The precarious nature of the near-past's completion and the possibility of its return and continuation is emphasized by Levi's use of the continuous past tense, the imperfect, to describe occurences which remind him of his time in the camps: 'Il freddo era intenso; il cielo, fittamente stellato, si andava schiarendo a levante, a promessa di una di quelle meravigliose aurore di pianura a cui, al tempo della nostra schiavitú, *assistevamo* interminabilmente dalla piazza dell'appello del Lager' (The cold was intense; the sky, thick with stars, was lighting slowly in the east, promising one of those marvellous dawns of the plain which, during the time of our slavery, we *used to attend* interminably in the roll-call square of the *Lager*) (*LT*, I, p. 226, my italics). Frequent reminders like this of the fact that the past is still very much present at this point in Levi's mind, serve to keep the near-past closer to the present, and also, therefore, to bring *Se questo è un uomo* closer to *La tregua*.

In stark contrast to Levi's first text, however, the actual present tense is absent here from the narration of events, and is only employed authorially as commentary when the narrator's voice, distinct from that of Levi's narrative persona, reflects with hindsight, for example, that 'è questo il tremendo privilegio della nostra generazione e del mio popolo' (this is the tremendous privilege of our generation and of my people) (*LT*, I, p. 206), or that 'non è dato all'uomo di godere gioie incontaminate' (man is not given to enjoying uncontaminated happiness) (*LT*, I, p. 366). The implied present tense of *La tregua*, which exists in a literal sense as the past tense yet which is symbolic of the present in the temporal setting of the text, is unambiguous: it is the post-Auschwitz time, the *tregua*, and the journey home, which occupy the greater part of Levi's attention here. It is not a forward-looking present, however, as any notion of the future is somewhat complicated by the fact that the very future to which the survivors are returning is also their past. Their entire journey is an act of *getting back* as well as literally returning, in the desperate hope of finding something when they return that will resemble their former lives. Any anticipation of or speculation about their future lives is shadowy and vague. It is the ultimate aim of all the ex-deportees and yet it is rarely specified or clarified in any way; the text and the people within it are focussed on the moment of arrival home, 'Che cosa avremmo ritrovato a casa?' (What would we find at home?) (*LT*, I, p. 394) but no further into the future than that. This future is as ambivalent as the pre-Auschwitz ancient past, and again is similarly remarkable for its nonappearance.

The most noteworthy aspect of this analysis of the symbolic tenses of *La tregua* is their connection to *Se questo è un uomo*. In spite of the time difference that separates these two works, their author's perceptions, experiences and writing of time in the two texts is unaltered. Sixteen years after the composition of *Se questo è un uomo*, Levi remains firmly within the confines of an identical time-zone: concepts of a pre-Auschwitz past and a post-Auschwitz future remain non-existent in *La tregua*, and Levi's focus continues to rest on the all-encompassing present moment. Notions of time are structured around the event of the concentration camp, 'la cesura di Auschwitz', which casts its shadow over the post-liberation present and which has only shifted ever so slightly by this second text, from present to near-past.

It is a minor and entirely logical shift in temporal perspective with regard to the concentration camp which is not invariably echoed by a comparable repositioning of other aspects of the second work. Levi continues to observe human behaviour from what is often a philosophical angle in *La tregua* which has much in common with his original investigation in *Se questo è un uomo* of 'alcuni aspetti dell'animo umano' (some aspects of the human mind) (*SQ*, I, p. 5). Levi retains his interest in and fascination with anthropology, in effect extending his examination of the 'comportamento dell'animale-uomo di fronte alla lotta per la vita' (behaviour of the human animal faced with the battle for life) (*SQ*, I, p. 83) through his stance in *La tregua* where he observes, for example of those who had managed to obtain positions of power in the refugee camps, that 'L'assistere al comportamento dell'uomo che agisce non secondo ragione, ma secondo i propri impulsi profondi, è uno spettacolo di estremo interesse, simile a quello di cui gode il naturalista che studia le attività di un animale dagli istinti complessi' (Witnessing the behaviour of a man who acts not according to reason, but according to his own profound impulses, is an extremely interesting spectacle, similar to that enjoyed by the naturalist when studying the activities of an animal with complex instincts) (*LT*, I, p. 250). Correspondingly constant is the positioning of Levi's autobiographical persona in the relating of his experiences, for here, as in *Se questo è un uomo*,

Levi's narrative persona effectively effaces himself from events. Yet whereas in *Se questo è un uomo* Levi's authorial voice was often inconspicuous due to its place within the collective and multiple narrating voices, existing only implicitly as part of the first-person plural, in *La tregua* Levi removes himself more from the action of the text's episodes rather than from the relating of events. He is both in the midst of the text as well as paradoxically somewhat absent, following what is, in Marcus' theories, the conventional function of memoir writers who 'efface themselves within the histories they observe and record'.[8] Levi places himself precisely in the role of observer and recorder, not always participating in the events occurring around him, choosing instead to narrate these incidents as though he were a by-stander. In the episodes recounted, Levi's narrative persona often deliberately decides to be a spectator, rather than to actively partake and engage in the action; it is a position exemplified by Levi's comments on il Tenente's dance lessons where he states that 'lo spettacolo di queste lezioni mi interessava talmente, che trovai modo di assistervi, infilandomi per gli strani meandri della Casa Rossa e appiattandomi in un angolo scuro' (the spectacle of these lessons interested me so much that I found a way to watch them, slipping through the strange labyrinth of the Red House and hiding myself in a dark corner) (*LT*, I, p. 359). Levi's narrative persona is primarily an observer of many of the collective, group events, only reluctantly joining in, as Levi indeed affirms, 'di mala voglia' (unwillingly) (*LT*, I, p. 239). Yet this is not entirely a stance of disconnection or distance from the episodes of the text since Levi's observing, philosophical and anthropological approaches to the relating of events are not accompanied by any degree of emotional detachment. There are forty-eight occasions within the text on which Levi explicitly specifies his own, personal emotional state, as distinct from that of the other ex-deportees and his descriptions of their collective emotions.[9] Any detachment is therefore restricted to the disengagement of Levi's narrative persona from the events described and is not applicable to Levi as author, whose emotional connection with the episodes portrayed is, as with *Se questo è un uomo*, clearly specified whenever necessary.

The observational aspects to Levi's writing are continued with regard to his characterization of the people he encounters throughout the course of *La tregua*. Whereas in *Se questo è un uomo* Levi's character descriptions often contained references to the prisoners' pre-concentration camp existences through the mention of their nationality and place of origin as well as, on occasion, the disclosure of their previous career,[10] for the ex-deportees in *La tregua* the past Levi focusses on primarily in his descriptions is that of their recent past in the camps. Their most significant features for Levi are therefore no longer references to lives prior to deportation, but to experiences of the camps: the frequent mention of the names of concentration camps reverberate throughout Levi's depictions of character and again serve to maintain the proximity and presence of the camps themselves. To provide but a few of the multitude of potential examples, Frau Vita appears to us, 'dal corpo disfatto e dal dolce viso chiaro, era una giovane vedova di Trieste, mezza ebrea, reduce da Birkenau [...] ferita profondamente, ulcerata da quanto aveva subito e visto in un anno di Lager' (with her ruined figure and her sweet clear face, a young widow from Trieste, half Jewish, a survivor of Birkenau [...] deeply wounded, ulcerated by what she had undergone and seen in a year of the *Lager*) (*LT*, I, p. 222); Henek 'era stato catturato, e deportato ad Auschwitz con tutta la famiglia' (had been captured, and deported to Auschwitz with his whole family) (*LT*, I, p. 217); Olga 'era una donna di grande intelligenza e cultura, forte, bella e consapevole; deportata a Birkenau, vi aveva sopravvissuto, sola della sua famiglia (was a woman of great intelligence and culture, strong, beautiful and aware; deported to Birkenau, she had survived, the only member of her family to do so) (*LT*, I, p. 223), and Levi begins his narration of his encounter with Cesare 'nel campo di Buna' since 'avevo conosciuto Cesare negli ultimi giorni di Lager' (in the Buna camp since I had met Cesare in the last days of the *Lager*) (*LT*, I, p. 261). For the majority of people with whom Levi comes into contact in this text, the preponderance of whom are only minor characters, Levi's physical descriptions are brief, yet clear: they are almost photographic in their detail and in their ability to capture and convey the essence of a person's appearance. Thus the goalkeeper of the Polish football team is 'uno spilungone biondo, dal viso emaciato, dal petto concavo e dalle movenze da apache' (a blond beanpole, with an emaciated face, a concave chest and with the movements of an Apache) (*LT*, I, p. 283); Kleine Kiepura 'era cresciuto troppo e male: dal busto tozzo e corto sporgevano braccia e gambe lunghissime, da *ragno*; e di sotto il viso pallido, dai tratti non privi di grazia infantile, balzava in avanti una enorme mandibola, piú prominente del naso' (had grown too much, and badly: enormously long arms and legs sprouted from his squat, short body, *like those of a spider*; and below his pale face, with features which were not lacking in infantile grace, a huge jaw jutted out, more prominent than his nose) (*LT*, I, p. 219, my italics); Egorov is 'ubriaco fradicio, infilato in smisurati pantaloni la cui cintura gli arrivava alle ascelle, mentre la coda di rondine spazzava il pavimento' (blind drunk, slipped into ill-fitting trousers whose waistband came up to his armpits whilst its tails swept the floor) (*LT*, I, p. 280), and Mordo Nahum appears 'rosso di pelo e di pelle, aveva grossi occhi scialbi ed acquosi e un gran naso ricurvo; il che conferiva all'intera sua persona un aspetto rapace ed impedito, quasi di *uccello* notturno sorpreso dalla luce, o di *pesce* da preda fuori del suo naturale elemento' (red of hair and skin, he had large, pale and watery eyes and a huge curved nose, which gave his whole body a predatory and obstructed appearance, almost like a *nightbird* surprised by light, or a *predatory fish* outside its natural habitat) (*LT*, I, p. 228, my italics). Nor are Mordo Nahum and Kleine Kiepura the only characters to be compared to animals: Marja, the nurse, is 'simile a un *gatto* di bosco per gli occhi obliqui e selvatici, il naso breve dalle narici frontali, e le movenze agili e silenziose' (similar to a *forest cat* with her oblique and wild eyes, her short nose with flared nostrils, and her agile, silent movements) (*LT*, I, p. 252); Cesare is 'vispo come un *grillo*' (lively as a *grasshopper*) (*LT*, I, p. 262), and Noah is 'forte come un *cavallo*, [...] *uccello* d'alto volo' (strong as a *horse* [...] a high-flying *bird*) (*LT*, I, p. 221). Animal metaphors inundate Levi's depictions of human beings in this text, as they did in *Se questo è un uomo*, but the animal imagery which was so revealing in the former text as it helped to emphasise the prisoners' transformation from rational, thinking men into beasts, has changed its form in this text. In *La tregua* Levi's frequent comparisons of humans with animals are no longer employed to highlight degradation but are here used exclusively as a descriptive tool, with none of the previous negative connotations. The animals Levi selects for his metaphors have also altered: men are no longer compared to worms, insects or starving beasts, but to horses, cats and birds, a wholly different category of animal. So whilst Levi writes of the Ucrainian women returning *en masse* from Germany that 'di animali umiliati e domati erano la loro inerzia, il loro appartarsi, la loro mancanza di pudore' (their inertia, their aloofness, their lack of modesty were those of humiliated and broken-in animals) (*LT*, I, p. 310), it is to show what imprisonment in the concentration camps did to human beings: here he is comparing them to animals in exactly the same way as he did of himself and the other prisoners in *Se questo è un uomo*. This quotation in fact serves as a contrast between the two texts and a reminder of precisely what has changed. For the 'animali umiliati' belong to the previous text, to the ex-prisoners' near past, and they emphasise these survivors' transformation, highlighting the fact that from their devolution into beasts they are now re-evolving back into thinking, feeling, civilised men.

This evolution is a slow process which is reflected within the animal metaphors and their progressive alteration throughout the text. At the beginning of *La tregua*, there is little development or change from the animal imagery contained within *Se questo è un uomo*: the first two chapters of the text contain similes and metaphors such as 'come bestie feroci e vili' (like worthless and ferocious beasts) (*LT*, I, p. 210); 'da topo' (like a mouse) (p. 213); 'animaletti selvaggi' (wild little creatures) (p. 218), and 'da ragno' (like a spider) (p. 219). Yet as the temporal distance between the ex-prisoners and their lives in the concentration camp increases, the types of creature to which Levi compares them begins to differ more clearly from his earlier text. It is a distance of time rather than a physical, geographical detachment from the *Lager* which is significant here for even from the end of the second chapter, 'Il Campo Grande', which is set geographically in Auschwitz itself rather than in the satellite camp of Buna, we begin to see 'come un cavallo' (like a horse) (*LT*, I, p. 221); 'simile a un gatto' (similar to a cat) (p. 252); 'come un'allodola' (like a lark) (p. 256); 'come un toro' (like a bull) (p. 267), and 'come un orso' (like a bear) (p. 273). These are still interspersed with the occasional animal metaphor with a negative connotation ('come cani feroci' [like ferocious dogs] [p. 287], or 'stupido come un gallo' [as stupid as a rooster] [p. 315]) but for the most part the animal analogies are used comically here as is revealed when they are considered in their full context: 'gli occhi, infossati sotto enormi archi ciliari come cani feroci in fondo alle loro tane' (his eyes, sunken under enormous eyebrows like ferocious dogs at the back of their lair) (p. 287), and 'un generale magiaro in alta uniforme, litigioso e variopinto e stupido come un gallo' (a Magyar general in full uniform, as quarrelsome, gaily coloured and stupid as a rooster) (p. 315). There is a conscious evolution here in Levi's choice of metaphors for his depiction of character, and the metaphors selected for the composition of *La tregua* indicate both continuities with *Se questo è un uomo*, in the use of animal metaphors, at the same time as a distancing from certain elements of the first text through the gradual alteration of the tropes.

This alteration to the language of *La tregua* is accompanied by a similarly notable development in the role of language itself. The concentration camp in which 'la confusione delle lingue è una componente fondamentale del modo di vivere di quaggiú' (the confusion of languages is a fundamental component of the way of life down here) (*SQ*, I, p. 32) and where language and the ability or inability to communicate are sources of either great misery or salvation, of complete isolation or as an invaluable means of attaining human contact, has been transformed here. In *La tregua* language remains a vital issue, but here many of the problems connected with the multilingual nature of the camps disperse. Although the post-war setting of *La tregua* is at least as multilingual an environment as the concentration camps, we are no longer presented with 'la perpetua Babele' (the perpetual Babel) (*SQ*, I, p. 32) of a multilingual chaos, but rather with a sense of joy at the possibility of communication. The act of communicating is here portrayed as an essential step towards re-becoming human, and any degree of success is perceived with delight as the satisfaction of a basic, human need. Thus Levi, who returns from a market in Cracow having picked up a smattering of Polish, declares that these 'brandelli di informazione [...] mi riempivano di una gioia insulsa e puerile' (scraps of information [...] filled me with an inane and puerile joy) (*LT*, I, p. 239) and, after managing to communicate in Latin with a priest in the marketplace in Cracow, remarks that, 'avevo del tutto dimenticato la fame e il freddo, tanto è vero che il bisogno di contatti umani è da annoverarsi fra i bisogni primordiali' (I had completely forgotten the hunger and the cold, in fact the need for human contact ought to count among the primordial needs) (*LT*, I, p. 241). All the people Levi depicts here speak a variety of European languages, a prime example being Mordo Nahum who 'oltre alla sua lingua, parlava spagnolo [...], francese, un italiano stentato ma di buon accento, e, seppi poi, il turco, il bulgaro e un po' di albanese' (as well as his own language spoke Spanish [...], French, a stilted Italian but with a good accent, and, I found out later, Turkish, Bulgarian and a bit of Albanian) (*LT*, I, p. 227-8), and communication and conversation encounter no insurmountable barriers. The only exception is Hurbinek, the Auschwitz baby, whom nobody had taught to speak, who remains a strong symbol of the aftermath of the concentration camp system, an emblem of both its continuity and its inescapability as his inability to communicate persists after liberation, until his death. Against the figure of Hurbinek, the occasional linguistic problem which does arise for the other, adult ex-deportees is portrayed as comical, as in the depiction of Levi and Cesare's exploits in the chapter entitled 'Una curizetta'; incomprehension and a lack of a common language in which to communicate have lost their menacing urgency and their capacity to alienate and isolate, for here, failing to comprehend is no longer a matter of life or death. In *La tregua* communication is now both possible and necessary: possible because these are now free men, and necessary precisely in order to feel both free and human again.

The reconstruction of the ex-prisoners' humanity is central to the development of *La tregua*, and the developments in language and communication here closely follow the internal advancement of the survivors themselves as their voyage home becomes a journey of rediscovery and rebecoming; an inner journey to re-establish their own identities that occurs simultaneously to the external, physical odyssey back home.[11] The original loss of identity, the anonymity and namelessness of the concentration camps is often recalled through the recurrence of the word 'anonimo' (anonymous) (*LT*, I, pp. 219, 222, 234, 282, 312) as the ex-prisoners struggle to re-affirm their individual identities. An important factor in the survivors' rediscovery, reassertion and recuperation of themselves and their humanity is manifested in the exercising of the freedom of choice now granted to them. Although the ex-inmates are shunted from one refugee camp to another throughout the course of *La tregua*, they are granted many of the same choices as free men as to how to spend their time, and are able, like Velletrano in 'Il bosco e la via', to construct alternative living arrangements if they so wish.

Yet it is vital not to mistake the occasionally happier aspects of the survivors' lives here for a greater positivity in the text as a whole, for the brighter and more optimistic elements of some parts of this work do not endure and neither do they extend to the language of the text itself. Jane Nystedt was one of the first to undertake a detailed study of the language of Levi's *oeuvre*, and she noted that whilst the word *pericolo* (danger) is entirely absent from this text, the word *angoscia* (anguish) recurs eight times, compared to only five within *Se questo è un uomo*, and *minaccia* (threat) emerges on seven occasions here and only four times within the previous text.[12] Close examination of Levi's choice of adverbs and adjectives is equally revealing: many individual words, in particular adjectives, employed in *La tregua* are strongly reminiscent of *Se questo è un uomo*.[13] Adjectives, and their variations, such as 'spaventoso' (frightening) (*LT*, I, pp. 205, 229, 277, 335, 377, 395); 'terribile' (pp. 209, 231, 378, 386); 'triste' (sad) (pp. 216, 242, 245, 250, 252, 270, 287, 298, 375, 383, 387, 389); 'violento' (pp. 205, 237, 311, 335, 338, 374, 377, 380, 386); 'doloroso' (painful) (pp. 259, 310, 316, 342, 385) and 'barbarico' (pp. 248, 266, 288, 325) echo those used to depict Levi's Auschwitz experiences, and are prominent throughout *La tregua*. Analogously, the recurrence of adverbs such as 'brutalmente' (brutally) (pp. 230, 241, 304, 395); 'confusamente' (confusedly) (pp. 241, 328, 348); 'penosamente' (painfully) (pp. 323, 362) and 'ferocemente' (ferociously) (pp. 248, 330), to provide just a few examples, contains clear traces of the language and issues of the former text. The effects of some of the adjectives that are particularly evocative of the *Lager* are at times emphasised still further by their juxtaposition with a noun, or other adjective, that often seems out of place, and is therefore particularly conspicuous: 'pantomima sinistra' (sinister pantomime) (p. 362); 'mostruoso cuore' (monstrous heart) (p. 293); 'satanica proposta' (satanic proposal) (p. 289); 'barbarica dignità' (barbaric dignity) (p. 288); 'con orrenda e macabra esitazione' (with horrendous and macabre hesitation) (p. 362), and 'filtro infernale' (infernal filter) (p. 305). The metaphor 'come un incubo' (like a nightmare) (pp. 214, 304, 318) also recurs frequently enough to remind us of Levi's previous nightmarish existence. There are, correspondingly, many instances in *La tregua* when a virtually unconnected event reminds Levi of the concentration camps: being outside one cold, frosty morning reminds him of how, during his imprisonment, he would be kept standing 'interminabilmente dalla piazza dell'appello del Lager' (interminably in the roll-call square of the *Lager*) (*LT*, I, p. 226); Levi's way of falling asleep whilst travelling he describes as exactly 'come si impara a fare in Lager' (as one learns to do in the *Lager*) (*LT*, I, p. 231), and his description of his train journey south from Russia to Romania, in which there were between twenty and twenty-five men in each wagon, 'alla luce delle nostre molte esperienze ferroviarie precedenti, voleva dire un viaggiare comodo e riposante' (in the light of our many previous rail experiences meant a comfortable and restful journey) (*LT*, I, p. 368-9). Much of the language of this text, as well as the events themselves, are, therefore, not merely tainted with sadness and with a pervading air of melancholy, but are also shadowed by the persistent spectre of the horror, terror and misery of the survivors' recent past: 'il dolore dell'esilio, della casa lontana, della solitudine, degli amici perduti, della giovinezza perduta, e dello stuolo di cadaveri intorno' (the pain of exile, of a distant home, of loneliness, of lost friends, of a lost youth, and of the crowd of corpses around) (*LT*, I, p. 209) which darkens every moment of potential contentment post-liberation.[14]

Levi's remark at the beginning of *La tregua* that 'nulla mai piú sarebbe potuto avvenire di cosí buono e puro da cancellare il nostro passato, [...] i segni dell'offesa sarebbero rimasti in noi per sempre, [...] è una inesauribile fonte di male' (never again could anything happen which was good and pure enough to cancel out our past, [...] the signs of the offence would remain in us forever, [...] it is an inexhaustible source of pain) (*LT*, I, p. 206) is therefore proved by the conclusion of the text. The concentration camps are consistently portrayed here as a never-ending source of pain, as a poison in the blood ('il veleno di Auschwitz' [the poison of Auschwitz] [*LT*, I, p. 394]), and as a debilitating suffering from which the ex-deportees will never truly recover. The imagery of disease recurs frequently, with the consequences of imprisonment referred to as 'l'infezione del Lager' (the infection of the *Lager*) (*LT*, I, p. 220), the *Lager* itself as 'un male irreparabile e definitivo, presente ovunque, annidato come una cancrena nei visceri dell'Europa' (an irreparable and definitive evil, ever-present, harbouring like a cancer in the intestines of Europe) (*LT*, I, p. 389), and the ex-prisoners as 'appestati' (plagued) (*LT*, I, p. 228) by their experiences. The ongoing suffering of the survivors finds a parallel in the similarly scarred and devastated Europe that provides the backdrop for the events of the text. It is both an environment and a situation that bears little relation to the *tregua* of the title, the lack of which is exemplified on two occasions in the chapter entitled 'Il greco' as Levi writes:

> La libertà, l'improbabile, impossibile libertà, cosí lontana da Auschwitz che solo nei sogni osavamo sperarla, era giunta: ma non ci aveva portati alla Terra Promessa. Era intorno a noi, ma sotto forma di una spietata pianura deserta. Ci aspettavano altre prove, altre fatiche, altre fami, altri geli, altre paure. (*LT*, I, p. 230)

(Freedom, the improbable, impossible freedom, so far from Auschwitz that we only dared hope for it in our dreams, had arrived: but it had not brought us to the Promised Land. It was all around us, but in the form of a merciless, deserted plain. Other trials, exhaustions, hungers, frosts and fears awaited us.)

> In quei giorni e in quei luoghi, poco dopo il passaggio del fronte, un vento alto spirava sulla faccia della terra: il mondo intorno a noi sembrava ritornato al Caos primigenio, e brulicava di esemplari umani scaleni, difettivi, abnormi; e ciascuno di essi si agitava, in moti ciechi o deliberati, in ricerca affannosa della propria sede, della propria sfera. (*LT*, I, p. 226)

(In those days and in those parts, shortly after the passing of the front, a high wind was blowing over the face of the earth; the world around us seemed to have returned to primeval Chaos, and it was swarming with scalene, defective, abnormal human specimens, and each of these clamoured, with blind or deliberate movements, in anxious search of his own place, his own sphere.)

As in *Se questo è un uomo*, the setting of much of *La tregua* is that of an upside-down, chaotic world, the 'Caos primigenio', although here it is the confusion of the aftermath, rather than the chaos of the camps themselves. By the final chapter of *La tregua*, 'Il risveglio', any notion of a period of respite is over: the interval of the journey itself is completed, terminating in the arrival home, and yet the rational expectation of this return culminating in the ultimate moment of liberation also ends here as the respite of freedom was never more than a brief respite, a *tregua*. The text both begins and ends with imprisonment since in the concluding dream Levi remains inside the prison camps:

> È un sogno entro un altro sogno, vario nei particolari, unico nella sostanza. Sono a tavola con la famiglia, o con amici, o al lavoro, o in una campagna verde: in un ambiente insomma placido e disteso, apparentemente privo di tensione e di pena; eppure provo un'angoscia sottile e profonda, la sensazione definita di una minaccia che incombe. E infatti, al procedere del sogno, a poco a poco o brutalmente, ogni volta in modo diverso, tutto cade e si disfa intorno a me, lo scenario, le pareti, le persone, e l'angoscia si fa piú intensa e piú precisa. Tutto è ora volto in caos: sono solo al centro di un nulla grigio e torbido, ed ecco, io *so* che cosa questo significa, ed anche so di averlo sempre saputo: sono di nuovo in Lager, e nulla era vero all'infuori del Lager. Il resto era breve vacanza, o inganno dei sensi, sogno: la famiglia, la natura in fiore, la casa. Ora questo sogno interno, il sogno di pace, è finito, e nel sogno esterno, che prosegue gelido, odo risuonare una voce, ben nota; una sola parola, non imperiosa, anzi breve e sommessa. È il comando dell'alba in Auschwitz, una parola straniera, temuta e attesa: alzarsi, "Wstawać". (*LT*, I, p. 395)

(It is a dream within a dream, varied in detail, one in substance. I am sitting at a table with my family, or with friends, or at work, or in the green countryside, in short in a peaceful, relaxed environment, apparently without tension or pain; yet I feel a subtle and deep anguish, the definite sensation of an impending threat. And indeed as the dream proceeds, slowly or brutally, each time in a different way, everything falls and disintegrates around me, the scenery, the walls, the people, and the anguish becomes more intense and more precise. Now everything has changed to chaos: I am alone in the centre of a grey and turbid nothing, and see, I *know* what this means, and I also know that I have always known it: I am once more in the *Lager*, and nothing was true outside the *Lager*. The rest was a brief holiday, a deception of the senses, a dream: my family, nature in bloom, my home. Now this internal dream, the dream of peace, has finished, and in the external dream, which continues icily, I hear a well-known voice resound: a single word, not imperious, but brief and subdued. It is the dawn command in Auschwitz, a foreign word, feared and expected: get up, "Wstawać".)

This haunting conclusion sheds more light upon the text's title. For if nothing is real outside the *Lager*, then any respite is nothing more than a brief holiday, a deception of the senses, or a dream within a dream, that is, a *tregua*. This concluding word, 'Wstawać', echoes not only from *Se questo è un uomo* but also from the poem which opens *La tregua*, '11 gennaio 1946', which concludes in an identical way. The repetition of this word, the reverberation and recurrence of the language of the concentration camps, is acting as a frame or background for the main body of this text. What appears to be a post-Auschwitz text both begins and ends with its author inside Auschwitz. The post-Auschwitz, *tregua* world, which was originally referred to in the text as 'il Lager a rovescio' (*LT*, I, p. 232) has re-become 'il mondo alla rovescia' (the world overturned).[15] It is a re-becoming and a regression which is reflected in the connections which link the structures of the two works, with the seventeen chapters of *Se questo è un uomo* mirrored in the symmetrical seventeen chapters of *La tregua*. The circular progression of *La tregua* ends, not back at home, not in a new life of freedom, but back in the true home of the concentration camps, in the real world of no illusions and no respite. This is the true reality: Levi's *risveglio* of the concluding chapter is precisely an awakening to discover that the rest of the world is a dream, and only the nightmare of Auschwitz is real. The world of the concentration camps is not, therefore, over: liberation is an illusion and escape from the camps a delusion. As Levi wrote in *Se questo è un uomo*, which appears in retrospect to anticipate this moment of *La tregua*, 'guai a sognare: il momento di coscienza che accompagna il risveglio è la sofferenza piú acuta' (woe betide you if you dream: the moment of consciousness which accompanies the awakening is the most acute suffering) (*SQ*, I, p. 38).

Notes

1. 'Prefazione all'edizione scolastica di *La tregua*', in *Pagine sparse*, I, pp. 1141–1145 (p. 1145).
2. In his interview with Philip Roth entitled 'Salvarsi dall'inferno come Robinson', Levi specifically mentions his desire, whilst composing *La tregua*, to 'divertirmi scrivendo e divertire i miei futuri lettori', alluding also to *La tregua*'s emphasis on 'gli episodi piú strani, piú esotici, piú allegri' for the benefit of the readers. (*La Stampa*, 26 November 1986)

3. Fiora Vincenti, *Invito alla lettura di Primo Levi*, 1973, p. 100.
4. As Levi points out, *La tregua* was a unique text in its time since 'Nessuno aveva mai scritto che cos'era l'Unione Sovietica allora. Era una terra di nessuno, calpestata, distrutta, incendiata, torturata, devastata, massacrata nei suoi villaggi e nelle sue comunità, ma prodigiosamente ricca e feconda di fermenti come la terra dopo il diluvio. Per molti anni, dopo la guerra, nessuno ci era potuto andare; a nessuno era stato lecito guardare intorno e capire. A me era successo di vedere dal di dentro quell'immenso paese ubriaco di vittoria, pur con i suoi venti milioni di morti alle spalle'. (Taken from a typed outline of answers Levi gave at a conference at Zurich University, Switzerland, 8–12 November 1976, transcribed by Poli and Calcagno, 1992, p. 25).
5. My figures, not including the vast number of people who pass unnamed through the course of the text. Significantly, though, this is less than the number of named people to feature in *SQ* who total 89.
6. Poli and Calcagno, 1992, p. 95. The text is taken from a speech given by Levi at a conference in the Teatro Carignano, Turin, 19 November 1976.
7. There is only one contradiction to this which occurs when Levi strikes up a conversation, in Latin, with a priest in Cracow, of which he writes that: 'venimmo confusamente a parlare di tutto, dell'essere io ebreo, del Lager, [...] e di innumerevoli altre cose, a cui l'inusitata veste della lingua dava un curioso sapore di trapassato remoto'. (*LT*, I, p. 241) This is the only occasion in which the concentration camps are given a sense of belonging to the remote past, and since Levi himself attributes this to the ancient language he was using at the time, this quotation has been discounted from the theory outlined above as the evidence points almost unerringly towards the depiction of Auschwitz as belonging to the very recent past.
8. Laura Marcus, *Auto/biographical Discourses: Criticism, Theory, Practice* (Manchester: Manchester University Press, 1994) p. 151. What is, for some critics, Levi's 'detachment' has also been described as his 'incapacità di lasciarsi andare al presente' since Levi 'assiste alle storie *de haulte graisse* e le racconta, ma non le vive' (Cesare Cases, 'L'ordine delle cose e l'ordine delle parole', *Opere: Volume primo*, 1987, and Ferrero, ed., 1997, p. 23), and 'il narratore compare in queste pagine come un occhio che vede, un corpo che soffre, una mente che ironizza e giudica, ma non è mai protagonista' (Paolo Milano, 'La guerra quella di sempre', 21 April 1963).
9. Figures are my own. Descriptions of collective emotions run throughout the text.
10. See, in particular, Steinlauf, *SQ*, p. 35, Alfred L., pp. 89-90, and Jean, p. 105.
11. Along similar lines Fiora Vincenti writes of *LT* as: 'il libro del ritorno, inteso come travaglio interiore, lotta contro le memorie, resurrezione alla vita, dove gli episodi, i personaggi, gli incontri, le stesse tappe del viaggio stanno ad illustrare, in chiave emblematica, i momenti cruciali di quel doloroso itinerario che è appunto il recupero dell'io, della propria integrità umana, calpestata e avvilita dalle tremende ferite che ha dovuto subire' (1973, p. 100).
12. Jane Nystedt, 1993, p. 38. Nystedt provides the figures for these particular linguistic comparisons but does not provide any interpretation or analysis of these facts.
13. The figures that follow, and all remaining figures, calculations and analyses are my own.

14. It is important to note that even the moment of liberation from the concentration camps is not portrayed by Levi, or by many other survivors, as a happy one: Levi writes that 'l'ora della libertà suonò grave e chiusa'. (*LT*, I, p. 206); Elie Wiesel writes that 'strangely, we did not "feel" the victory. There were no joyous embraces, no shouts or songs to mark our happiness, for that word was meaningless to us. We were not happy. We wondered whether we would ever be'. (*All Rivers Run to the Sea*, 1997, p. 96), and André Laithier testifies that 'Il ricordo tragico dei nostri compagni perduti ci tolse la gioia della liberazione' (Vincenzo Pappalettera, ed., *Nei Lager c'ero Anch'io*, 1973, p. 386).
15. Levi's words to refer to the concentration camps, taken from Levi's preface to Bravo and Jalla, eds., *La vita offesa: Stora e memoria dei Lager nazisti nei racconti di duecento sopravvissuti*, 1988, p. 8, also in *Pagine sparse*, II, pp. 1347–50.

3
Storie naturali and *Vizio di forma*: 'I mostri generati dal sonno della ragione'[1]

The collections of short stories which constitute *Storie naturali* and *Vizio di forma* are Levi's first works of fiction. Although published in 1966 and 1971 respectively, the stories have wide-ranging dates of composition and were, in many cases, written long before their publication in these collections. Whilst the stories contained in *Vizio di forma* were written slightly nearer to the time of their publication, between 1968 and 1970, from the *Storie naturali* collection, 'I mnemagoghi' was composed in 1946; 'Il Versificatore', 'Censura in Bitinia' and an early version of 'Quaestio de Centauris' entitled 'Il centauro Trachi' were published in *Il Mondo* between May 1960 and August 1961; 'L'amico dell'uomo' appeared in *Il Mondo* in January 1962 and 'Angelica Farfalla' in August 1962; the five remaining NATCA stories were published individually in *Il Giorno* between 1964 and 1966; 'Il sesto giorno' was begun in 1946 and completed in 1957, and 'La bella addormentata nel frigo' finished in 1952.[2] Many of these stories therefore overlap in part with the composition of both *Se questo è un uomo* and *La tregua*, with the majority of the *Storie naturali* written prior to the publication of *La tregua*. Their date of publication as part of the *Storie naturali* is therefore deceptive as their inception, composition and, often, their previous publication is in the years immediately following *Se questo è un uomo*. The temporal contiguity of these works is fundamental in the tracing of the thematic echoes between them.

This chapter will examine *Storie naturali* and *Vizio di forma* together since they not only follow one another chronologically, in terms of publication, but also thematically, and have been published together, since 1996, as part of Levi's *I racconti* collection. The stories contained in the two texts are, on a superficial level, extremely different in content, tone and style from both *Se questo è un uomo* and *La tregua*. The autobiographical nature of Levi's writings has gone, to be replaced with works of invention, fantasy and, for the most part, futuristic fiction, a development which has necessitated an alteration of genre. The genre selected is that of the short story, a genre 'inherently suited to dealing with the unconventional, in relationships, in attitudes, in behaviour […], encouraging improvisation and experimentation'[3] which traditionally 'breaks up the familiar life-world of the everyday, defamiliarizes our assumption that reality is simply the conceptual construct we take it to be'.[4] Levi's charting of 'a reality which is essentially alien and baffling', which both confronts and challenges 'the 'irreality' of modern existence by positing alternative worlds'[5] to draw attention to the *vizi di forma* of contemporary life is therefore most aptly done through the medium of the short story. Whilst Levi's short stories often appear superficially light and playful, the apparently less sombre nature of these two collections may be due in part to the transition from testimony to fiction as well as to the contrast provided by previous knowledge of *Se questo è un uomo*. Levi's own comments about the stories encourage readers not to take them too seriously, describing them in Ernesto Ferrero's introduction to *Storie naturali* as 'racconti-scherzo' (joke-stories) (p. xii), yet the subject matter is not to be taken at face value since even a cursory reading of the stories would reveal their more serious side. Levi's treatment of this subject matter, his tone, manner and style of writing, often create the impression of playfulness, and what appears to be a lighter tone frequently comes through Levi's parody of styles and his ironic manipulation of other literary genres. In the *Storie naturali*, for example, 'Cladonia rapida' parodies scientific reports; 'L'ordine a buon mercato' mimics sales language; 'Il versificatore' mocks both the language of salesmen and the composition of poetry; 'Quaestio de centauris' parodies classical literary styles, and 'Il sesto giorno' satirizes formal business meetings. In *Vizio di forma*, 'Visto di lontano' mocks a scientific style of writing; 'Le nostre belle specificazioni' makes a mockery of bureaucratic language; the two 'Recuenco' tales provide ironic, futuristic stories of third world charity; 'Procacciatori d'affari' parodies the language of salesmen, and 'Lumini rossi', 'I sintetici', 'In fronte scritto' and 'Ottima è l'acqua' are ironic, futuristic horror stories.[6] Whilst this parody of different literary styles is occasionally interspersed with stories that cannot be interpreted ironically, and which are entirely sombre in their message, such as 'I mnemagoghi', 'Angelica farfalla', 'Versamina', 'Verso occidente' and 'Vilmy', the effect of Levi's use of parody throughout both collections is to create an air precisely of 'racconti-scherzo', of playfulness and frivolity.

In spite of the seemingly dramatic differences in content and style between the *Storie naturali*, *Vizio di forma* and Levi's two previous texts, the very fact that the composition of all these texts coincides offers 'a line of continuity between Levi's literary documents witnessing the Holocaust and his creations of fantasy'.[7] Thematic continuities between these collections and Levi's earlier works are, in places, evident; Levi was frequently asked whether *Storie naturali* and *Vizio di forma* were an allegorical or symbolic continuation of his writing on the concentration camps, but he tended to reply that he did not believe the works were connected, remarking, on different occasions, that:

> Io credo che c'entri in fondo abbastanza poco il fatto del Lager rivisitato, il fatto che i miei racconti riproducano, vogliano riprodurre

il mondo del Lager ravvisato nel mondo di oggi [...] può darsi che ci sia un [...] collegamento, ma non è che volessi farlo.[8]

(I believe that, all things considered, the issue of the *Lager* revisited has relatively little to do with it, the issue of whether my stories reproduce, or want to reproduce the world of the *Lager* perceived in today's world. [...] perhaps there is a [...] connection, but it is not deliberate.)

Le mie miniere sono piú d'una e diverse. [...] Certo, Auschwitz in certi racconti riaffiora, ma come eredità del profondo, non come deliberato proposito.[9]

(My sources are more than one and they vary. [...] Of course, Auschwitz resurfaces in some stories, but as a legacy from the depths, not as a deliberate intention.)

Molti mi hanno chiesto se nel dare forma narrativa alle smagliature piccole o grosse del nostro mondo e della nostra civiltà io volessi alludere di nuovo al Lager. Posso rispondere: deliberatamente no di certo; nel senso che scrivere deliberatamente di una realtà in termini simbolici non è nel mio programma.[10]

(Many people have asked me whether in giving narrative form to the faults both large and small in our world and our civilisation I wanted to allude to the *Lager* once more. In response I can say that deliberately, certainly not, in the sense that deliberately writing about a reality in symbolic terms is not part of my plan.)

However, whilst these collections of stories are by no stretch of the imagination merely a patent return to the issues raised in *Se questo è un uomo*, they do contain strong resonances of certain aspects of the Holocaust experience as portrayed within Levi's first text. Whether or not these echoes of his earlier text were deliberate or even conscious is immaterial, and also unprovable by the evidence available to us. The vital issue is whether there is enough evidence of them within the texts to bring *Se questo è un uomo* back from being an *eredità del profondo* into the forefront of the reader's mind again, operating as hypotext for these collections.

Storie naturali

Fifteen individual stories, highly varied in both style and genre, constitute the

Storie naturali, an obviously ironic title as indicated by the quotation from Rabelais' *Gargantua* which serves as epigraph to this collection. Levi's reference to Pliny's *Naturalis historia*, telling of 'des enfantements estranges et contre nature' (strange and unnatural births) (*SN*, I, p. 399), anticipates the real theme of Levi's short stories: the unnatural rather than the natural, a distortion in our moral universe and offences against the natural order of the world. Often considered as science fiction, the role of science is all-important in these stories, yet this is not a scientist's enthusiastic portrayal of the future wonders of technology. Instead, the *Storie naturali* portray characters whose lives have been, sometimes subtly, sometimes overtly, subverted by the scientific inventions and the technological developments which have occurred in this mainly futuristic setting. Levi's science here is warped and twisted, corrupt and corrupting, not striving to enhance human life or to uncover new mysteries of life or the universe, but rather to create anomalies of nature and aberrations of reason.

The science of the *Storie naturali* is often employed for profit, which in turn frequently culminates in the destruction of some elements of the characters' humanity. The six Simpson, or NATCA, stories which lie at the heart of the work emphasise this point as they highlight the dangers of the application of science for profit and the abuse of technological inventions designed to enhance human life. There is a progression through the course of these stories in the scale of the abuse, beginning with the relatively harmless over-reliance on the latest gadgetry, and culminating in the loss of all typically human characteristics after the inventions take over and destroy a life completely. Thus 'Il versificatore' assumes the human characteristic of poetic creativity precisely at the expense of the poet himself whose over-reliance on the machine leads to his inability to function without it, and in 'L'ordine a buon mercato' and 'Alcune applicazioni del Mimete' a sense of conscience is lost: 'Chi può vietarmi di infilare nel Mimete qualche grammo di atomi di carbonio, di riordinarli in onesto assetto tetraedrico, e di vendere il risultato? Nessuno: non la legge, e neppure la coscienza.' (Who can prevent me from slipping a few grams of carbon atoms into the Mimete, from reordering them into an honest tetrahedrical order and from selling the result? Nobody: neither the law nor my conscience) (*SN*, I, p. 451). It is precisely this lack of conscience that is at the root of the scientific disasters Levi describes: the innovations themselves are not necessarily unethical, immoral or evil, although realistically they are open to abuse, but they fall into the hands of fallible and corruptible men, men like Gilberto, who is 'un uomo pericoloso, un piccolo prometeo nocivo [...]. È un figlio del secolo [...], anzi, è un simbolo del nostro secolo' (a dangerous man, a harmful little Prometheus [...]. He is a child of our century [...], in fact, he is a symbol of our century) (*SN*, I, p. 461), the average man, acting predictably under the given circumstances. On taking possession of the *Mimete*, Gilberto is depicted as

Godlike and omnipotent, his acts of creating, or rather duplicating, described with Biblical references: 'il giorno seguente [...], il giorno dopo [...], il quarto giorno [...], il quinto giorno [...], il sesto giorno [...]', up to 'il settimo giorno mi riposai' (the following day; the day after; the fourth day; the fifth day; the sixth day; on the seventh day I rested) (*SN*, I, p. 451-3) as he employs the machine to duplicate first his wife and then himself, thus bypassing all natural, Divine laws. The invention in 'La misura della bellezza', the *Calometro*, prescribes beauty, thereby removing the natural act of decision-making from the observer, replacing it with a biassed judgement of what ought to be considered perfect, and therefore functioning mainly, as the narrator's wife comments, as a 'misuratore di conformità' (measurer of conformity) (*SN*, I, p. 502); in 'Pieno impiego' humans become abusers as Levi describes a situation in which, given the opportunity, another normal, unexceptional man can become an enslaver of whatever or whomever is considered to be a lesser or inferior species, even convincing themselves, as Simpson does here, that the enslaved are happy with their lot, that he is living in harmony with a lesser species, and that these creatures 'non sono condizionate: sono al mio servizio. Anzi, piú esattamente: abbiamo concluso un accordo' (they are not dependent: they are at my service. On the contrary, to be more precise, we have reached an agreement) (*SN*, I, p. 520). By the last of these six stories, 'Trattamento di quiescenza', the circle is complete as it is Simpson himself who is enslaved, the victim of the *Torec*, unable to continue his existence without it: 'senza Torec sarebbe perduto, col Torec è perduto ugualmente' (without the Torec he would be lost, with the Torec he is lost just the same) (*SN*, I, p. 567).

The science and technology of these stories are used for no positive ends, indeed the function and role of science throughout many of the *Storie naturali* is distorted. Levi's belief in the potential of science, 'la scienza, come figlia della ragione, può liberare l'umanità da buona parte delle sue sofferenze'[11] (science, as the daughter of reason, can liberate humanity from a good deal of its suffering) is here overturned as science causes rather than relieves much of mankind's suffering. The aberrant and morally questionable science of the *Storie naturali* is a science *alla rovescia* paradigmatic of 'il mondo alla rovescia' (the world overturned) of the concentration camps. There is considerable evidence to connect the perverted depiction of science *alla rovescia* here with that of the concentration camps, whether this be the distorted role of the prisoner-scientists in the camp's rubber factory which never produced an ounce of rubber,[12] or the scientific invention of the gas chambers. Levi's comment that 'siamo figli di quell'Europa dove è Auschwitz: siamo vissuti in quel secolo in cui *la scienza è stata curvata*, ed ha partorito il codice razziale e le camere a gas'[13] (we are the children of that Europe containing Auschwitz: we have lived in that century in which *science has been bent* and has produced the racial code and the gas chambers) is therefore applicable to the twisted role of science in the *Storie naturali*. Science remains *curvata* here, as one of the many after-effects of witnessing the unethical application of science for the destruction of humanity. The thematic recurrence of man's abuse of scientific developments in the *Storie naturali* must clearly be viewed as a continuation of an aspect of Levi's Holocaust experiences, then, for Levi's rewriting in this text of science *alla rovescia* is strongly linked to the aftermath of having experienced the application of science for evil within the concentration camp system.[14]

Similarly connected to Levi's previous experiences is another theme which recurs throughout a number of Levi's short stories here, that of slavery. The characters in twelve of the fifteen stories are enslaved in some way, whether they be slaves to the latest technology and gadgetry as in the six Simpson stories, slaves to the past as in 'I mnemagoghi', physically enslaved or imprisoned as in 'Censura in Bitinia', 'Angelica Farfalla', 'La bella addormentata nel frigo' and the centaur in 'Quaestio de centauris', or slave to a drug or chemical as in 'Versamina', highlighting not only the continuing importance of the issue of slavery in Levi's mind but also the fact that 'se rimangono decisive le sue [Levi's] testimonianze sugli orrori di Auschwitz, non è meno importante, oggi, denunciare il nuovo lager, nel quale l'uomo moderno sta imprigionando se stesso, insieme con il proprio universo'[15] (if Levi's testimonies to the horrors of Auschwitz remain crucial, it is no less important, today, to denounce the new *Lager*, in which modern man is imprisoning himself, together with his own universe). Like *Se questo è un uomo*, each of the tales dealing with aspects of enslavement here also shows the loss of some aspects of the humanity of those subjugated. This loss of the human in turn reflects the process of dehumanization Levi first described in *Se questo è un uomo*. The compromise and subsequent loss of the ability to create poetry in 'Il versificatore' is an extension of Levi's inability to recall and recite Dante's *Inferno* as portrayed within *Se questo è un uomo*. When the machine becomes indispensable to the poet, just as when the ability to assess beauty for oneself in 'La misura della bellezza' has been lost, it is as though 'non si può piú pensare, è come già essere morti' (one can no longer think, it is like being already dead) (*SQ*, I, p. 16), for the loss of the power of thought was, in *Se questo è un uomo*, one of the first steps towards the demolition of the prisoners' humanity. The loss of individual physical identity in 'Alcune applicazioni del Mimete', with the identical sets of duplicated Emmas and Gilbertos, is reminiscent of the indistinguishable appearance of the prisoners ('non c'è ove specchiarsi, ma il nostro aspetto ci sta dinanzi, riflesso in cento visi lividi' [there is nowhere to look at our reflection, but our appearance is right in front of us, reflected in a hundred livid faces] [*SQ*, I, p. 20]), whilst Simpson's sacrifice of 'le api, il lavoro, il sonno, la moglie, i libri' (the bees, his work, sleep, his wife, his books) (*SN*, I, p. 566), alongside his own identity and life to the *Torec* in 'Trattamento di quiescenza' constitutes a total loss of the self, strongly evocative in the advancement of his physical and mental degeneration of Levi's description of the typical camp prisoner, 'un uomo vuoto, ridotto a sofferenza e bisogno, dimentico di dignità e discernimento, poiché accade facilmente, a chi ha perso tutto, di perdere se stesso' (an empty man, reduced to suffering and need, oblivious to dignity and discernment, since it happens easily that he who has lost everything loses himself) (SQ, I, p. 21). Correspondingly dehumanised and likewise reduced to a state of 'sofferenza e bisogno' are the imprisoned victims of 'Angelica Farfalla' who undergo a similar transformation to that of the prisoners of the concentration camps, from men into beasts, in this case into vulture-like, enchained creatures, referred to as 'bestiacce' (foul beasts) (SN, I, p. 439), and in 'Versamina', as Kleber's addiction to the drug starts to take hold, he too adopts bestial behaviour, scratching himself 'in un modo feroce, come un cane' (in a ferocious manner, like a dog) (SN, I, p. 473). The physically imprisoned Patricia in 'La bella addormentata nel frigo' has her humanity compromised by her treatment at the hands of her 'owners', viewed as an object in the eyes of her guardians, whilst the guests who attend her annual birthday defrosting do so out of curiosity, firing questions at her as soon as she regains consciousness, enjoying her existence as an exhibition rather than as human life ('Si può guardare dallo spioncino del frigo?' [Can we look through the peep hole of the freezer?] [SN, I, p. 483]) and thus echoing, although to a lesser extent, Levi's treatment 'come [...] un cadavere in sala anatomica' (as [...] a cadaver in anatomical theatre) (SQ, I, p. 43) at the hands of his oppressors who referred to the prisoners simply as 'pezzi' (pieces) (SQ, I, p. 10).

The human characteristics lost in the *Storie naturali* are therefore lost in favour of a descent into a lower, more bestial state. There is a clear connection and continuity with *Se questo è un uomo* here, particularly in the stories which emphasise a process of metamorphosis through the characters' loss of human traits in favour of more animalistic characteristics. Whereas before it was the concentration camp system which brought about the metamorphosis of human beings into a primitive, degraded condition, in the *Storie naturali* it is often the over-dependence on, or blatant abuse of technology which brings about this de-evolution of man.

Levi is again focusing, then, on the dual nature of man, 'l'animale-uomo' (the human animal) (SQ, I, p. 83), as embodied in the figure of the centaur in 'Quaestio de centauris'. The convergence between the animate and inanimate, as well as between the human and the bestial, reverberates throughout the text, in various forms: 'Cladonia rapida' deals with the 'conturbante problema della convergenza in atto fra il mondo animato e il mondo inanimato' (the disturbing problem of the convergence underway between the animate world and the inanimate world) (SN, I, p. 446) and of the difficulties which arise when there is a 'sovrapposizione di una rudimentale volontà (o iniziativa) della macchina sulla volontà (o iniziativa) umana' (superimposition of a machine's rudimentary will (or initiative) over human will (or initiative) (*SN*, I, p. 445); in 'Quaestio de centauris' the fusion between the animate and the inanimate takes the form of hybrid creations as dolphins are born of a tuna fish and a cow, flies and flowers produce butterflies, toads and rocks engender turtles, and owls and mice create bats (*SN*, I, p. 506) alongside the hybrid centaur, Trachi, exemplar of the human/bestial divide. The inclusion of 'Quaestio de centauris' in this collection is also indicative of Levi's tendency to invert normal or accepted meanings, as with his transposition of the role of science. For here the Greek myth of the centaurs is turned *alla rovescia*: the centaur Eurytus' attempt to rape the Lapith bride has been reversed by Levi since in his tale it is a human who steals the object of a centaur's affections, human actions which provoke violence.[16] The figure of Trachi as a centaur is especially significant in this collection: not only does he personify the human-bestial conversion but he is also representative of Levi himself as suggested by Levi's frequent references to himself as a centaur:

> Io sono un anfibio, un centauro. [...] Io sono diviso in due metà. Una è quella della fabbrica, sono un tecnico, un chimico. Un'altra, invece, è totalmente distaccata dalla prima, ed è quella nella quale scrivo, rispondo alle interviste, lavoro sulle mie esperienze passate e presenti. Sono proprio due mezzi cervelli.[17]

> (I am an amphibian, a centaur. [...] I am divided into two halves. One half is that of the factory: I am an engineer, a chemist. The other half, however, is totally separate from the first, and is the half in which I write, respond to interviews, work on my experiences, past and present. They are really two half brains.)

The divided nature of the centaur is therefore emblematic of both Levi's professional partitioning and of the notion of human/bestial convergence common to much of Levi's writing.

The loss of the human in favour of the bestial continues to be one of the central themes in 'Angelica Farfalla' which takes this connection between animals and humans, as well as the theme of scientific abuse one step further. The failure of Professor Leeb's attempts at an enforced state of human evolution, and his deliberate misapplication of science which reduces the subjects concerned to a state of total bestiality, is perhaps Levi's most patent example of the consequences of the abuse of scientific knowledge. The irony of Levi's reversal of Dante's reference to 'l'angelica farfalla, / che vola a la giustizia sanza schermi'[18] (the angelic butterfly, / which flies unshielded to justice) to instead highlight the capacity of human beings to evolve in reverse away from the divine, back to a state of bestiality, is again a rewriting of his concentration camp experiences. Leeb is playing God, transgressing the boundaries of both his scientific knowledge and natural and ethical laws by employing genetic engineering to speed up the evolutionary process. This is an issue common to much of the text, for 'la lotta per la vita' (the battle for life) (*SQ*, I, p. 83) of *Se questo è un uomo* is here transformed into what is, for many of the characters, a struggle to control life, rather than to survive it, to reduce the bad in life and to enhance the good by any possible means. The characters in eleven of the fifteen stories are all pushing in different ways and with various means to make human life better, faster, easier, more efficient or longer. Thus Montesanto in 'I Mnemagoghi' is struggling to enhance his memory through smell; the chickens in 'Censura in Bitinia' work more efficiently than humans would in their place; the poet in 'Il versificatore' wishes to free himself from his boring tasks by using the computer instead of his own brain; Professor Leeb in 'Angelica Farfalla' wants to speed up the evolutionary process; the *Mimete* machine in both 'L'ordine a buon mercato' and 'Alcune applicazioni del Mimete' grants the power to duplicate quickly and with the minimum of effort; the *versamina* substance is intended to improve life by removing pain; Patricia in 'La bella addormentata nel frigo' has her life-span lengthened considerably while she is conscious of only the most interesting parts of it; the machine in 'La misura della bellezza' enables its owner to make rapid judgements; many of the insects in 'Pieno impiego' are employed to relieve Simpson of his gardening tasks, and the *Torec* in 'Trattamento di quiescenza' uses virtual reality to make available, again with the minimum of effort, the full range of human experiences and emotions. Instead of the battle for survival as depicted in *Se questo è un uomo*, *Storie naturali* portrays struggles to improve the level of survival itself.

However, the very blindness of this striving to improve and control the standard of life consistently comes, as we have seen, at the expense of the characters themselves, as they each, to a greater or lesser extent, compromise some element of their humanity. In the *Storie naturali*, many of the characters have lost sight of their conscience and have allowed the tools available or invented to improve their quality of life to be consistently over-used, against what ought to have been their better judgement. They have not used their power of reason or employed their scientific abilities morally and ethically to the benefit of the planet as a whole, instead their focus has been almost entirely on their own individual interests: Simpson, who succumbed to the lure of the *Torec* in spite of the guidelines for limits on its usage; the chickens in 'Censura in Bitinia', who are hired to help with the massive task of censorship, only to be allowed to take over entirely; or Gilberto's inability and unwillingness to resist the obvious temptations of the *Mimete* in 'Alcune applicazioni del Mimete'. It is precisely this lack of Aristotelian rationality and better judgement which confirms the loss of what Levi considered to be vitally and essentially human. The importance of the power of reason for Levi is highlighted most patently in the stories in which the characters' abuse of reason is punished most harshly. Such is the case in 'Versamina' in which 'questi credono di liberare l'umanità dal dolore, quelli di regalarle l'energia gratis, e non sanno che niente è gratis, mai: tutto si paga' (some believe they can liberate humanity from pain, others that they can bestow energy for free, and they do not realise that nothing is free, ever: everything must be paid for) (*SN*, I, p. 471) and in this instance the price paid is life. This chemical compound which upsets the natural order of life through the reversal of human reactions to pleasure and pain, intended as serious and important scientific research, culminates in the destruction of the human and animal lives it was intended to improve. The inventor of the *versamina* witnessed the devastating and horrific effects of his drug on animals and yet, against the advice of his colleagues to whom 'pareva che ce ne fosse abbastanza per andare cauti' (it appeared that there was enough reason to be cautious) (*SN*, I, p. 473), still takes the drug himself, just as Simpson was aware that 'occorre volontà e buon senso per non lasciarsi sopraffare' (it requires will and common sense to not allow yourself to be overwhelmed) (*SN*, I, p. 553) with the *Torec* but chooses to disregard the time limits at great personal cost.

It is not the science or technology that is always wrong in these stories, then, for the fault lies only too frequently with man and his use or abuse of the tools granted to him. It is precisely due to a lack of reason that many of the *Storie naturali*'s disastrous consequences occur, and Levi's depiction here of mankind in a state of degradation arises precisely through the Kantian philosophy that man's dignity comes through his ability to use practical reason, and to employ autonomy of will, which many of Levi's characters here are unable or unwilling to do. The stories' emphasis on the individual repercussions of the indiscriminate application of science, alongside the absence of reason which leads to the abuse of technology in the first place, is another factor which connects these stories to Levi's experiences in the concentration camps. In the *Storie naturali* Levi retains his initial commitment to showing the worst excesses mankind is capable of, to demonstrating the need for restraint and, above all, for reason:

> Del mio primo libro io mi servo per dimostrare dove si arriva quando s'imbocca la strada dell'intolleranza, quando s'incomincia a violentare l'uomo, quando le coscienze si lasciano sedurre e oscurare, quando si delega la propria volontà e si abdica al proprio giudizio e al proprio senso morale davanti al principio di autorità.[19]

(From my first book onwards I have worked to show where you end up when you turn down the street of intolerance, when you start to use violence against mankind, when consciences allow themselves to be seduced and obscured, when you delegate your own will and abdicate your own judgement and sense of morality when faced with the principle of authority.)

Scurani's comment that 'il campo di concentramento Levi lo ha sentito come un sistema quasi perfetto di condizionamento per ridurre l'uomo al 'sonno della ragione''[20] (Levi felt the concentration camp to be an almost perfect system of conditioning to reduce man to a 'sleep of reason') is also applicable here where the hunger for new technological developments leads to a comparable state of 'sonno della ragione'. The product of what was, for Levi, the ultimate 'sonno della ragione', the concentration camps, is evident in the thematic echoes of issues originally raised in *Se questo è un uomo* which recur here throughout this collection. The reappearance of the theme of imprisonment and of separation by a barbed-wire fence from the rest of the free world is a pivotal example. Montesanto in 'I Mnemagoghi' has, by choice, spent 22 years of his life detached from society without emerging from the darkened, isolated house where he carries out his research alone, without any form of human contact, whilst the characters in 'Il sesto giorno' are equally disconnected, in a different dimension to that of the planet whose species they are designing. In 'Trattamento di quiescenza' Simpson is enclosed in the 'virtual' prison contained within the *Torec*, and the victims of the experimentation in 'Angelica Farfalla' are physically imprisoned in a room, unable to communicate with their neighbours even through the window since this is kept firmly covered. The greatest degree of isolation, however, belongs to Patricia in 'La bella addormentata nel frigo', frozen for eternity for the benefit of scientific research, and defrosted once a year on special occasions so that she might bear witness to these memorable events in the future.

'La bella addormentata nel frigo' also serves as an example of the continuation of another of *Se questo è un uomo*'s themes, that of the sterility of time. For the 'tempo sterile e stagnante' (sterile and stagnant time) (*SQ*, I, p. 113) of the concentration camps, where 'il tempo passa goccia a goccia' (time passes drop by drop) (*SQ*, I, p. 16), 'giorni e mesi si riversavano torpidi dal futuro nel passato' (days and months flowed, turgid, from the future into the past) and 'la storia si era fermata' (history had stopped) (*SQ*, I, p. 113) is continued in several of the stories here. For Patricia, in the freezer, time is, quite literally, frozen: of her one hundred and sixty-three years of age, only twenty-three have been lived normally, the other one hundred and forty spent in a state of hibernation in which she has no sense of time passing, 'quanto al tempo trascorso in frigo, passa per noi, non per lei. In lei non lascia traccia, né nella memoria, né nei tessuti' (as for the time spent in the freezer, it passes for us, not for her. In her it leaves no trace, neither in memory nor in the tissues) (*SN*, I, p. 485), closely echoing Levi's words in *Se questo è un uomo* that 'Anche oggi [...], già non è piú un giorno, non ha lasciato traccia nella memoria di nessuno' (Even today [...], is already no longer a day, it has left no trace in anyone's memory) (*SQ*, I, p. 129). Simpson, in 'Trattamento di quiescenza' is also left with no sense of time as he lives his life vicariously through the cassettes in the *Torec*, and Montesanto in 'I Mnemagoghi' passes his life of semi-obscurity with no distinction between day and night, in a desperate attempt to recapture the past and relive it in the present: instead of experiencing the loss of a concept of future time, like the prisoners of the *Lager*, Montesanto makes deliberate efforts to twist the present into the past, to reverse the passage of time and recover his past. For many of the characters here, the phenomenon of futurelessness continues to be very much present.[21]

Without an awareness of the issues of atemporality and the lack of any possible future as they appear in *Se questo è un uomo*, the theme of futurelessness here would not be so evident or so pertinent. For the future, which in *Se questo è un uomo* 'ci stava davanti grigio e inarticolato, come una barriera invincibile' (faced us, grey and inarticulate, like an invincible barrier) (*SQ*, I, p. 113), is still unfeasible and even impossible in the *Storie naturali*. It is as though much in this third work of Levi's is still heading 'in viaggio verso il nulla, in viaggio all'ingiú, verso il fondo' (journeying towards nothingness, journeying downwards, towards the bottom) (*SQ*, I, p. 11), at the bottom of which lies the same probability of death Levi felt in the camps. However, whereas in *Se questo è un uomo* questions such as 'Quanti fra noi giungeranno vivi al nuovo anno? Quanti alla primavera?' (How many of us will make it alive to the new year? How many to spring?) (*SQ*, I, p. 132) indicate that any future was measured against the probability and proximity of death, this is clearly not the case in *Storie naturali*. Here futurelessness is measured against the quality of the future itself. Thus in those stories in which the quality of any future existence is seriously damaged, as in 'I mnemagoghi', 'Versamina', 'Il sesto giorno' and 'Trattamento di quiescenza', death appears as the often inevitable outcome of choices made. Kleber took the *versamina* fully aware that 'un grammo basta per rovinare un uomo' (one gram is enough to ruin a man) (*SN*, I, p. 473) and that there would be no prospect of his long-term survival; in the case of Simpson, 's'avvia verso la morte, *lo sa*' (he is heading towards death, *he knows it*) (*SN*, I, p. 567, my italics), but he is unable to end his addiction to the *Torec*; for Montesanto there is not even the desire to possess a future since 'non posso pensare che con orrore all'eventualità che anche uno solo dei miei ricordi abbia a cancellarsi' (I can only contemplate with horror the eventuality that even just one of my memories will be erased) (*SN*, I, p. 405), and at the end of 'Il sesto giorno' we are left with the distinct impression that there can be no hope of the survival of the newly-created human species since the choice which occurred here was to not consult the advisors. It is such a degree of choice which distinguishes this recurrent theme between the two texts, for whilst death and futurelessness hang as a permanent threat in *Se questo è un uomo*, here any lack of future is not enforced by others or by chance but appears as a direct consequence of a decision.

In the *Lager* 'il perdere la nozione del passato e del futuro' meant that 'si viveva all'istante, in un modo abbastanza animalesco'[22] (losing the notion of the past and the future meant that one lived in the instant, in a manner quite animalesque). Man cannot, in either *Se questo è un uomo* or *Storie naturali*, exist fully without the prospect of a tangible future. The lack of a full existence manifests itself in this text as a portrayal of mankind *alla rovescia*, as the characters in these stories are turned into a parody of their former selves. Thus the creation of Emma II and Gilberto II in 'Alcune applicazioni del Mimete' is a grotesque parody not only of the original two characters, but also of creation itself; when the roles of pain and pleasure are reversed in 'Versamina', Kleber becomes a poor imitation not merely of his former self but also of a human being; by the end of 'Il versificatore', the poet is only mimicking his former profession as he no longer writes poetry himself; Patricia makes a farce of life by living only the good parts and excluding the bad in 'La bella addormentata nel frigo'; and 'Il sesto giorno' makes a mockery of the creation of man, leaving mankind's invention to the whim of those at a board meeting. The degradation of man originally outlined in *Se questo è un uomo* is still, therefore, in evidence here as Levi 'in nome dell'umanesimo si oppone alla cosificazione e distruzione dell'uomo, ieri perpetrate in termini mostruosi dal nazismo e dalla Guerra, oggi, in forme di "assured" civiltà dalla scienza e dalla tecnica'[23] (in the name of Humanism places himself in opposition to the objectification and destruction of man, carried out yesterday by Nazism and the war, and commited today in the shape of the 'assured' civility of science and technology).

As in *Se questo è un uomo*, this distorsion of mankind and humanity is brought about through circumstances of violence and abuse, although here it is often a discreet, less apparent violence which suggests a continuation between the *Storie naturali* and *Se questo è un uomo*:

> Certamente un nesso c'è [fra le opere], anche se non è molto apparente. [...] E il nesso è l'uomo violentato. Violentata è la bella nel frigo: perché è nel frigo, perché è ridotta allo stato di un pezzo di ghiaccio e aspetta, una volta all'anno, di ritornare alla consapevolezza, alla coscienza. Violentato è l'uomo, a priori, ne Il sesto giorno [...] perché viene trattato come se fosse un motore d'automobile.[24]

> (Certainly there is a link [between the works], even if it is not very apparent. [...] And the link is mankind violated. The beauty in the freezer is violated: because she is in the freezer, because she is reduced to the status of a block of ice and she waits, once a year, to return to awareness, to consciousness. Man is also violated a priori in 'Il sesto giorno' [...] because he is treated as if he were a car engine.)

The violence and abuse against almost all the creatures mentioned throughout the stories does not stop at the examples given by Levi above. For Trachi, the centaur in 'Quaestio de Centauris', has his emotions violated by the owner with whom he has grown up; the creatures Simpson trains to work for him in 'Pieno impiego' have their independence stolen from them as they are treated like slaves; Simpson himself is abused by the company he spent his life working for when the present they give him as a retirement gift becomes his downfall, and the women at whom Simpson aims his camera in 'La misura della bellezza' have their privacy violated and invaded, to name but a few more examples. The acts of violence within the text are complex and take many forms, ranging from the subtle to the outrageous. Yet what is significant is not only that these differing degrees of violence are still present in Levi's work at this point, but that the aspects of human or animal life violated here are identical to those violated in the concentration camps. The themes within the *Storie naturali* of the exploitation of labour ('Censura in Bitinia' and 'Pieno impiego'), the violation of privacy ('La misura della bellezza'), the treatment of humans as objects ('Il sesto giorno' and 'La bella addormentata nel frigo'), death through scientific experimentation ('Angelica Farfalla'), the loss of the innate human gifts of creativity and reason ('Versamina', 'La misura della bellezza' and 'Trattamento di quiescenza') and the violent transformation of men into beasts ('Angelica Farfalla' and 'Versamina') are all, as they occur in this text, fictional extensions of the real-life issues raised in *Se questo è un uomo*. Levi's subject matter has not altered significantly, it has merely changed form, from autobiographical to fictional, from the issues of the concentration camp world to similar issues arising in a highly credible, fictitious world.

The *Storie naturali* provide another picture of mankind abused and violated, existing in a society pervaded by an accepted evil, in this case technology, which systematically destroys man. Here man is not so much mistreated by his fellow man, as in the case of *Se questo è un uomo*, but is rather defiling his own dignity, or allowing it to be defiled, by science and by new machines rather than by 'la grande *macchina* del Lager' (the great *machine* of the *Lager*) (SQ, I, p. 152, my italics). The *Storie naturali* are therefore a continuation of Levi's original depiction of mankind in crisis: not only has the natural order of things been disturbed in each of these stories, but somewhere along the line man has always allowed his judgement to be swayed, and his sense of conscience to be overtaken by a desire and a passion for science. The concluding quotation of 'Versamina', 'fair is foul, and foul is fair' (SN, I, p. 476), a key theme of so many of the *Storie naturali*, is also precisely the line which most irrevocably connects *Storie naturali* to *Se questo è un uomo*: the world of reversals, of abnormality and of transgressions of ethics and values, a world turned upside down, is a continuing portrayal of 'il mondo alla rovescia'.

Vizio di forma

The principal themes of *Vizio di forma* do not differ greatly from those of *Storie naturali*. Comparable misapplications of science occur here in the twenty stories which constitute the *Vizio di forma* collection, which occasionally expand in scope to embrace the collective repercussions, for both society and the planet, as well as the wider-ranging and potentially catastrophic ecological and humanitarian effects of Levi's original ideas. Levi's focus remains strongly on the human as he continues his exploration of 'alcuni aspetti dell'animo umano' (some aspects of the human mind) (*SQ*, I, p. 5): in *Vizio di forma*, as in *Storie naturali*, the repercussions for humanity of the abuse of reason with regard to science and technological progress take priority over the importance of the inventions or developments taking place. As with the previous collection, the stories of *Vizio di forma* contain a range of thematic continuities with *Se questo è un uomo*, more patent and often more significant in some stories than in others. The themes of the concentration camps which resonate in this collection are not identical to those in *Storie naturali*: several of the vaguer thematic echoes to recur in *Storie naturali*, such as slavery, imprisonment, a sense of timelessness and the loss of human characteristics are here, in the later collection, frequently more focussed on increasingly precise issues like tattoos ('In fronte scritto'), starvation (the two 'Recuenco' stories) and the potentially harmful effects of various food sources ('Vilmy', 'Ottima è l'acqua', 'Recuenco: il rafter'). It is worth examining in detail those stories here which contain both the more general and the specific resonances of the concentration camps.

In the first story in the collection, 'Protezione', Levi depicts a population apparently at constant risk from falling meteorites, surviving in the obligatory armour legislated by the government for protection. The echoes of Levi's first text are particularly in evidence here: the characters are living in a state of perpetual nervous tension with the tangible danger of the meteorites, akin to Levi's statement in *Se questo è un uomo* that 'mi sento minacciato, insidiato, ad ogni istante sono pronto a contrarmi in uno spasimo di difesa' (I feel threatened, besieged, ready at any moment to draw myself into a spasm of defence) (*SQ*, I, p. 32), and the effect of the *corazza* regulation is one of uniformity, with the entire population dressed identically, much resembling the world where 'tutti sono vestiti a righe' (everyone is dressed in stripes) (*SQ*, I, p. 27). The underlying issue is again one of abuse, in this case the violation of people's rights. For with a total lack of concrete evidence of any real danger from the meteorites, the need for *corazzas* is legislated primarily for the financial profit of the manufacturers; mankind here is manipulated and controlled by those in power, living with the fear of both possible meteorites and potential punishment for failing to comply with legislation.

Several of the stories in this collection echo this theme of human lives being subjected to the dominance of others, whether it be the domination of the red lights in 'Lumini rossi', the assumption of control by the inanimate telephone network in 'A fin di bene', the tyranny of the *vilmy* over its owner, or the manipulation and destruction of a starving population in the two Recuenco stories. The characters in these tales have little personal power over important decisions in their lives since their rights are violated by the people, animals, or objects with supremacy over them. Just as in the *Storie naturali* Simpson was a slave to the *Torec* and Kleber to the effects of the *versamina*, in *Vizio di forma* Paul Morris is enslaved to the whims and milk of the *vilmy* as much as Luigi is at the mercy of the lights and Maria of the inspections in 'Lumini rossi'. They are all, in their different ways, entrapped, and are as incapable of free choice as those whose 'ogni [...] azione è, a tempo e luogo, sensibilmente l'unica possibile' (every [...] action is, given the time and place, the only one possible) (*SQ*, I, p. 94).

'Verso occidente' and 'Procacciatori d'affari' are the antitheses of these other tales, both featuring characters who make independent, positive choices about their own lives.[25] Paradoxically, these characters bear comparison to Levi's depiction of concentration camp prisoners to the same extent as those deprived of choices outlined above. The issue of the right to make decisions in one's own life as demonstrated here (in 'Procacciatori d'affari' the decision of the as-yet-unborn spirit to be born fairly, randomly and without preferential treatment, and in the case of 'Verso occidente' the preference of the Arunde tribe to decline medical and chemical intervention with their suicidal tendencies) are examples of precisely the rights of choice denied prisoners in the concentration camps. The members of the Arunde tribe who reject the scientists' offer of a drug to relieve their suicidal tendencies, declaring that 'preferiamo la libertà alla droga, e la morte all'illusione' (we prefer freedom to drugs, and death to illusion) (*VF*, I, p. 587) have the freedom to select life or death for themselves: the continuation of their existence is, as much as possible, of their own choosing. Similarly, the spirit in 'Procacciatori d'affari' opts for no advantageous circumstances of birth, choosing to live by chance and at random, but beyond external control, making the positive choice, like the narrator of 'Il fabbro di se stesso', to 'costruirsi dalle radici' (build himself up from the roots) (*VF*, I, p. 625), freely and independently. To those in power in 'Procacciatori d'affari', human bodies are merely a marketable item to be sold to the souls: human beings here are perceived and treated as objects, with human bodies described as 'la veste umana', 'abito umano' (the human garment; human clothing) (*VF*, I, p. 624), echoing the 'pezzi', or 'merce di dozzina' (pieces; cheap merchandise) of *Se questo è un uomo* (*SQ*, I, p. 10-11). It is an objectification of humanity which occurs more than once in *Vizio di forma* and which has its roots firmly in Levi's experiences of dehumanisation in the *Lager*. Its clearest manifestation is perhaps in 'Psicofante' where the eponymous machine analyses and categorises the party guests, classifying them as a variety of things from a plate of food, to a cloud or a pot of paint, thus transforming what it judges to be the essence of a human being into an object. It is interesting to note that the party guests here behave in a similar manner to those in 'La bella addormentata nel frigo' in *Storie naturali* in the sense that they too are unaware of any process of dehumanisation at work and are ignorant of the act of violence implied by this machine that they are employing for entertainment.

In the two stories that follow 'Psicofante', 'Recuenco: la Nutrice' and 'Recuenco: il rafter', human beings are again dealt with as though insignificant. As alternative sides of the same tale, it is the second perspective, 'il rafter', which is particularly significant as we see how the priorities on the mission are apparently wrong: the 'rafter costa piú di una missione lunare, e il latte costa quasi niente' (the *rafter* costs more than a mission to the moon, and the milk costs almost nothing); and the workers are given 'solo tre minuti per scaricarlo [il latte]: anche se se ne spreca un poco, non importa; l'essenziale è che non si perda tempo' (only three minutes to unload it [the milk]: even if a little gets spilt, it doesn't matter; the important thing is that you don't waste time) (*VF*, I, p. 699). There is no compassion on the part of those working on the *rafter* towards the starving villagers; they are portrayed as insects, as 'formiche in un formicaio scoperchiato' (ants in an uncovered anthill) (*VF*, I, p. 700) and their human rights are completely disregarded. Yet those distributing the milk are simply doing their job, with as little care as the prison guards at Auschwitz who were also merely performing 'il loro ufficio di ogni giorno' (their everyday duty) (*SQ*, I, p. 14). The echoes in the Recuenco stories of Levi's experience in the concentration camps are not limited simply to the inhumane treatment of the starving. It is also significant that the over-consumption of this creamy milk, the very thing which is supposed to act as a form of nourishment, swells up the stomach and results in death. Levi provides us in these tales with a picture of milk turned bad, poison instead of nourishment which precisely equates with the meaning of the pseudonym Levi originally employed for the publication of *Storie naturali*, Damiano Malabaila. Not only is the depiction here of the starving devouring the milk, 'tutti lo ingoiavano avidamente, raccogliendolo da terra con le mani, con le pale, con foglie di palma' (they all swallow it avidly, gathering it up from the ground with their hands, with their shovels, with palm leaves) (*VF*, I, p. 693), reminiscent of Levi's descriptions of eating in Auschwitz, where the prisoners ate 'in piedi, furiosamente, scottandoci la bocca e la gola, senza il tempo di respirare' (on our feet, furiously, burning our mouths and throats, without time to breathe) (*SQ*, I, p. 71), but it provides another example of food which does not perform its basic task of providing nourishment: like the daily soup in the camps, it is worthless and deprived of its fundamental role.

Equally deprived of its function as a sustainer of life is the water in 'Ottima è l'acqua', steadily contaminated until its viscosity increases to the point where it causes plantlife and humans to die. In *Se questo è un uomo* water has a similarly sinister role to play, causing identical symptoms to those in the two Recuenco stories: severe diarrhoea and swelling of the stomach, resulting in dehydration and often death. The water here 'emanava il solito leggero odore palustre' (emanated the usual light swamp-like odour) (*VF*, I, p. 735), whilst that of Levi's first work 'è inquinata', 'non è potabile', and 'ha odore di palude' (is poisoned; is not drinkable; has the odour of a swamp) (*SQ*, I, p. 16), exactly the same smell Boero describes in 'Ottima è l'acqua' and the same term as is employed in 'Verso occidente' with reference to the sea, 'la palude' (the swamp) (*VF*, I, p. 587). The sources of water described in both *Vizio di forma* and *Se questo è un uomo* are therefore identical: corrupted and impure, harmful rather than beneficial and essential to human life, our very lifeforce gone bad. The water of *Vizio di forma* can therefore have greater meaning conferred upon it precisely in the light of Levi's first text. The toxicity of these waters consistently creates an infernal image of the world: in *Se questo è un uomo* Levi's discovery that the camp water is undrinkable coincides exactly with his conclusion that 'questo è l'inferno' (this is Hell) (*SQ*, I, p. 16) and by the end of 'Ottima è l'acqua', when waters are contaminated the world over, we are left a similarly infernal image of the world, with the survival of the whole planet in question.

The 'incertezza del domani' (uncertainty of tomorrow) (*SQ*, I, p. 11) as portrayed in *Se questo è un uomo* is echoed here, then, for it can only be a matter of time before life as portrayed in 'Ottima è l'acqua' rushes headlong into extinction. In 'Vilmy' also, time is ticking away until death; the *vilmy* are 'affascinati dagli orologi' (fascinated by clocks) (*VF*, I, p. 633) and Paul Morris, drugged by the power of the *vilmy*'s milk, yet another example within *Vizio di forma* of a destructive and deadly milk, will be addicted 'per tutti gli anni che [...] restano, che non possono essere tanti' (for all his remaining years, which cannot be very many) (*VF*, I, p. 633). 'Nel Parco' deals with a similar theme, but in this case time is non-existent as the literary characters exist in a kind of limbo which is unlikely to become a permanent state of being unless they or their authors are particularly famous. Once forgotten they fade, quite literally, into oblivion, with no prospect of any future. As was the case for both *La tregua* and *Storie naturali*, any concept of a future here in *Vizio di forma* often remains improbable, short-lived, and barely anticipated. This concept of time, the inability to perceive future time, or to dare to trust in its possibility, is a clear consequence of the concentration camp system.

'Nel Parco' and its precursor, 'Lavoro creativo', contain some of the clearest thematic connections with *Se questo è un uomo*. When Antonio's fictional character, James Collins, pays him a visit in 'Lavoro creativo', he tells of the Parco Nazionale, a world for literary characters where he and his contemporary characters are always 'ultimi alla distribuzione degli abiti e delle scarpe, ultimi all'assegnazione dei cavalli, ultimi alla coda della biblioteca, delle docce e della lavanderia' (last for the distribution of clothes and shoes, last for the allocation of horses, last in the queue for the library, the showers and the laundry) (*VF*, I, p. 653), the act of queueing for clothes, shoes and showers reflecting the world where 'bisogna mettersi in fila per cinque, a intervalli di due metri fra uomo e uomo' (you need to put yourselves in lines of five, with a distance of two metres between each man) (*SQ*, I, p. 16). In the Parco Nazionale, there is a lack of food, as well as levels of hierarchy which mirror those of the camp system. In the park, as in the concentration camp, there are officials in military dress, ration cards for food, clothes, shoes and cigarettes and a guarded perimeter fence, although the fence here appears to serve a protective rather than an oppressive function. In both the *Lager* and the park new arrivals need to undergo an initiation procedure before admittance to their new world; both locations are totally cut off from an outside world that knows nothing of their existence; there is no escape from either place except through death: either a physical death, or a metaphorical death in the memory of those outside; and there are frequent disappearances. The park is a similarly incomprehensible, upside-down world in which, as in Auschwitz, new arrivals are advised that 'è meglio che lei non cerchi qui un'immagine del mondo che ha lasciato' (it is better that you don't search for an image of the world left behind here) for this is a 'variopinta, pigmentata e distorta' (multi-coloured, pigmented and distorted) (*VF*, I, p. 676) version of Antonio's previous existence, another 'mondo alla rovescia'. The Parco Nazionale is a rewriting of the concentration camp: a fictional, alternative variation, removed of the horrors of Levi's previous, original version, but one which still functions within many of the same parameters.

It is along similar lines that two of the other stories from *Vizio di forma*, 'I sintetici' and 'In fronte scritto', proceed. Whilst dealing, to a lesser extent, with issues that arose in *Se questo è un uomo*, these stories also provide fictitious surroundings for an alternative interpretation of certain aspects of Levi's concentration camp experience. 'In fronte scritto', in which a young couple have their foreheads tattooed for marketing purposes, expands on the issue of the tattoos enforced upon the prisoners of the camps. Whilst the characters in this story make the choice to be tattooed, in effect renting out their foreheads, they are still described as 'marcata come si fa coi vitelli' (branded as you do with calves) (*VF*, I, p. 728) and 'gente segnata' (marked people) (*VF*, I, p. 730), indicating an act of dehumanisation which to a certain extent reflects that of the prisoners. The experience of this marketing experiment is not easily forgotten: the scars and, in some cases the original tattoo, remain even after their attempted removal, and children subsequently born to the tattooed couple are born 'marked' too, with parallels which can be drawn with the children of concentration camp survivors, comparably marked by their parents' past. In 'I sintetici', the young boy at the heart of the story, Mario, is singled out for precisely the opposite, for being 'unmarked' by his lack of a navel. He suffers a gradual progression of discrimination and isolation, until he eventually becomes a total outcast, simply because of the circumstances of his allegedly unnatural conception in a test tube. Mario is treated as an inferior being by his classmates because of his origins, an experience which is overtly and transparently connected to Levi's own life. Mario's classmates view him as an interesting biological experiment ('Mario mi interessa. Mi interessa vedere quello che fa', [Mario interests me. I'm interested in seeing what he does] [*VF*, I, p. 593]), evocative of both 'La bella addormentata nel frigo' and of Levi's description of his own treatment in the concentration camp hospital. In this tale, as in *Se questo è un uomo* and in so many of the short stories examined thus far, characters are dehumanised through the treatment they suffer at the hands of others, reduced to lesser beings in the eyes of their fellow creatures as if they were truly unreal, inferior and 'synthetic' as the title of this story suggests.

Mario, like numerous other characters within *Vizio di forma*, is detached from a collective, united society, living instead alone and 'different', in a society of individuals. As Walter commented in 'Verso occidente': 'l'umanità ha voltato le spalle alla natura, da un pezzo: è fatta di individui, e punta tutto sulla sopravvivenza individuale' (humanity turned its back on nature some time ago: it's made up of individuals, and focuses everything on individual survival) (*VF*, I, p. 583). Aside from the conditions of life itself, there is little difference between the society portrayed here and that of the concentration camps where 'ognuno è disperatamente ferocemente solo' (everyone is desperately ferociously alone) (*SQ*, I, p. 84). It is this aberrant and anomalous society that constitutes the *vizio di forma* of the title and which provides much of the air of rarely specified unease in the stories. It is, in fact, precisely as though 'qualcuno da qualche parte ha sbagliato, ed i piani terrestri presentano una faglia, un vizio di forma' (someone somewhere made a mistake, and the earthly plains are showing a fault, a procedural flaw) (*VF*, I, p. 623), for the worlds portrayed here all have 'qualche smagliatura' (some defects) (*VF*, I, p. 617). Our planet described from afar in 'Visto di lontano' refers to the 'periodo anomalo' (anomalous period), from 1939-1945, which 'è stato caratterizzato da numerose deviazioni dalla norma terrestre' (is characterised by numerous deviations from the earthly norm) (*VF*, I, p. 607) and deviations from the norm are the main topic of *Vizio di forma*. These anomalies are at times downright disastrous, as in 'Ottima è l'acqua', and at others merely disconcerting, as in 'Ammutinamento' where the trees agree to rebel against humans and to uproot themselves, seeking freedom away from mankind's neglect and abuse. The characters living alongside these aberrations are lost and confused, struggling to cope and unable to work together for their common good. They are not at all dissimilar from Levi's earlier description of himself and his fellow prisoners: 'siamo rotti, vinti: anche se abbiamo saputo adattarci' (we are broken, beaten: even if we have learnt how to adapt) (*SQ*, I, p. 146).

In *Vizio di forma*, as in *Se questo è un uomo*, it is the deviant conditions of life which frequently culminate in the ultimate loss of man's dignity, as mankind is compelled to shed something of its humanity in order to continue to adapt and survive. As Santagostino has noted, it is not just that the human characters in these stories have lost elements of their humanity, for there is a parallel process at work here through which the forfeiture of human characteristics results in the animation and progressive humanisation of the previously inanimate.[26] Thus the telephone network in 'A fin di bene' changes from an anonymous system to la Rete, endowed with its own name, powers of thought and authority; the trees in 'Ammutinamento' learn to communicate amongst themselves and make the decision to move away from mankind; in 'Psicofante' the machine has the power to assess and categorise human beings, and the *Golem* in 'Il servo' has a brain as complex as that of its inventor. The investment of inanimate objects with human qualities which occurs simultaneously with the dehumanisation of living beings is precisely what occurred in *Se questo è un uomo* also. In the former text, Levi's portrayal of machinery and the camp itself as more alive than the prisoners, resounds throughout *Se questo è un uomo*, exemplified by statements such as 'nulla è vivo se non macchine e schiavi: e più quelle di questi' (nothing is alive except for machines and slaves, and the former more so than the latter) (*SQ*, I, p. 67), by the fact that the paths and buildings of the camp are invested with identical names to those of the prisoners, that is numbers, and by the prisoners' perception of the dredger performing the human act of eating (*SQ*, I, p. 69). In both *Vizio di forma* and *Se questo è un uomo*, then, humanity's degradation is often accentuated precisely through the animation of the inanimate.

The process of mankind's debasement here, as in the *Storie naturali*, offers another picture of both life and the human species parodied: the figure of the *Golem* in 'Il servo' is a mechanical extension of the duplication of Emma and Gilberto by the *Mimete* machine: it is an obscene parody of any natural process of creation, whilst the futuristic vision of life in 'Protezione' and 'Lumini rossi' makes a mockery of any quality of existence. The characters struggle to retain their dignity and battle through differing levels of degradation to, again, 'salvare almeno lo scheletro, l'impalcatura, la forma della civiltà' (save at least the skeleton, the scaffolding, the shape of civilisation) (*SQ*, I, p. 35). Yet Levi frequently reiterates that we do not have to give our consent to living this way: we do not have to live a life controlled by those in a position of power (as in 'Protezione', 'Lumini rossi' 'Recuenco: La nutrice' and 'Recuenco: il rafter'), or make bad, irreversible choices in an attempt to make life better ('Vilmy', 'In fronte scritto'), for we have the ability to make positive, free choices (as in 'Verso occidente', 'Procacciatori d'affari', 'Il fabbro di se stesso', and 'Il servo'). Levi's belief in the power of man's reason remains strong in this collection: we do not have to march on slowly and unthinking, taking 'un passo avanti' (a step forwards) ('Eran cento', epigraphic poem to *Vizio di forma*, p. 569) regardless of where these steps will end, for we are, still, in possession of 'la facoltà di negare il nostro consenso' (the power to withhold our consent) (*SQ*, I, p. 35), and can choose, protest and object to our fate, much like the *Golem* who rejects certain tasks, accepting only those which 'richiedono coraggio e valentia' (require courage and ability) (*VF*, I, p. 714). It is, in fact, precisely when we consent to the deviations from the norm as revealed within *Vizio di forma*, and when we continue to march on regardless, that 'al termine della catena, sta il Lager' (at the end of the chain is the *Lager*) (*SQ*, I, p. 5), the greatest *vizio* of all. Levi himself remarked of the stories in *Vizio di forma* that:

> Non le pubblicherei se non mi fosse accorto [...] che fra il Lager e queste invenzioni una continuità, un ponte esiste: il Lager, per me, è stato il piú grosso dei "vizi", degli stravolgimenti [...], il piú minaccioso dei mostri generati dalla ragione.[27]
>
> (I would not publish them if I hadn't realised [...] that a bridge, a continuity exists between the *Lager* and these inventions: the *Lager*, for me, was the biggest of all "faults", of all distortions [...], the most threatening of all the monsters generated by reason.)

Vizio di forma is therefore another version of mankind surviving, or attempting to survive, in the conditions created by the aberration of reason which was, as referred to in this text, the 'cumuli di cadaveri scheletriti ai piedi di un rogo, in una tetra cornice di fumo e di filo spinato' (masses of skeletal corpses at the foot of a pyre, in a dismal frame of smoke and barbed wire) (*VF*, I, p. 624). The concentration camp is simply the most extreme example of the *vizi di forma* Levi is outlining here. The basic, fundamental idea remains the same: man abused by man, as well as by his own creations, and by his mistreatment of the world around him. *Vizio di forma* is an extension of *Se questo è un uomo*'s representation of man's existence and ability to cope in extreme circumstances, and his skill in adapting to these conditions at the expense of human nature itself. As such, *Vizio di forma* is both a continuation and a fictional rewriting of Levi's original portrayal of mankind in crisis. The inspiration for writing persists unaltered here, for the 'mondo alla rovescia' (the world overturned) has not been righted yet and the fact that mankind appears not even to notice is, in itself, a *vizio di forma*.

Notes

1. Sections of this chapter have been previously published in 'The Perversion of a Fairy Tale: Primo Levi's 'La bella addormentata nel frigo'', *Modern Language Review*, April 2005.
2. These dates of publication and composition are provided by Marco Belpoliti in the *Note ai testi* of *Opere 1*, pp. 1375-1469.
3. Valerie Shaw, *The Short Story: A Critical Introduction*, 1983, p. 223.
4. Charles E. May, 'The Nature of Knowledge in Short Fiction', in Charles E. May, ed., *The New Short Story Theories*, 1994, pp. 131-43, p. 137.
5. Shaw, 1983, p. 229.
6. Several of these examples have been previously noted by Pier Vincenzo Mengaldo, 'Lingua e scrittura in Primo Levi', introduction to Levi's *Opere III.*, 1990, p. LVI, and in Ferrero, ed., 1997, p. 215-216.
7. Klein, Ilona, '"Official Science Often Lacks Humility": Humor, Science and Technology in Levi's *Storie naturali*', published in Tarrow, 1990, pp. 112-126, p. 113. Several critics have already focussed, to a greater or lesser extent, on some of the aspects of *SN* and *VF* which echo elements of *SQ*. (See, in particular, Santagostino's 'Nuove prospettive nell'interpretazione della narrativa fantascientifica di Primo Levi', *Narrativa*, January 1993, and Walter Mauro's 'Primo Levi: La sorte dell'uomo, dalla testimonianza dei Lager nazisti al futuro della civiltà tecnologica nella satira fantascientifica', in Grana, ed., *Letteratura italiana. Novecento: I contemporanei, VII*, 1979.) This chapter will endeavour to expand these ideas and to provide further, original suggestions of the ways in which these aspects recur.
8. Grassano, 1981, p. 10, and in Belpoliti, 1997a, p. 176.
9. Levi's words spoken at a conference in Zurich, 8-12 November 1976, entitled 'Esperienze di uno scrittore', transcribed in Poli and Calcagno, 1992, p. 54-5.
10. Levi's words spoken at a conference at the Teatro Carignano, Turin, 19 November 1976, transcribed in Poli and Calcagno, 1992, p. 96.
11. Levi's words to Claudio Toscani, 'Incontro con Primo Levi', *Il Ragguaglio Librario*, no. 3, 1972.
12. See *SQ*, I, p. 137.
13. Levi's words spoken at a conference entitled 'Deportati anniversario' in 1955, published in Cavaglion, ed., *Primo Levi per l'Aned: l'Aned per Primo Levi*, 1997, p. 19, my italics.
14. Levi is not the only survivor to have written of the perversion of science for evil in the concentration camps. Physicians Lucie Adelsberger and Olga Lengyel also write in their testimonies of how medicine and medical research were distorted, abused and mis-used in the camps.
15. Giorgio Calcagno, 'Ancora un Lager per Primo Levi', *Il nostro tempo*, 18 April 1971.
16. This reversal of the Greek myth has also recently been noted by Bianchini, 2000, p. 70.
17. Edoardo Fadini, 'Primo Levi si sente scrittore 'dimezzato'', *l'Unità*, 4 January 1966, also published in Belpoliti, 1997a, pp. 106-109.
18. *Divina Commedia, Purgatorio*, Canto X, 125-6.
19. Levi's words to Paolo Spriano, 'L'avventura di Primo Levi', *l'Unità*, 14 July 1963.

20. Alessandro Scurani, 'Primo Levi', *Scrittori italiani*, 1983, p. 48. Also published as 'Le tre anime di Primo Levi' in *Letture*, 38, 1983.
21. Mauro writes that 'La prospettiva del futuro in sfacelo pertanto diventa un tema di fondo sul quale la fantasia poetica di Levi cerca di esercitarsi, fornendo dati di sostegno, ma al contempo definendo la posizione dell'intellettuale traumatizzato da eventi sconvolgenti che la razionalità del chimico non solo non riesce ad eliminare, ma addirittura utilizza come esasperazione e dilatazione del reale.' (Walter Mauro, 'Primo Levi: La sorte dell'uomo, dalla testimonianza dei Lager nazisti al futuro della civiltà tecnologica nella satira fantascientifica', in Grana, ed., *Letteratura italiana: Novecento*, 1979) p. 6892.
22. Levi's words from a television interview with Beniamino Placido, 27 October 1983, transcribed by Poli and Calcagno, 1992, p. 186.
23. Armando La Torre, 'La fantascienza umana di Primo Levi', in *Letteratura e communicazione*, 1971, p. 274.
24. Levi's words spoken in an interview with Ugo Buzzolan, 'Primo Levi: Come scongelare la bella ragazza dopo cent'anni', *La Stampa*, 13 January 1978. It must also be significant that several of the acts of violence ('La bella addormentata nel frigo', 'Angelica Farfalla' and 'Versamina') take place in Germany, 'il paese della violenza [...] è proprio, come dire [...] una vendetta che mi sono preso'. (This is part of Levi's answer to the question of why he chose to site the most violent of these *storie* in Germany. Taken from 'Primo Levi: Conversazione con Daniela Amsallem, [Turin: 15 July 1980], published in Belpoliti, 1997b).
25. 'Verso occidente' is an unusual case since it features both characters who make the positive choices referred to above as well as the character of Walter who does not choose his own death but has it forced upon him by the lemmings he is attempting to save.
26. See Santagostino, 'Nuove propettive nell'interpretazione della narrativa fantascientifica di Primo Levi', *Narrativa*, 1993, pp. 13, 14, 18-23.
27. Ernesto Ferrero, Introduction to *I Racconti: Storie naturali, Vizio di forma, Lilit*, p. xiii.

4
Il sistema periodico:
'L'uomo salvato dal suo mestiere'[1]

It was 1959 by the time the English scientist Charles Percy Snow's paper on 'The Two Cultures' had been translated into Italian, setting in motion a polemic which was to feature strongly in literary and scientific debates for more than a decade. Snow's insistence that science and the humanities were two separate, entirely oppositional, cultures, and that the former was inherently superior to the latter was vehemently contested by Frank Raymond Leavis only a couple of years later who maintained the opposite, that is, that the two cultures complemented each other and ideally ought to be considered as one. By 1966, Levi had already established his bipolar position[2] within the debate with his combined career as writer and scientist and with the publication of the literary and scientific *Storie naturali*. Levi's remarks to Giuseppe Grassano, published in 1981, are a case in point:

> Se viviamo in un mondo impregnato di tecnologia e di scienza, è sconsigliabile ignorarlo, anche perché la Scienza, con la S maiuscola, e la Tecnologia, con la T maiuscola, sono delle formidabili fonti d'ispirazione. Oltre che esistere e dover pure rispecchiarsi in qualche modo nella parola scritta, sono, a mio parere [...] degli stimoli formidabili.[3]

> (If we live in a world permeated with technology and science, it is unadvisable to ignore it, also because Science, with a capital S, and Technology, with a capital T, are tremendous sources of inspiration. Besides existing and therefore needing to be reflected in some way in the written word, they are, in my opinion [...] tremendous stimuli.)

At the time of publication in 1975[4] *Il sistema periodico* was celebrated for its success in bridging these two normally distant cultures.[5] Indeed Levi's publication of *Il sistema periodico* is confirmation of his stance over the debate: if *Storie naturali* and *Vizio di forma* were evidence that scientific knowledge could inspire fictional literature, then *Il sistema periodico* exists as proof that a specific science, chemistry, could be written about in a literary fashion, that the two cultures of science and literature are not mutually exclusive. The majority of critics have tended to focus either on the literary versus the scientific merits of *Il sistema periodico*, within the context of the two cultures debate, or on the previously obscure autobiographical elements of the text, both before and after the composition of *Se questo è un uomo*.[6] To judge from previous studies on *Il sistema periodico*, then, there would appear to be very little to say from a literary angle about the thematic and stylistic echoes of *Se questo è un uomo* here. This chapter will attempt to prove otherwise, providing new insights into *Il sistema periodico* and drawing novel conclusions on the connections between the two texts.

Il sistema periodico, like so many of Levi's other writings, does not conform to any one literary genre, but is rather a combination of styles from Levi's previous works, a synthesis of autobiographical elements along similar lines to *Se questo è un uomo* and *La tregua* and of fictional chapters comparable to those contained within the *Storie naturali* and *Vizio di forma*. As Levi comments in the final chapter of the text, 'questo non è un trattato di chimica. [...] Non è neppure un'autobiografia, [...] ma storia in qualche modo è pure. È, o avrebbe voluto essere, una microstoria, la storia di un mestiere e delle sue sconfitte, vittorie e miserie' (this is not a chemistry treatise. [...] It is not even an autobiography, [...] but it is history in some way nevertheless. It is, or it would have liked to be, a microhistory, the story of a career and its defeats, victories and trials) (*SP*, I, p. 934). Laura Marcus' statement that 'autobiography is itself a major source of concern because of its very instability in terms of the postulated opposites between self and world, literature and history, subject and object'[7] is relevant here with reference to the tensions within Levi's text between autobiography and fiction, history and the personal, chemistry and literature. In spite of the variety of genres employed in *Il sistema periodico*, sixteen of the chapters, therefore the majority, are autobiographical, with the exceptions of the fictional 'Mercurio', 'Piombo', 'Zolfo', 'Titanio' and 'Carbonio'. The autobiographical chapters are arranged chronologically, covering a narrative period from 1935 to 1967, and therefore embracing the greatest historical period of all Levi's narrative as well as being the most specifically scientific of all his works, founded on Levi's career as a chemist and the experiences of his profession. His choice of subject matter was based on the fact that 'mi sentivo in debito verso il mio mestiere quotidiano; mi sembrava di aver sprecato un'occasione a non parlare dell'esperienza di un lavoro che molti pensano arido, misterioso e sospetto'[8] (I felt indebted to my everyday career; I seemed to have wasted an opportunity in not speaking about my experience of a profession which many consider arid, mysterious and suspicious) and also that 'io volevo solo far capire come *nessuna esperienza umana sia indegna di attenzione* [...] anche l'esperienza di una carriera che vista dal di fuori è arida, faticosa, difficile anche, deludente e frustrante; cioè la carriera del tecnico di fabbrica'[9]

(I only wanted to convey how *no human experience is unworthy of attention* [...] even the experience of a career which, seen from the outside, is arid, tiring, also difficult, disappointing and frustrating; in other words the career of a factory engineer). The phrase 'nessuna esperienza umana sia indegna di attenzione' is significant, for whilst here Levi is referring to his experiences as a chemist, he employs virtually identical words in *Se questo è un uomo* with reference to his concentration camp experiences, stating that 'noi siamo infatti persuasi che nessuna umana esperienza sia vuota di senso e indegna di analisi' (we are indeed convinced that no human experience is without sense and unworthy of analysis) (*SQ*, I, p. 83). Levi's first text is therefore strongly recalled in his own comments about the composition of this, his fifth. For although Levi stated that 'Auschwitz non si dimentica, non si cancella facilmente, ma non avrei voluto che il centro di gravità di questo libro [*Il sistema periodico*] fosse spostato sui campi di concentramento'[10] (Auschwitz is not forgotten, is not easily erased, but I would not have wished for the centre of gravity in this book to be transferred onto the concentration camps), the centre of *Il sistema periodico* is precisely there, in Auschwitz. Of the twenty-one chapters which constitute the text, the central chapter, 'Cerio', with ten chapters on either side, is set exclusively in the concentration camp. Placed in the physical heart of the text, then, Levi's time in the *Lager* would appear to be quite literally central to the development both of his professional career as a chemist and of the text itself. Precisely half of *Il sistema periodico* is set pre-Holocaust, pre-*Se questo è un uomo*, whilst the other half is post-*La tregua*, post-return. The structure of the text is divided exactly into two, even taking into account the fictional tales included in the collection, consequently resulting in the fact that everything within this text is situated either pre- or post-Auschwitz, a narrative structure that recalls Levi's remarks within *La tregua* of how 'Auschwitz [...] spaccava in due la catena dei miei ricordi' (Auschwitz [...] split in two the chain of my memories) (*LT*, I, p. 375). This split of both Levi's memories and the text coincides with another image frequently evoked by Levi, that of the centaur. It was Levi himself who remarked that 'io sono un anfibio, un centauro. [...] Io sono diviso in due metà. Una è quella della fabbrica. [...] Un'altra [...] è quella nella quale scrivo, rispondo alle interviste, lavoro sulle mie esperienze passate e presenti. Sono proprio due mezzi cervelli'[11] (I am an amphibian, a centaur. [...] I am divided into two halves. One half is that of the factory. [...] The other half [...] is the one in which I write, respond to interviews, work on my experiences both past and present. They are really two half brains). These two halves: half human, half horse in the figure of the centaur, but also half writer, half chemist in the case of Levi; as well as half survivor, half scientist; half man, half beast in the camps; then half pre-deportation and half post-Auschwitz in *Il sistema periodico*, is therefore a dividing factor that runs throughout much of Levi's literary output, not simply coinciding with the structural schism in this text.

Another dividing factor at work within this text is the tension between the 'microstoria' (microhistory) (*SP*, I, p. 934) of Levi's narrative persona and the wider historical picture: a tension, that is, between the autobiographical, first-person narrative of the text and the narration of historically-based experiences. Similar divisions were at work in *Se questo è un uomo* with Levi alternating between bearing witness for himself and a universal testimony highlighted by his use of the first-person plural. This is an issue common to much of Levi's writing: in his own words, 'fin dal mio libro *Se questo è un uomo*, ho desiderato che i miei scritti, anche se li ho firmati io, fossero letti come opere collettive, come una voce che rappresentasse altri voci'[12] (right from my first book, *Se questo è un uomo*, I have wanted my writings, even if they are published in my name, to be read as collective works, as one voice which represents other voices). In *Il sistema periodico*, however, the variation between the first-person singular and the first-person plural narration changes with even greater frequency than in *Se questo è un uomo*, and the implied 'we' or the other voices represented here are not always clearly identifiable. 'Argon' is narrated in the third person, sometimes plural and sometimes singular, as this is 'their' story, the story of Levi's ancestors; 'Idrogeno' alternates between Levi's narrative persona expressing himself in the first-person singular, and in the plural 'we' embracing Levi and his classmate, Enrico; 'Zinco' opens with an unspecified 'noi' only clarified much later in the chapter, interspersed with narrative in the third person, and later contrasted against the personal, first-person tale; 'Ferro' begins similarly with a vague 'noi', which progresses to 'io' versus the 'noi', then assumes the form of a 'we' constituting Levi and Sandro; 'Potassio' talks of 'la nostra patria vera', 'le nostre radici' and 'la nostra generazione' (our true homeland; our roots; our generation) (*SP*, I, p. 783) yet this 'our' is constantly changing between 'our generation', 'we Italians' and 'we Jews' before limiting itself to Levi's personal story again; 'Nichel' is narrated in the first-person singular from the onset, with only occasional flashes of others' tales; the fictional 'Piombo' and 'Mercurio' are told from the point of view of a fictitious first-person narrator; 'Fosforo' is solely in the first-person singular; 'Oro' embraces 'we' friends from Turin, 'we' partisans and 'we' prisoners before becoming the 'I', Levi prisoner; 'Cerio' is the tale of 'I' the chemist-writer-survivor, 'we' prisoners and then a 'noi' which includes only Levi and Alberto; 'Cromo' is in the first-person singular except for a brief passage where the 'noi' welcomes Levi's wife-to-be, Lucia; the fictional 'Zolfo' and 'Titanio' are written from the third-person viewpoints of Lanza and Maria; 'Arsenico' and 'Azoto' are both narrated almost exclusively in the first-person singular; the 'noi' in 'Stagno' is Levi and his colleague Emilio; 'Uranio' is in the first-person singular; 'Argento' begins as Levi's story, then changes to the third person of Cerrato which then becomes Cerrato's 'io' as he narrates his tale; in 'Vanadio' the 'we' is those who worked at the same factory as Levi, which then flashes back to being 'we prisoners in the *Lager*' before using the first-person singular; and in 'Carbonio' the 'we' embraces Levi and his readers, 'our' element of carbon, and then the third person of the element itself. The 'noi' form of *Se questo è un uomo* which, although frequently embracing different people in allowance for new arrivals and deaths, always clearly referred to the prisoners, is variable in this later text, referring to a wide variety of different groups of people. The ever-varying narrating point of view in *Il sistema periodico* highlights the fact that yet again this text is not restricted to being Levi's story: it is not exclusively or strictly autobiographical, but is a collective, changeable, plural narrative, variable in each chapter.

The twenty-one chapters of *Il sistema periodico* are each named after a chemical element of the Periodic Table. However, whereas Mendeleev's Periodic Table contains one hundred and ten elements ordered according to their atomic weight, Levi selects only twenty-one elements whose selection and sequence have no identifiable pattern.[13] Mendeleev's Periodic Table is not, therefore, a strict metatextual framework for Levi's text[14] and nor is it the case that, 'la celebre Tavola di Mendeleev è diventata il sistema attraverso cui Levi riesce a tenere insieme la sua materiale, a dare una parvenza d'ordine all'intero edificio narrativo'[15] (Mendeleev's famous Table is the system through which Levi manages to hold his material together, to give an appearance of order to the entire narrative edifice). Mendeleev's Periodic Table does, in fact, grant merely a 'parvenza d'ordine' (an appearance of order), for Levi has not maintained any of Mendeleev's original, logical order. Although Levi commented that:

> Dopo Mendeleev ci si accorge che la materia è ordinata, non è disordinata e quindi si ha ragione di supporre che l'intero universo sia ordinato e non disordinato. Per questo mi è piaciuto questo ambiguo titolo [*Il sistema periodico*], anche se non dice molto a molti, e l'ho scelto come *ordinatore* di questi racconti.[16]

(After Mendeleev we are aware that matter is ordered; matter is not disordered and therefore we have reason to suppose that the entire universe is ordered and not disordered. It is for this reason that I liked this ambiguous title [*The Periodic Table*], even if it does not convey much to many people, and I chose it as *organiser* of these stories.)

Mendeleev's Periodic Table in which 'il caos dava luogo all'ordine, l'indistinto al comprensibile'[17] (chaos gave way to order, confusion to comprehension) is not actually employed as *ordinatore* here and has in fact been overturned as Levi's chaotic, illogical positioning of the chemical elements in the stucture of his text appears to deliberately upset Mendeleev's *sistema* and its imposition of order. Gone are the 'poesia, piú alta e piú solenne di tutte le poesie digerite in liceo' (poetry, higher and more solemn than all the poems digested at school) (*SP*, I, p. 775) and the 'rima' (rhyme) of Mendeleev's Table in which 'ogni riga termina con la stessa 'sillaba'', and through which 'diventava possible [...] individuare caselle vuote che avrebbero dovuto essere riempite, dato che "tutto ciò che può esistere esiste"; cioè fare opera profetica'[18] (every line ends with the same 'syllable'; it became possible [...] to determine the empty slots which ought to be filled, given that 'everything which can exist exists': in other words, to carry out prophetic work). Riatsch and Gorgé write that 'l'assenza di una struttura fa sì che la serie di elementi del *Sistema periodico* si presenti come semplice e casuale parte di un tutto (la tavola di Mendeleev)'[19] (the absence of a structure means that the series of elements in *Il sistema periodico* presents itself as a simple and casual part of a whole that is Mendeleev's Table) but it is more than this. Through chemistry the young Levi aspired to 'arrivare molto in là, di giungere a possedere la chiave dell'universo'[20] (to go a long way, to get as far as possessing the key to the universe) and Mendeleev's Table 'che, se cercava il ponte, l'anello mancante, fra il mondo delle carte e il mondo delle cose, non lo doveva cercare lontano: era lí' (which, if you were looking for the bridge, the missing link, between the paper world and the concrete world, you didn't have to look very far: it was there) (*SP*, I, p. 775). The Periodic Table is clearly and undoubtedly a source of inspiration for this text and yet its equally patent distortion would suggest that this text is not merely part of a whole. Levi has, in fact, created a new version of chemistry, a new Periodic Table, only this is *Il sistema periodico* 'alla rovescia' (overturned), instead of 'il mondo alla rovescia' (the world overturned), transforming something comprehensible into the incomprehensible in much the same way as, upon release from the concentration camps, 'il mondo intorno [...] sembrava ritornato al Caos primigenio' (the world around [...] seemed to have returned to primeval Chaos) (*LT*, I, p. 226). The concentration camp world is reflected here in the tensions between an imposition of order, that of Mendeleev's structuring of the Periodic Table, and Levi's rebellion against this through his decision to *rovesciarlo*: the very subversion of this previously established way of ordering the chemical world reflects a return to the chaos from which Levi has physically escaped. There is further evidence that the concentration camps function as the source of this chaos here, for the chapter dedicated to Levi's time in Auschwitz, 'Cerio', is not just central physically and metaphorically, but also mathematically. The atomic numbers of the chemical elements Levi chooses as chapter headings also make 'Cerio' the pivotal chapter. The sum of the atomic numbers in the first half of Levi's work, from 'Argon' to 'Oro' total three hundred and seventy eight, a total mirrored exactly by the sum of those in the second half, from 'Cerio' to 'Carbonio': from 'Argon' to 'Oro' the atomic numbers are 18, 1, 30, 26, 19, 28, 82, 80, 15 and 79 (total 378); from

'Cerio' to 'Carbonio' the atomic numbers are 58, 24, 16, 22, 33, 7, 50, 92, 47, 23 and 6 (also total 378). There is a degree of symmetry, then, in Levi's ordering of his chapters and the atomic weight of their elements, but it is a symmetry which is divided at the point of 'Cerio', making 'Cerio' the turning point of the text. With the first half of the 'centaurian' division of this text representing the build-up to Levi's time in Auschwitz, and the second half as the aftermath, the content and structure of *Il sistema periodico* revolve around the concentration camp, an experience which brought chaos into Levi's life and reflects its chaos onto Levi's portrayal of the Periodic Table here.

The chemical elements of the Periodic Table are at times applied metaphorically in Levi's stories to the characters or themes contained within the chapter itself. Thus in 'Argon', Levi's ancestors are 'inerti' like the 'cosiddetti gas inerti' especially 'l'argon, l'Inoperoso' (inert, like the so-called inert gases especially Argon the Inactive) (*SP*, I, p. 741) and in 'Zinco' Jews, in particular Levi's own autobiographical persona, are 'l'impurezza che fa reagire lo zinco' (the impurity which causes zinc to react) (*SP*, I, p. 769). In other chapters, the chemical element itself is the protagonist, forming a vital part of the experiences recounted. In 'Arsenico', for example, arsenic is the element contaminating the sugar sample Levi has been investigating, and 'Carbonio' describes the possible adventure of an atom of carbon in which the atom itself is the central character. Whilst the Periodic Table itself has been overturned here, the role of science, itself 'alla rovescia' in the *Storie naturali* and *Vizio di forma*, has altered in this text, for this is no longer a science of errors and the resulting consequences. Here science is used for positive, constructive ends rather than as a source of man's downfall as in the *Storie naturali* and *Vizio di forma*, or as a method of mass destruction as in *Se questo è un uomo*. In *Il sistema periodico*, chemistry 'si presenta invece come una scienza vitale e demiurgica che insegna le arti del rigore, dell'industriosità, della sopravvivenza, che risolve enigmi e problemi polizieschi'[21] (instead presents itself as a vital and demiurgic science which teaches the arts of rigour, industriousness and survival, which resolves enigmas and detective problems). With chemistry as a solver of 'problemi polizieschi', Levi himself often plays the role of the detective, even describing himself as 'mezzo chimico e mezzo poliziesco' (half chemist, half detective) (*SP*, I, p. 872), investigating and analysing substances to uncover their hidden mysteries. Thus in 'Cromo' we see Levi battling to find the cause of and a remedy for the mysteriously congealed paint; in 'Arsenico' the chemist has to ascertain the hidden substance in the sugar sample; in 'Potassio' 'il colpevole era trovato' (the culprit had been found) (*SP*, I, p. 791), and in 'Uranio' he unravels the true identity of the so-called Uranium rock. Yet it is not simply a detective story element which features in many of these chapters, rather that each of the stories, with the exceptions of 'Argon', 'Carbonio', 'Mercurio' and 'Titanio', contains its own battle or challenge of some kind that Levi-the-chemist (or the protagonist of the fictional tales) has to overcome. 'Idrogeno' is the adolescent Levi's struggle to prove himself as a future chemist; 'Zinco' reveals Levi's endeavours to survive the initiation procedure into the laboratory in his early University years and his battle to overcome his shyness with the opposite sex in order to strike up friendships; 'Ferro' shows Levi fighting to survive both racial discrimination and the mountains; 'Potassio' is a battle to find a suitable mentor willing to supervise his studies, and the challenge of experiments; 'Nichel' portrays the difficulties in extracting the nickel in question; in 'Piombo' the fictional Rodmund has to struggle to unearth the sources of lead he requires; in 'Fosforo' Levi contends with an incredibly boring job in the difficult surroundings of his new laboratory conditions and laws; in 'Oro' Levi is struggling as a partisan and faces prison for the first time; 'Cerio' is Levi battling for life itself in the concentration camp; 'Cromo' is a kind of appendix to *La tregua*, depicting the trials of finding work upon return to Turin, the composition of *Se questo è un uomo*, plus the complications that need solving at work; the fictional 'Zolfo' contains a challenge for Lanza to unearth the problems with this experiment; 'Arsenico' is the challenge of discovering the hidden substance; 'Azoto' portrays the dilemma Levi faced in extracting organic nitrogen; 'Stagno' reveals Levi struggling to make a living; 'Uranio' contains both the test of becoming a salesman and that of discovering what the 'uranium' really was; 'Argento' tells of an ex-school friend's professional challenges, and 'Vanadio' is the struggle to overcome and forgive the past. *Il sistema periodico* is not, therefore, merely a collection of Levi's professional experiences, is not simply 'la storia di un mestiere' (the story of a career) (*SP*, I, p. 934), but rather a collection of his professional trials and difficulties, interspersed with fictional tales along similar lines. As such, this text is conveying a life of challenges and the lessons learned as a consequence, this time through the learning experience beset with trials of his career as a chemist, rather than through 'la seconda università'[22] (my second university), Auschwitz.

Whereas the primary challenge of *Se questo è un uomo* manifested itself as 'la lotta per la vita' (the battle for life) (*SQ*, I, p. 84-5) against human adversaries, *Il sistema periodico* deals with a Darwinian survival of the fittest between man and nature or Matter. There are several references to Darwin in Levi's work, a number of which are worth mentioning here in relation to their connections with both *Il sistema periodico* and *Se questo è un uomo*. Levi's words to describe Darwin's work in his personal anthology, *La ricerca delle radici*, that 'dal groviglio estrae l'ordine' (extracts order from confusion) (*RR*, II, p. 1383), closely echo a phrase he used to describe Mendeleev's Periodic Table, in which 'il caos dava luogo all'ordine'[23] (chaos gave way to order). Both the Table of chemical elements and Darwin's research, from Levi's perspective, seek to bring order to an otherwise chaotic world. Levi also alluded to Darwin's theories on natural selection in *Se questo è un uomo*, writing that 'questo spietato processo di selezione naturale si sarebbe potuto leggere nelle statistiche del movimento dei Lager' (this relentless process of natural selection could have been read in the statistics of Lager movement) (*SQ*, I, p. 85), and in *Il sistema periodico* Darwin is mentioned in 'Cerio', the chapter set in Auschwitz, with reference to Levi's realisation that he was undergoing the same 'involuzione-evoluzione di un famoso cane per bene, un cane vittoriano e *darwiniano*' (involution-evolution of a famous respectable dog, a Victorian and *Darwinian* dog) (*SP*, I, p. 861, my italics). These brief allusions to Darwin therefore both recur in and connect *Il sistema periodico* to *Se questo è un uomo*: in the autobiographical chapters of *Il sistema periodico* set in the period before deportation 'learning through trial and error is constructed as an individualistic, Darwinian process';[24] there is often a degree of experimenting, of failed endeavours and struggles which culminate in the outcome of the story, and precisely in order for the fittest to emerge as survivor. Thus 'Idrogeno' shows the adolescent Levi and his schoolfriend battling against 'il primo nostro avversario' (our first adversary) (*SP*, I, p. 760), attempting to bring about, through various methods, 'almeno uno dei fenomeni che si trovavano descritti con tanta disinvoltura sul nostro testo di chimica' (at least one of the phenomena described with such ease in our chemistry textbook) (*SP*, I, p. 761); in 'Zinco' the chemistry laboratories are a place where 'si impara per strada, le esperienze degli altri non servono, l'essenziale è misurarsi' (one learns along the way, others' experiences are of no use, the important thing is to measure oneself) (*SP*, I, p. 766); in his later University years recounted in 'Ferro', 'si contasse sull'opera della *selezione naturale* per eleggere fra di noi i piú adatti alla sopravvivenza fisica e professionale' (you counted on the work of *natural selection* to chose from our ranks those most suited to physical and professional survival) (*SP*, I, p. 772, my italics) and Sandro and Levi's conquering of the mountains in the same chapter are a true test of their survival instincts; in 'Potassio' Levi and his contemporaries unwittingly employ trial-and-error techniques to 'conoscere i nostri limiti' (know our limits) (*SP*, I, p. 784), subjecting themselves to tests of strength and endurance; in 'Nichel' the method of extracting the nickel itself is performed through 'un gioco sottile di ragione, di prove e di errori' (a shrewd game of reason, trial and error) (*SP*, I, p. 801); in the fictional 'Piombo' Rodmund has to use trial and error tactics to discover new sources of lead to convert into gold and therefore make his living; in 'Fosforo' Levi has to exercise trial and error in his experiments with plants and rabbits; and in 'Oro' the partisans are merely beginning to learn how to survive when they are captured. These trial-and-error aspects of the learning process depicted in the text prior to 'Cerio' reflect the opening chapters of *Se questo è un uomo* in which Levi has to discover, by himself and often precisely through trial and error, the rules of life in the camp, essential to having any remote chance of survival. Yet this feature of the first half of *Il sistema periodico* is also a direct reversal of the initiation procedures of *Se questo è un uomo*, just as *Se questo è un uomo* is, in many ways, a complete overturning of Darwin's theories; in both cases because Darwin's theory of the process of natural selection contrasts entirely with the unnatural selections of the camps, where, as outlined by Levi in the chapter entitled 'I sommersi e i salvati', the 'best' did not always survive and the choice between life and death was no longer natural but entirely in the hands of men. Chemistry, as portrayed in the early chapters of this text, allows for mistakes, and, more importantly, it permits chemists to learn from their errors, and to progress and develop throughout their period of initiation/training; the 'Iniziazione' chapter of *Se questo è un uomo* granted no such luxuries. Here, logic and reason can dominate and allow man to successfully overcome an initiation into chemistry; the unnatural, illogical and incomprehensible world of the camps did not allow for survival on the basis of superior intellect. The reverberations of Darwinism and reversed Darwinism throughout these works therefore serve to emphasise precisely what has altered in Levi's experience. This particular aspect of 'il mondo alla rovescia' has been righted in this text: after the destruction of all that is human in the camps, including the evolution of man, in *Il sistema periodico*, through the depiction of his own human, rational side at work professionally, Levi can re-establish his position as a man and right the evolutionary process.

The humanity of Levi's narrative persona is further emphasised within *Il sistema periodico* by the emotionally-charged focus of the text and by Levi's direct reference to his feelings at the time of experience.[25] Thus Levi's comments that: 'provavo paura retrospettiva e insieme una certa sciocca fierezza'; 'mi sentivo curioso, [...] e vagamente scocciato'; 'mi sentivo frustrato e sfidato'; 'mi sentivo disperato'; 'mi sentivo sui carboni ardenti'; 'mi sentivo ilare e vittorioso', and 'mi sentivo invincibile e tabú, anche di fronte ai nemici vicini' (I felt a retrospective fear and, at the same time, a certain foolish pride; I felt curious, [...] and vaguely annoyed; I felt frustrated and challenged; I felt desperate; I was on hot coals; I felt cheerful and victorious; I felt invincible and taboo, even faced with my close enemies) (*SP*, I, pp. 763, 767, 769, 769, 770, 770, and 807 respectively) are particularly significant when compared to Levi's first text, firstly because the emotions specified in this text are almost exclusively Levi's own, as opposed to the multiple, collective emotions of testimony, and secondly because they indicate such a strong return to the human domain of feelings and emotions, a true distancing from Levi's statement in *Se questo è un uomo* that 'da molti mesi non conoscevo piú il dolore, la gioia, il timore, se non in quel modo staccato e lontano che è caratteristico del Lager' (I had not known pain, joy, fear for many months, except in that detached and distant way which is characteristic of the *Lager*) (*SQ*, I, p. 148). Even when Levi's feelings are not always directly specified, there is often no actual need to express them, for his words are clear enough to convey the intended emotion:

con addosso una cappa quasi tangibile di scoramento e di amarezza (*SP*, I, p. 785);

(wearing an almost tangible cloak of disheartenment and bitterness)

pensavo di aver aperto una porta con una chiave, e di possedere la chiave di molte porte, forse di tutte (*SP*, I, p. 806-7);

(I thought I had unlocked a door, and that I possessed the key to many doors, perhaps all of them)

mi sentivo invadere da un odio assurdo per il rivale mai conosciuto (*SP*, I, p. 846);

(I felt myself invaded by an absurd hatred for the rival I had never met)

mi sentivo crescere dentro, forse per la prima volta, una nauseabonda sensazione di vuoto (*SP*, I, p. 847);

(perhaps for the first time, I felt a nauseating sensation of emptiness growing inside me)

portare in canna una ragazza che si desidera, ed esserne talmente lontani da non potersene neppure innamorare: portarla in canna in Viale Gorizia per aiutarla ad essere di un altro, ed a sparire dalla mia vita (*SP*, I, p. 847);

(carrying a girl you long for on your crossbar, and being so far from her that you could never even fall in love with her; carrying her on your crossbar to Viale Gorizia to help her become another's, and to disappear from my life)

eravamo usciti distrutti, destituiti, desiderosi che tutto finisse e di finire noi stessi (*SP*, I, p. 853);

(we came out destroyed, destitute, longing for everything to finish and to finish off ourselves)

il giorno seguente il destino mi riserbasse un dono diverso ed unico: l'incontro con una donna, giovane e di carne e d'ossa, calda contro il mio fianco attraverso i cappotti, allegra in mezzo alla nebbia umida dei viali, paziente sapiente e sicura mentre camminavamo per le strade ancora fiancheggiate di macerie. In poche ore sapemmo di appartenerci, non per un incontro, ma per la vita, come infatti è stato. In poche ore mi ero sentito nuovo e pieno di potenze nuove, lavato e guarito dal lungo male, pronto finalmente ad entrare nella vita con gioia e vigore. (*SP*, I, p. 872)

(the next day destiny kept a different and unique gift for me: an encounter with a woman, young and of flesh and blood, warm by my side through our coats, happy in the middle of the damp fog of the avenues, patient, wise and secure whilst we walked through the streets still lined with rubble. Within a few hours we knew we belonged to each other, not for one date, but for life, as indeed it has been. Within a few hours I had become new and full of new powers, washed and healed of my long suffering, finally ready to enter into life with joy and vigour.)

Il sistema periodico is really, then, 'tremando per l'emozione' (trembling with emotion) (*SP*, I, p. 770) rather than devoid of emotion. The chapter 'Vanadio' provides an interesting example of both the existence of emotion in this text and of Levi's strategies for conveying anger and passing judgement for the events of the concentration camps. 'Vanadio' contains references to strong emotions: the very recollection of Dr Müller 'mi aveva precipitato in una eccitazione violenta' (had plunged me into a violent fervour) (*SP*, I, p. 925); upon receipt of Müller's letter 'adesso toccava a me rispondere, e mi sentivo imbarazzato' (now it was my turn to respond, and I felt uncomfortable) (*SP*, I, p. 927), and at the suggestion of a reunion 'avevo paura [...] non mi sentivo capace di rappresentare i morti di Auschwitz' (I was afraid [...] I didn't feel capable of representing Auschwitz's dead) (*SP*, I, p. 928). Yet feelings of anger are not specified directly, and any urge or desire for revenge, as stated in relation to Levi's recurring dreams of confronting those in power from the concentration camp, were motivated 'non per fare vendetta [...] Solo per ristabilire le misure, e per dire "dunque?"' (not to take revenge [...] Only to restore the balance, and to say "Well?") (*SP*, I, p. 925). An explicit judgement exists, however, within the text. Müller's letter, his excuses for his behaviour, his '*wishful thinking* postumo' (posthumous wishful thinking), and in particular his creation of 'un passato di comodo' (a comfortable past) (*SP*, I, p. 930) do not excuse his actions or redeem him in Levi's eyes. Levi in fact condemns Müller outright:

Mi dichiaravo pronto a perdonare i nemici, e magari anche ad amarli, ma solo quando mostrino segni certi di pentimento, e cioè quando cessino di essere nemici. [...] Quanto al giudizio specifico sul suo comportamento, che Müller implicitamente domandava, citavo discretamente due casi a me noti di suoi colleghi tedeschi che nei nostri confronti avevano fatto qualcosa di ben piú coraggioso di quanto lui rivendicava. Ammettevo che non tutti nascono eroi, e che un mondo in cui *tutti* fossero come lui, cioè onesti ed inermi, sarebbe tollerabile, ma questo è un mondo irreale. Nel mondo reale gli armati esistono, costruiscono Auschwitz, e gli onesti ed inermi spianano loro la strada; perciò di Auschwitz deve rispondere ogni tedesco, anzi, ogni uomo, e dopo Auschwitz non è piú lecito essere inermi. (*SP*, I, p. 932-3)

(I declared myself ready to forgive my enemies, and maybe even to love them, but only when they show certain signs of repentance, therefore when they cease to be enemies. [...] As for a specific judgement on his behaviour, which Müller was implicitly asking for, I tactfully cited two cases known to me of German colleagues of his who had done something rather more courageous towards us than what he claimed to have done. I admitted that not everyone is born a hero, and that a world in which *everyone* was like him, honest and helpless, would be tolerable, but that this is a dream world. In the real world the armed exist, they build Auschwitz, and the honest and helpless pave the way for them: therefore every German must answer for Auschwitz, indeed every man, and after Auschwitz it is no longer permissible to be helpless.)

Levi's response to his previous enemies, with remarks such as, 'l'avversario mi distrae, mi interessa piú come uomo che come avversario, lo sto a sentire e rischio di credergli' (the adversary distracts me, I am more interested in him as a man than as an adversary, I stop to listen to him and I risk believing him) (*SP*, I, p. 928) is indicative of the root of his lack of anger, and is further evidence of his human side which rationalises and struggles to understand everything, including his enemies' motives. Levi's quest to comprehend, to understand chemistry, life, human nature, and the many unanswerable whys of Auschwitz is a continuing thread throughout his works.[26] For whilst he commented to Tullio Regge that 'adesso so che non c'è, il perché delle cose'[27] (I now know that there is no reason for things) in *Il sistema periodico* he is still searching to comprehend precisely this, 'il perché delle cose' (the reason for things). Whereas in *Se questo è un uomo* 'la nostra saggezza era il "non cercar di capire"' (*SQ*, I, p. 112) because 'Hier ist kein Warum – (qui non c'è perché)' (*SQ*, I, p. 23) (our wisdom lay in "not trying to understand" because here there is no why), in *Il sistema periodico* Levi's 'fame di capire' (hunger to understand) (*SP*, I, p. 778) is transferred, for the most part, to Matter and chemistry since 'vincere la materia è comprenderla, e comprendere la materia è necessario per comprendere l'universo e noi stessi' (beating matter is understanding it, and understanding matter is necessary in order to understand the universe and ourselves) (*SP*, I, p. 775).

This process of Levi-the-chemist's learning and understanding often comes through the role played by each of the actual elements, as every element is represented in the chemist-writer's mind as a source of knowledge, with the stories focusing on what the individuals concerned, or Levi himself, learn from their contact with an element. Thus the element zinc:

> Il cosí tenero e delicato zinco, cosí arrendevole davanti agli acidi, che se ne fanno un solo boccone, si comporta invece in modo assai diverso quando è molto puro: allora resiste ostinatamente all'attacco. Se ne potevano trarre due conseguenze filosofiche tra loro contrastanti: l'elogio della purezza, che protegge dal male come un usbergo; l'elogio dell'impurezza, che dà adito ai mutamenti, cioè alla vita. [...] Perché la ruota giri, perché la vita viva, ci vogliono le impurezze, e le impurezze delle impurezze. [...] Ci vuole il dissenso, il diverso, il grano di sale e di senape: il fascismo non li vuole, li vieta, e per questo tu non sei fascista; vuole tutti uguali e tu non sei uguale. (*SP*, I, p. 768)
> Sono io l'impurezza che fa reagire lo zinco, sono io il granello di sale e di senape. L'impurezza, certo: poiché proprio in quei mesi iniziava la pubblicazione di "La Difesa della Razza", e di purezza si faceva un gran parlare, ed io cominciavo ad essere fiero di essere impuro. (*SP*, I, p. 769-70)

(Zinc, so soft and delicate, so yielding towards acids, which devour it in just one mouthful, behaves in a quite different manner when it is very pure: then it obstinately resists attack. Two opposing philosophical conclusions can be drawn from this: in praise of purity, which protects from harm like a shield; in praise of impurity which gives rise to changes, and therefore to life. [...] In order for the wheel to turn, in order for life to be lived, impurities are required, and impurities of the impurities. [...] Dissent, differences, the grain of salt and of mustard are needed: fascism doesn't want them, it forbids them, and for this reason you are not fascist; it wants everybody the same and you are not the same.

I am the impurity which makes zinc react, I am the little grain of salt and mustard. Impurity is the right word since just in those last months the publication of "The Defence of the Race" began, and everyone was talking about purity, and I began to be proud of being impure.)

Chemistry itself is therefore a learning process as:

> La materia è anche una scuola, la vera scuola. Combattendo contro di lei si matura e si cresce. In questo combattimento si vince o si perde e a volta a volta la materia è sentita come astuta o come ottusa, senza che ci sia contrasto, perché sono due suoi aspetti diversi.[28]

(Matter is also a school, your true school. Fighting against matter you mature and grow. You either win or lose this battle and matter was felt to be at once astute and obtuse, without there being any conflict between the two, because they are both two of its different aspects.

Chemistry, then, is a *combattimento* against matter itself. The battle in Levi's first text, of man against man, has here been transformed into man against matter, echoing the words of Mordo Nahum in *La tregua*, 'guerra è sempre' (war is always) (*LT*, I, p. 242). It is worth citing a number of examples in full to substantiate this point:

> Il rapporto con la Materia [...] diventava dialettico: era una scherma, una partita a due. Due avversari disuguali: da una parte, ad interrogare, il chimico implume, inerme, con a fianco il testo dell'Autenrieth come solo alleato [...]; dall'altra, a rispondere per enigmi, la Materia con la sua passività sorniona, vecchia come il Tutto e portentosamente ricca d'inganni, solenne e sottile come la Sfinge. (*SP*, I, p. 772)

> The relationship with Matter [...] became dialectical: it was fencing, a game for two. Two unequal adversaries: on the one side, interrogating, the unfledged, unarmed chemist, with the Autenrieth textbook by his side as his only ally [...]; on the other side, responding only with enigmas, Matter with her sly passivity, as old as the universe and prodigiously full of tricks, solemn and penetrating as the Sphinx.)

> Siamo chimici, cioè cacciatori [...]; non ci si deve arrendere alla materia incomprensibile, non ci si deve sedere. [...] Non ci si deve mai sentire disarmati: la natura è immensa e complessa, ma non è impermeabile all'intelligenza; devi girarle intorno, pungere, sondare, cercare il varco o fartelo. (*SP*, I, p. 804)

> (We are chemists, or rather hunters [...]; one must not surrender to incomprehensible matter, one must not be seated. [...] One must never feel unarmed: nature is immense and complex, but it is not impermeable to intelligence; you must go all around, pierce, probe, look for the opening or make one yourself.)

> L'avversario era sempre ancora quello, il non-io, il Gran Curvo, la Hyle: la materia stupida, neghittosamente nemica. (*SP*, I, p. 873)

> (The adversary was always the same, the not-me, the *Gran Curvo*, the *Hyle*: stupid matter, indolently inimical.)

> Era scoccata l'ora dell'appuntamento con la Materia, la grande antagonista dello Spirito (*SP*, I, p. 767)

(The time had struck for the appointment with Matter, the great antagonist of Spirit)

Qui la faccenda si faceva seria, il confronto con la Materia-Mater, con la madre nemica, era piú duro e piú prossimo. (*SP*, I, p. 771)

(Here the issue became serious, the confrontation with Materia Mater, with the enemy mother, was harder and closer.)

Ti dànno l'impressione di combattere un'interminabile guerra contro un esercito avversario ottuso e tardo, ma tremendo per numero e peso; di perdere tutte le battaglie, una dopo l'altra, un anno dopo l'altro. (*SP*, I, p. 914)

(They give you the impression of fighting an interminable war against an enemy army which is obtuse and slow but tremendous in number and in weight, the impression of losing every battle, one after the other, year after year.)

Penso che il mio mestiere sia bello e intelligente, anche se l'avversario può divenire pericoloso. E che sia una battaglia che non finisce mai.[29]

(I think my profession is beautiful and intelligent, even if the adversary can become dangerous. And that it is a never-ending battle.)

Throughout *Il sistema periodico* Levi provides a portrayal of a 'chimico militante' (militant chemist) (*SP*, I, p. 791) who employs chemistry as his defence, his arms against Matter. The autobiographical chapters of *Il sistema periodico* are not merely about the professional struggles of Levi as a chemist, then, for they also encompass aspects of *Se questo è un uomo*, that is man's struggle against an enemy, in this case Matter. The tale of Levi's professional survival, contained in the autobiographical chapters of *Il sistema periodico*, therefore mirrors some aspects of his portrayal of his concentration camp experience; the very retelling of this professional survival is only made possible by Levi's previous survival experience. Indeed, prior knowledge of both the camps and *Se questo è un uomo* in particular is taken for granted in this text: it is essential for an understanding of 'Cerio', set in the camp; of 'Cromo', dealing with the trials of life upon return to Turin and the composition of *Se questo è un uomo* itself; 'Azoto', in which Levi's career as a chemist is referred to as 'fortificato [...] dall'esperienza di Auschwitz' (fortified [...] by the experience of Auschwitz) (*SP*, I, p. 895) and in which Levi describes himself as the 'autore sfiduciato di un libro [*SQ*] che a me sembrava bello, ma che nessuno leggeva' (the disheartened author of a book [*SQ*] which to me seemed good, but which nobody read) (*SP*, I, p. 897);

'Uranio', in which both *Se questo è un uomo* and Levi's actual experiences are commented on, and 'Vanadio' which contains a flashback to the *Lager*, triggered by the contact with Dr Müller. On a variety of occasions Levi specified that his physical survival of the camps was due in good part to chemistry itself:

> Al mio mestiere devo la vita. Non sarei sopravvissuto ad Auschwitz, se dopo dieci mesi di dura manovalanza non fossi entrato in un laboratorio, dove ho continuato a fare il manovale, ma al coperto. La qualifica di chimico, l'essere inserito col mio nome di allora, cioè con un numero, nell'organico della fabbrica di Buna che dipendeva dall'IG Farben Industrie, mi ha messo forse anche al riparo dalle "selezioni", perché, come chimici, eravamo considerati "formalmente utili".[30]

> (I owe my life to my profession. I would not have survived Auschwitz if, after ten months of hard manual labour, I hadn't entered the laboratory where I continued the manual work, but under cover. The qualification of chemist, being placed with the name I had then, in other words with a number, into the staff of the Buna factory which was under the supervision of IG Farben Industries, perhaps sheltered me from the "selections" because, as chemists, we were considered "officially useful".)

Il sistema periodico therefore elaborates on the 'Die Drei Leute Vom Labor' chapter of *Se questo è un uomo*, set in the Buna factory, as it provides a background as to how and why Levi could be saved by chemistry in the first place, and expands on his career post-Auschwitz in other laboratories. Whilst in the passages of *Se questo è un uomo* set in the laboratory Levi can begin to 'sentirsi uomo' (feel himself a man) (SQ, I, p. 138), *Il sistema periodico* demonstrates the professional, rational side to this man in a working environment. *Il sistema periodico* is thus evidence of the re-creation of the *uomo* in Levi, the proof of the successful re-establishment of his dignity after its annihilation in the camps.

Through *Il sistema periodico* Levi provides an elaboration on and an extension of one of the contributing factors towards his very survival: his professional career. Since *Se questo è un uomo* detailed how Levi's chemistry training was one of several determinants of his survival, *Il sistema periodico* is building precisely upon this text. Here, Levi is writing, perhaps even explaining or justifying how, pre-Auschwitz, he would come to be a chemist, how he would begin this career which would differentiate him from the other prisoners of the concentration camp and provide him with work in the camp's laboratory, thereby contributing towards the continuation of his very existence: Levi is rewriting the reasons for his survival, and he is drafting a tale of how, post-Auschwitz, this career helped restore him to humanity. Levi is rewriting issues of survival and surviving in this text, providing a history of battles, both personal and professional, which feature in the background and in the aftermath to *Se questo è un uomo*. *Il sistema periodico* offers a portrait of a life at work, but both this man's life and his work revolve around the central event and the central chapter of this text, that of Auschwitz.

Notes

1. An earlier, abridged version of this chapter is published as 'L'uomo salvato dal suo mestiere: Aspects of *Se questo è un uomo* Revisited in Primo Levi's *Il sistema periodico*', *Italian Studies*, 56, 2001.
2. See Giancarlo Borri, 'Primo Levi tra scienza e letteratura', in Ioli, ed., 1995, p. 209.
3. Grassano, 1981, p. 8.
4. SP was first published in its entirety in 1975, but at least four chapters had been published previously: 'Titanio' as 'Maria e il cerchio', *L'Italia socialista*, 19 September 1948; 'Zolfo' as 'Turno di notte', *L'Unità*, 31 August 1950; 'Carbonio', *Uomini e libri*, 1972; and an abridged version of 'Oro', *Il mondo*, 18 July 1974. (Belpoliti, *Opere I, Note ai testi*, pp. 1447-1448).
5. Critics commenting on this aspect include M. Piattelli Palmarini, 'Quando il romanzo "parla" la scienza', *Corriere della sera*, 17 August 1979; Mario Porro, 'Scienza', in Belpoliti, ed., 1997b; R. Pierantoni, 'Il sistema Aperiodico', in Cavaglion, ed., 1993; Borri, *Le divine impurità: Primo Levi tra scienza e letteratura*, 1992, and JoAnn Cannon, 'Chemistry and Writing in *The Periodic Table*', in Tarrow, ed., 1990, to name but a few.
6. The autobiographical elements of SP have been the main focus of Alberto Papuzzi, 'L'alpinismo? È la libertà di sbagliare', in Belopliti, ed., 1997a, and Cavaglion, 'Argon e la cultura ebraica piemontese (con l'abbozzo del racconto)', in Cavaglion, ed., 1993.
7. Marcus, 1994, p. 7.
8. Levi's words from an interview with Gabriella Poli, 'L'alfabeto della chimica', *La Stampa*, 6 December 1976.
9. Levi's words from an interview with Lorenzo Mondo, broadcast on Rai 2, 15 September 1975, transcribed in Poli and Calcagno, 1992, p. 73, my italics.
10. Rai 2 interview with Lorenzo Mondo, transcribed in Poli and Calcagno, 1992, p. 72.
11. Fadini, Edoardo, 'Primo Levi si sente scrittore "dimezzato"', *l'Unità*, 4 January 1966.
12. Levi's words spoken at the conference given at the Storia Vissuta convention, published in Cavaglion, ed., 1997, p. 67.
13. Critics who agree with this include Cicioni, 1995, p. 70, and Riatsch and Gorgé, 'Né sistema né periodico: appunti per la lettura di *Il sistema periodico* di Primo Levi', 1991, p. 66 who write that the 21 elements chosen by Levi 'non rispecchiano nessun ordine riconducibile ad un qualsiasi principio classificatorio della tavola di Mendeleev'. In fact Levi has not even arranged his chapters in order of the atomic weight of the elements in question, selecting, as he has, the elements with the atomic weight of 18, 1, 30, 26, 19, 28, 82, 80, 15, 79, 58, 24, 16, 22, 33, 7, 50, 92, 47, 23, and 6, with no correlation between these weights.
14. As Riatsch and Gorgé write ('Né sistema né periodico: appunti per la lettura di *Il sistema*

periodico di Primo Levi', 1991), although 'la citazione del titolo propone il testo di Levi come *metatesto* (che si occupa della tavola di Mendeleev in quanto "testo") e come *ipertesto* (che si occupa dello stesso *contenuto* della famosa tavola)', *Il sistema periodico* 'non è un metatesto che [...] "include" il suo ipotesto, bensì un *ipertesto* che se ne allontana attraverso una serie di *selezioni* e profonde *trasformazioni*'. (p. 66).

15. Belpoliti, Marco, 1998, p. 158. Along similar lines Grassano also writes of 'la tabella di Mendeleev, che offre struttura e titolo al volume' (Grassano, 1981, p. 99).
16. Interview with Lorenzo Mondo, broadcast on Rai 2, 15 September 1975, and transcribed in part by Poli and Calcagno, 1992, p. 71, my italics.
17. These are Levi's own words employed to describe the Periodic Table, as spoken to Tullio Regge in Ferrero, *Dialogo*, 1984, p. 9.
18. Levi's words, in Ferrero, ed., 1984, p. 9-10.
19. Riatsch and Gorgé, 1991, p. 67.
20. Ferrero, ed., *Dialogo*, 1984, p. 13.
21. Belpoliti, 1998, p. 46.
22. Levi's words from his interview with Giuseppe Grassano (Grassano, 1981, p. 14).
23. Levi's words to describe the Periodic Table, in Ferrero, ed., *Dialogo*, 1984, p. 9.
24. Cicioni, 1995, p. 74.
25. A number of critics would disagree with this. Cicioni, for example, writes that 'the consistent focus of Levi's self-representation is the narrated self as an Italian Jew, as a survivor of Auschwitz and as a chemist: the private self is excluded or marginalized' (1995, p. 70-71) and that 'the sole emotions to be disclosed, besides the recurring ones of the Auschwitz survivor, are those connected with the discourses of the chemist and writer' (p. 72). Similarly, Grassano writes of 'una evidente carica di partecipazione emotiva' in this text (Grassano, 1981, p. 113). There is, however, sufficient evidence to disprove these statements.
26. Mattioda in particular writes that 'come pochi altri, Primo Levi ha tentato di trovare delle spiegazioni razionali alle concretizzazioni dell'esperienza vissuta'. (Mattioda, 1998, p. 51) To Spadi's question of 'che cos'è nella coscienza dell'uomo laico la memoria dell'offesa? Come si riscatta? Il religioso perdona attraverso un sentimento di "pietà", che aiuta, forse, a riscattare anche che ci fa del male; ma per il laico è forse piú difficile sviluppare una sensazione, un sentimento di perdono?' Levi responded that 'Io penso che per l'uomo laico, quale io sono, l'essenziale sia capire e far capire'. (Spadi, 1997, p. 16).
27. Ferrero, 1984, p. 13.
28. Levi's words taken from an interview with Gagliano, Ernesto and Giorgio De Rienzo, 'La ragione non può andare in vacanza', *Stampa Sera*, 13 May 1975, also in Belpoliti, ed., 1997a, 115-7. It is interesting to note that whilst here Levi refers to Matter as a school, he also refers to the Lager as his true University, 'per me è stato una specie di università il Lager'. (Cavaglion, 1997, p. 74).
29. Interview with Gabriella Poli, 'L'alfabeto della chimica', *Tuttolibri*, *La stampa*, 6 December 1976.
30. Primo Levi, 'Lo scrittore non scrittore', a talk he gave at the Teatro Carignano, Turin, 19 November 1976, published in *La stampa* and Poli and Calcagno, 1992, pp. 92-98, p. 97. For Levi's alternative words on how chemistry 'mi ha salvato la vita' see Gagliano, E and G. De Rienzo, 13 May 1975, Mario Porro, 'Scienza', in Belpoliti, 1997b, p. 443, amongst others.

5
La chiave a stella: 'Arbeit macht frei'

La chiave a stella is Levi's sixth work, his first full-length fictional novel, as well as the first work to be composed in its entirety after Levi's retirement from his full-time career as a chemist. First published in December 1978, the character of the protagonist, Libertino Faussone, had appeared previously in a short story entitled 'Meditato con malizia' published in *La stampa* in March 1977, which was later to become the first chapter of *La chiave a stella*. Written in a period of disillusionment with working life, amid the prevailing belief that manual work was both oppressive and alienating, *La chiave a stella* is a clear reaction against many of the political and ideological debates of the time, and forms a stark contrast to the often negative and negating depictions of work in other contemporary writings. *La chiave a stella*'s controversial depiction of working life was at the basis of much debate surrounding its publication, and Levi himself was aware of its contentious subject matter:

> So che il mio libro è destinato a provocare qualche polemica, anche se non è nato con intento polemico. Certo, al giorno d'oggi il rifiuto del lavoro è addirittura teorizzato da componenti giovanili, ma anche senza giungere a queste posizioni estreme esiste in strati piuttosto diffusi una tendenza a sottovalutare la competenza professionale intesa come valore positivo in sé.[1]

> (I know that my book is destined to cause some controversy, even if it was not born of controversial intent. Of course, nowadays the rejection of work is even theorised by the young, but even without reaching these extreme positions there exists the rather widespread tendency to undervalue professional competence intended as a positive value in itself.)

La chiave a stella's reception by critics was often considered in the light of contemporary attitudes towards work. Corrado Stajano described *La chiave a stella* as a particularly interesting text on the grounds that 'affronta dall'interno il problema del rapporto tra l'uomo, le modalità del lavoro e l'oggetto del lavoro'[2] (it addresses from within the problem of the relationship between man, ways of working and the object of work); Giovanni Raboni considered Levi's conclusions to be 'affermazioni inconsuete, scarsamente alla moda, forse scandalose'[3] (unusual affirmations, barely in fashion, scandalous perhaps), words partly echoed in Gabriella Poli and Giorgio Calcagno's comments that *La chiave a stella* was '[una] sfida alla dilagante dissacrazione del lavoro [...]. Libro-scandalo insomma'[4] (a challenge to the rampant desecration of work [...]. In short, a scandal of a book), and Ernesto Ferrero wrote of how Levi's depiction of work as a means of attaining happiness was a provocatory assertion in the ideological climate of the late 1970s 'in cui il lavoro è visto come sofferenza, pura alienazione, esperienza disumanizzante'[5] (in which work was seen as suffering, pure alienation, a dehumanising experience). The attention of critics has, in general, tended to focus on three particular aspects of this text: its venture into the domain of manual work, Levi's linguistic experimentation, considered by many to be the greatest novelty here (Beccaria, 1993; Verdenelli, 1991; Mengaldo, 1990), and the text's affirmation that positive, free work represents one of the greatest approximations to wordly happiness attainable by mankind (Milano, 1979; Gramigna, 1978). Few connections have been made thus far, then, between the composition of *La chiave a stella* and Levi's experiences of slave labour in the concentration camp, between the work depicted in *La chiave a stella* and the horrendous 'Arbeit macht frei' (work makes you free) of Auschwitz and *Se questo è un uomo*. It is a significant oversight, particularly since, in the years both approaching and during the composition of *La chiave a stella*, Levi continued to write and publish a number of brief articles still specifically addressing the issues of the concentration camps: 'Un passato che credevamo non dovesse ritornare piú', *Corriere della Sera*, 8 May 1974; 'Così fu Auschwitz', *La Stampa*, 9 February 1975; 'Film e svastiche', *La Stampa*, 12 February 1977; 'I tedeschi e Kappler', *Ha Keillah*, October 1977; 'Donne da macello', *La Stampa*, 10 March 1978; 'Perché non ritornino le SS', *La Stampa*, 20 April 1978, and 'Jean Améry, il filosofo suicida', *La Stampa*, 7 December 1978. This chapter will address the connections between this text and Levi's Holocaust writings, investigating, not exclusively but in particular, the ways in which the labour of the camps and Levi's depiction of his experiences of work in *Se questo è un uomo* are revisited and reworked here in *La chiave a stella*.

La chiave a stella would appear to have little evident relationship to Levi's first text: as Levi himself commented, 'in questo mio ultimo libro, *La chiave a stella*, mi sono spogliato completamente della mia qualità di testimone e di ex deportato'[6] (in this most recent book of mine, *La chiave a stella*, I have completely stripped myself of my capacity as witness and ex deportee) and this is frequently referred to as Levi's only text 'su cui non si allunghi l'ombra del Lager'[7] (over which the shadow of the *Lager* is not stretched), where 'Auschwitz [is] no more than an occasional faint shadow'.[8] It ought to be noted, however, that the testimonial aspect of *Se questo è un uomo* remains here: not only has Levi in fact failed to shed himself of his 'qualità di testimone e di ex deportato', but the testimonial angle of *La chiave a stella* is still inseparably associated with the bearing witness of *Se questo è un uomo*. The association can be pinpointed to a precise moment in the text: at the beginning of the second chapter of *La chiave a stella* Levi's narrative persona has clearly been recounting to Faussone both his experiences in the concentration camps and his writing of *Se questo è un uomo*, since the chapter opens with Faussone's remark that '...Beh, è roba da non crederci: lo capisco che queste cose le è venuto voglia di scriverle. Sí, qualche cosa ne sapevo anch'io, me le raccontava mio padre, che in Germania c'era stato anche lui, ma in un'altra maniera.' (Well, it's unbelievable stuff: I understand that you wanted to write about these things. Yes, I knew a bit about it too, my father used to tell me things, he had been in Germany too, but in different circumstances) (*CS*, I, p. 952). This unnarrated but alluded-to conversation between Levi's narrative persona and his fictional creation creates a backdrop of intimacy between the two which is founded upon the relating of past experiences and in particular on Levi's role as survivor-testifier. Levi's statement shortly after the publication of the text that he intended to 'scrivere un racconto dove chi narrava fosse un testimone'[9] (write a story in which the narrator was a witness), reveals an objective which, as Belpoliti has observed, links *La chiave a stella* from a narrating viewpoint to the testimonial elements of both *Se questo è un uomo* and *La tregua*.[10] Through his choice of Faussone's profession, Levi wanted to 'dimostrare che anche il lavoro del "vile meccanico" può essere sorgente d'ispirazione e dunque di racconto. [...]. In questo senso, anche *La chiave a stella* può essere considerata una testimonianza'[11] (to show that even the job of a "worthless fitter" can be a source of inspiration and therefore also the source of a story. [...] In this sense, *La chiave a stella* can also be considered a testimony). Yet *La chiave a stella* is more than simply a testimony to a profession other than Levi's own, progressing from a text founded on Levi's own career, *Il sistema periodico*, to another, different kind of occupation. Levi's choice of narrative structure, to have the main character recount his own stories to a separate listener-narrator, rather than to narrate them directly to the reader through either a first- or third-person narrative, establishes a testifier-witness dynamic between the characters of Faussone and Levi's narrative persona, placing the latter in the role of witness to as well as the writer of Faussone's oral testimony. Written thirty years after Levi's original testimony to the horrors of the concentration camp world, *La chiave a stella* is still bearing witness, then, not to how man's humanity can be systematically destroyed, but to its restoration through the value and importance of work.

In a comparable manner, the linguistic experimentalism of *La chiave a stella*, Levi's use of Piedmontese for the voice of Faussone, has not only rendered Faussone's language typical of that of Turin's industrial workforce

(Beccaria, 1993), but also presents grounds for analogies with the language of *Se questo è un uomo*. Although much of Faussone's language is elucidated either by the narrator's demands for clarification, or by an explanation, ('questo termine, nel suo linguaggio, ha un significato vasto, equivalendo cumulativamente a remissivo, gentile, esperto, intelligente e coraggioso' [this term, in his language, has a wide range of meanings, being cumulatively equivalent to submissive, kind, expert, intelligent and courageous] [*CS*, I, p. 975] and 'Lui, veramente, aveva detto "'na fija", ed infatti, in bocca sua, il termine "ragazza" avrebbe suonato come una forzatura, ma altrettanto forzato e manierato suonerebbe "figlia" nella presente trascrizione.' [He had really said "'na fija", and actually, in his mouth, the term "ragazza" would have sounded forced, but "figlia" would sound just as forced and affected in the present transcription] [p. 979-80]), for any reader unfamiliar with Faussone's specific dialect and terminology this is still a less accessible language. It is a deliberate authenticity to the spoken word, justified by Levi's assertion that 'quelle storie [di Faussone] è molto difficile raccontarle in italiano; la loro lingua è questa. Ci sono termini tecnici, in italiano, che nessuno usa, e nemmeno capisce. L'uomo-fabbro parla la lingua degli uomini fabbri'[12] (it is very difficult to tell those tales [Faussone's] in Italian: this is their language. There are technical terms, in Italian, which nobody uses, and nobody understands. A man in manufacturing speaks the language of manufacturing men). It is precisely this faithfulness to the spoken idiom which reflects an element of *Se questo è un uomo*: the authenticity of Faussone's language is as vital to this text as the multilingual aspects of Levi's first work were to portraying the reality of the concentration camps. In both texts Levi employs language to increase the legitimacy, validity and accuracy of his writing to the situations he describes, be it the concentration camps or the adventures of Faussone's career.

The idea behind the character of Faussone was, according to Levi, conceived 'in Togliattigrad' where 'erano allora centinaia i Faussone, gente spedita dalla Fiat [...]. Erano tipi un po' speciali, quasi tutti piemontesi, operai che se la sapevano sbrigare in ogni situazione'[13] (there were hundreds of Faussones there then, people sent by Fiat [...]. They were a rather special sort, nearly all of them Piedmontese, workers who knew how to get through every situation). Levi's description of Alberto, his dear friend from *Se questo è un uomo*, is equally applicable to Faussone: Alberto, of whom Levi writes that 'il sangue delle sue vene è troppo libero perché [...] pensi di adagiarsi in un sistema [...], preferisce senza esitare gli incerti e le battaglie della "libera professione"' (the blood in his veins is too free for him to [...] consider making himself comfortable in a system [...], he unhesitatingly prefers the uncertainties and the battles of a "free profession") (*SQ*, I, p. 135) forms a basis for the character of Faussone whose 'battaglie della libera professione' are the subject matter here. Similar professional struggles were also at the heart of *Il sistema periodico*, and Levi-the-chemist's *misurarsi* through his battles against matter is continued here through the professional challenges Faussone faces. Parallels are drawn both between the careers of Levi and Faussone and, indirectly, between *La chiave a stella* and *Il sistema periodico* through the recurrence of the word *misurarsi* here:

> Tutti e tre i nostri mestieri, i due miei e il suo, nei loro giorni buoni possono dare la pienezza. Il suo, e il mestiere chimico che gli somiglia, perché insegnano a essere interi, a pensare con le mani e con tutto il corpo, a non arrendersi davanti alle giornate rovescie ed alle formule che non si capiscono [...] Siamo rimasti d'accordo su quanto di buono abbiamo in comune. Sul vantaggio di potersi *misurare*, del non dipendere da altri nel *misurarsi*, dello specchiarsi nella propria opera. (*CS*, I, p. 989, my italics)

> (All three of our professions, the two of mine plus his, can give a sense of fullness on their good days. His career, and the profession of chemist which resembles it, because both teach wholeness, teach you to think with your hands and with your whole body, to not surrender when faced with bad days or with formulas which can't be understood. [...] We agreed on how much good we have in common. On the advantage of being able to *measure yourself*, of not depending on others in this *self-measuring*, of being reflected in your own work.)

While each chapter of *Il sistema periodico* contained a challenge for Levi to overcome, in *La chiave a stella* it is Faussone's professional battles which constitute the focus of each chapter. Both Levi and Faussone struggle, through their respective professions, to *misurarsi*, for, as Levi writes in *L'altrui mestiere*, 'il misurarsi con la materia [...], è un'esperienza dolorosa ma salutare, senza la quale non si diventa adulti e responsabili' (measuring yourself against matter [...], is a painful but salutary experience, without which one does not become adult or responsible) (*AM*, II, p. 641-2), words echoed later, with reference to *La chiave a stella*, in his statement to Grassano that 'L'esercizio di se stessi, il confrontare se stessi con gli altri e con il mondo materiale, benché costi fatica e dolore, è indispensabile. Non si può pensare una vita senza confronto, e senza sconfitte quindi'[14] (Exerting oneself, comparing oneself to others and to the material world, although tiring and painful, is indispensable). For both Levi and Faussone, then, the process of measuring, comparing and assessing one's capabilities through work is a process of learning and growth, essential for becoming a fully-realized human being; the act of testing yourself through free, positive work heightens and strengthens the status of *man* in both *La chiave a stella* and *Il sistema periodico*.

It is a human and humanising aspect to work which is further emphasized through the terms Faussone employs to describe his constructions. In the chapter entitled 'Clausura', for example, both human and animate metaphors are repeatedly used to describe the construction of a distillation tower: 'mi sembrava di veder crescere un bambino, voglio dire un bambino ancora da nascere, quando è ancora nella pancia di sua mamma' (it was like I could see a baby growing, a baby as yet unborn, that is, when it is still in its mother's stomach) (*CS*, I, p. 953); 'come un albero abbattuto' (like a felled tree) (p. 954); 'sembrava la giungla di Tarzan' (it was like Tarzan's jungle) (p. 956); 'quella torre sembrava un bosco; e sembrava anche a quelle figure che si vedono nell'anticamera dei dottori, IL CORPO UMANO: una coi muscoli, una con gli ossi, una coi nervi e una con tutte le budelle' (that tower looked like a wood, and it also looked like those illustrations you see in doctors' waiting rooms, THE HUMAN BODY: one with the muscles, one with the bones, one with the nerves and all the bowels) (p. 957); 'anche la colonna stava facendo un discorso, e era proprio un po' come quando uno è malato e ha la febbre e dice delle goffate' (even the column was having a conversation, and it was really a bit like when someone is ill with a fever and they rant) (p. 958); 'come una gran bestia che gli mancasse il fiato' (like a great beast out of breath) (p. 959); 'come uno che a parlare non sia ancora buono ma si vede che ha male' (like someone who is not yet very good at speaking but you can see they are in pain) (p. 959); 'mi pareva che tutto l'impianto tirasse un respiro di sollievo, come quando uno sta male e allora gli dànno la morfina e lui si addormenta e per un poco ha smesso di soffrire' (it seemed to me that all the equipment was heaving a sigh of relief, like when someone is ill and then they give them morphine and they fall asleep and for a while have stopped suffering) (p. 960); 'come uno che soffra e non sia capace di parlare [...] come fanno i malati' (like someone who is suffering and is not able to speak [...] as the ill do) (p. 961), and 'a quel punto invece che un bambino quella colonna ammalata incominciava a sembrarmi una di quelle bestie' (at that point instead of resembling a baby the sick column started to look to me like one of those beasts) (p. 964). Levi's use of anthropic and living metaphors in such a way has several consequences: it highlights the degree of respect and dignity which Faussone affords his constructions, and accordingly also his work, and, perhaps more crucially, it draws the reader back to Levi's earlier texts, in particular to *Se questo è un uomo*, *Storie naturali* and *Vizio di forma*. Faussone's descriptions of so many of his constructions, throughout *La chiave a stella*, in human terms, of buildings and machinery invested with life, perceived as animate rather than inanimate, echo the *Versificatore*'s assumption of human qualities in *Storie naturali* as well as that of the *Rete* and the *Golem* of *Vizio di forma*. Most consequentially, however, the animation of edifices in particular as well as the blurring of the boundaries between the animate and the inanimate recalls Levi's portrayal of the *Lager* as a living organism, with its roads and buildings invested with numbers identical to the new 'names' of its human prisoners, who are, instead 'una sola grigia macchina' (just a single grey machine) (*SQ*, I, p. 45), and its dredger, more human than its audience, which appears to eat (*SQ*, I, p. 69). Levi's comment in *Se questo è un uomo* that 'nulla è vivo se non macchine e schiavi: e piú quelle di questi' (the only things alive are machines and slaves, and the former more than the latter) (*SQ*, I, p. 67) is therefore still partly true in *La chiave a stella*: the machines and buildings here continue to be portrayed as living; the most prominent distinction is that here the men are equally alive.

Faussone stands as the embodiment of professional and human dignity as the humanising factors of his work serve to elevate his sense of pride and self-worth. This professional dignity is central both to the text and to Faussone's way of life, for as he comments to the narrator of his stories: 'Se si escludono istanti prodigiosi e singoli che il destino ci può donare, l'amare il proprio lavoro (che purtroppo è privilegio di pochi) costituisce la migliore approssimazione concreta alla felicità sulla terra' (if you exclude the prodigious and unique instants that destiny can give us, loving your own job (which is, unfortunately, the privilege of the few) constitutes the best concrete approximation to earthly happiness) (*CS*, I, p. 1015). This work ethic is particularly significant when compared to Levi's earlier portrayals of work, for the notion of work revealed in *La chiave a stella* is comparable with that of Mordo Nahum in *La tregua* ('fondamento della sua etica era il lavoro, che egli sentiva come sacro dovere' [work, which he felt to be a sacred duty, was the foundation of his ethic] [*LT*, I, p. 237]) and is the very antithesis of that of *Se questo è un uomo*. *La chiave a stella* provides a picture of a free man whose life has been entirely of his own making and choice: 'io del mio destino non me ne sono mai lamentato, e del resto se mi lamentassi sarei una bestia, perché me lo sono scelto da me: volevo vedere dei paesi, lavorare con gusto, e non vergognarmi dei soldi che guadagno, e quello che volevo l'ho avuto' (I have never complained about my destiny, and, after all, I'd be a cretin if I complained because I chose my destiny all by myself: I wanted to see other countries, work tastefully, and not be ashamed of the money I earned, and I've got what I wanted) (*CS*, I, p. 967);[15] who not only lives freely but also works freely,[16] for as Levi's narrative persona remarks, 'il termine "libertà" ha notoriamente molti sensi, ma forse il tipo di libertà piú accessibile, piú goduto soggettivamente, e piú utile al consorzio umano, coincide con l'essere competenti nel proprio lavoro, e quindi nel provare piacere a svolgerlo' (the term "freedom" notoriously has many meanings, but perhaps the most accessible type of freedom, the type most subjectively enjoyed and most useful to human society corresponds with being competent in your own work, and therefore enjoying doing it) (*CS*, I, p. 1074). Faussone's work is patently antithetical to the senseless, horrendous parody of concentration camp work, designed to bring about suffering, degradation, depletion and ultimately death. The issue of work has therefore been transformed from 'una pura pena' (a pure punishment) in which 'mancava totalmente il rapporto tra causa e effetto, cioè il lavoro che ti dà sostentamento'[17] (the relationship between cause and effect was totally lacking, in other words work which provides sustenance) in *Se questo è un uomo*, into its rightful role in *La chiave a stella*, that of work which brings its own compensation, rewards and pleasure, so that Faussone can comment that 'ogni lavoro è come il primo amore' (every job is like your first love) (*CS*, I, p. 1048). The slave labour of Auschwitz, work *alla rovescia*, is righted here: whilst *Se questo è un uomo* outlined the alienating, debasing, humiliating and destructive effects of enforced labour, *La chiave a stella* reverses this, offering a representation of work as a defining aspect of this character's humanity and asserting mankind's dignity through work.

The work ethic of *La chiave a stella* is also reminiscent of the message behind *Storie naturali* and *Vizio di forma*. Tesio's definition of the morality of the two collections, in which 'occorre che ciascuno viva da uomo e agisca responsabilmente'[18] (everybody needs to live like a man and act responsibly) is reflected here where living and working as *da uomo* and *responsabilmente* is of the utmost importance. Levi's comparisons between his and Faussone's professions, which 'insegnano a essere interi, a pensare con le mani e con tutto il corpo, a non arrendersi' (teach you to be whole, to think with your hands and with your whole body, to not surrender) (*CS*, I, p. 989), depict a moral image of work which is both essential and advantageous to mankind. Throughout *La chiave a stella* work assumes an ethical role of particular benefit to Faussone who is able to indicate the personal gains to be had from productive, effective work. Thus in 'Senza tempo' Faussone affirms how his confidence in his work extends to other areas of his life: 'sta di fatto che dopo che ho preso sicurezza a saldare, ho preso sicurezza a tutto, fino alla maniera di camminare' (the fact of the matter is that after I became confident at welding, I became confident at everything, even in the way I walked) (*CS*, I, p. 1059); and in 'Acciughe I' the act of learning through work leads to personal growth: 'per me un uomo che non abbia mai avuto un collaudo negativo non è un uomo, è come se fosse rimasto alla prima comunione' (as far as I'm concerned a man who has never had a bad test is not a man, it is as if he remained at his first communion) (*CS*, I, p. 1083). The merits of the respective professions of both *La chiave a stella*'s storyteller and its narrator, ('tutti e tre i nostri mestieri, i due miei e il suo, nei loro giorni buoni possono dare la pienezza' [all three of our professions, the two of mine plus his, can give a sense of fullness on their good days] [*CS*, I, p. 989]), provide a feeling of *pienezza* which can only be gained through work. Throughout the course of *La chiave a stella*, Faussone's contentment with his work, in particular with work well done, prevails. Faussone's remarks that 'quando ho finito di metterla su [...] mi sentivo come se mi avessero fatto commendatore' (when I finished putting it up [...] I felt as if they had made me knight commander) (*CS*, I, p. 947), 'se ho fatto un lavoro [...], e non è troppo fuori mano, ogni tanto mi piace andarlo a trovare' (if I have done a job [...],and it is not too out-of-the-way, every now and again I like to go and visit it) (*CS*, I, p. 1063), and in particular that 'io l'anima ce la metto in tutti i lavori, lei lo sa, anche nei piú balordi, anzi, con piú che sono balordi, tanto piú ce la metto. Per me, ogni lavoro che incammino è come un primo amore' (I put my heart into every job, you know it, even into the more pointless ones, indeed the more pointless they are, the more effort I put in) (*CS*, I, p. 979) highlight the importance of his work to him. It is, perhaps unexpectedly, this theme of personal satisfaction with a job done to the best of one's ability which again links the storyteller of *La chiave a stella* to the author of *Se questo è un uomo*. The issue of personal contentment with work conscientiously and successfully performed was, improbably, first noted by Levi with reference to the concentration camps as he observed that:

> Il bisogno del "lavoro ben fatto" è talmente radicato da spingere a far bene anche il lavoro imposto, schiavistico. Il muratore italiano che mi ha salvato la vita, portandomi cibo di nascosto per sei mesi, detestava i tedeschi, il loro cibo, la loro lingua, la loro guerra; ma quando lo mettevano a tirar su muri li faceva dritti e solidi, non per obbedienza ma per dignità professionale.[19]

> (The need for "work well done" is so rooted in us that it drives us to perform even imposed, slave labour well. The Italian bricklayer who saved my life, secretly bringing me food for six months, hated the Germans, their food, their language, their war; yet when they put him to work building walls he built them straight and solid, not out of obedience but out of professional dignity.)

Levi's faith in the value of work, and in the moral benefits to be gained from work, perhaps indicate a determination to be unshaken by the experiences of slave labour. For Levi, work, after his experiences in Auschwitz, assumed a greater significance than it might otherwise have done:

> Sono ben consapevole che dopo il Lager il lavoro, anzi, i miei due lavori (la chimica e lo scrivere) hanno avuto, e tuttora hanno, un'importanza fondamentale nella mia vita. Sono convinto che l'uomo normale è biologicamente costruito per un'attività diretta a un fine, e che l'ozio, o il lavoro senza scopo (come l'*Arbeit* di Auschwitz) provoca sofferenza e atrofia.[20]

> (I am well aware that after the *Lager* work, in fact my two jobs (chemistry and writing) have had, and still have, a fundamental

importance in my life. I am convinced that normal man is biologically built for an activity directed towards an end, and that idleness, or aimless work (like the *Arbeit* of Auschwitz) provokes suffering and atrophy.)

If mankind is 'biologicamente costruito' to work then man's dignity through the fulfillment of this biological destiny, apparently destroyed forever in the camps, is definitively and categorically righted in *La chiave a stella*. Yet not only were Levi's notions of the value of work itself and the importance of work well done conceived with reference to the concentration camps: Levi's perceptions of work as a means of salvation are also grounded in his previous experiences. Levi referred to both of his professions as his lifelines: of his work as a chemist in the Buna factory he commented 'al mio mestiere devo la vita. Non sarei sopravvissuto ad Auschwitz, se dopo dieci mesi di dura manovalanza non fossi entrato in un laboratorio'[21] (I owe my life to my profession. I would not have survived Auschwitz if, after ten months of hard manual labour, I had not entered a laboratory); and to his work as a writer, with particular mention of the composition of *Se questo è un uomo*, 'Io penso che se mi sono "salvato" – e dico salvato nel senso vasto della parola – è perché ho scritto *Se questo è un uomo*'[22] (I think that if I am "saved", and I say saved in the widest sense of the word, it is because I wrote *Se questo è un uomo*). The inspiration for a character whose work is humanising, dignified and dignifying therefore has its roots precisely as a reaction to and against Levi's experiences and analysis of the concentration camps. *La chiave a stella*'s restoration of man's dignity through work is conclusively redressing the words placed above the gates of Auschwitz: the '*Arbeit Macht Frei*' of the concentration camp has here been righted and granted its true significance; work *can* make you free.

Notes

1. Levi's words cited in the preface to *La chiave a stella*, Einaudi 2nd edition of 1991, p. ii.
2. 'Il lavoro e la sua qualità', *Il Messaggero*, 11 December 1978, also published as an appendix to the 1991 Einaudi 2nd edition of *CS*.
3. 'Riesce a creare suspense col montaggio di una gru', *La Stampa*, 23 December 1978, also in Belpoliti, 1997b, pp. 128-9.
4. Poli and Calcagno, 1992, p. 124.
5. 'La fortuna critica' in Ferrero, ed., *Primo Levi: Un'antologia della critica*, 1997, pp. 303–384, p. 339.
6. Grassano, 1981, p. 3.
7. Poli and Calcagno, 1992, p. 161.
8. Mirna Cicioni, *Primo Levi: Bridges of Knowledge*, 1995, p. 86. Along similar lines, Jane

Nystedt also points out in her linguistic analysis of Levi's works that 'in *CS*, e in *CS* solo, mancano la 'violenza', la 'collera', il 'dolore', la 'strage'' (Nystedt, 1993, p. 38).

9. Levi's words to Francesco Poli, 'Tino Faussone, la storia di un operaio specializzato', *Quotidiano dei lavoratori*, 28 February 1979.
10. Belpoliti, *Note ai testi*, *Opere I*, p. 1455.
11. Levi's words to Antonio Debenedetti, 'Vincitore il romanzo', *Corriere della sera*, 4 July 1979.
12. Levi's words to Silvia Giacomoni, 'Il mago Merlino e l'uomo fabbro', *la Repubblica*, 24 January 1979, also in Belpoliti, ed., 1997a, pp. 118–22.
13. Levi's explanation of the idea behind the character of Faussone, given to Giorgio Manzini, 'Elogio del libero lavoro', *Paese Sera*, 11 December 1978.
14. Grassano, 1981, p. 9.
15. There is a clear comparison to be made here between Faussone and 'Il fabbro di se stesso' in *VF* whose life and evolution is also entirely of his own choice and design.
16. Faussone's work is free in the sense that it was entirely his own choice of career, and that he is 'non sotto padrone, non nella fabbrica, non a fare tutta la vita gli stessi gesti attaccato al convogliatore' (*CS*, I, p. 1017). However, he is not altogether liberated or unrealistically independent in his work, for 'dove mi mandano vado' (p. 975), 'quando hai fatto un contratto, dove ti mandano bisogna bene che ci vai' (p. 990) and occasionally his boss demands 'che mollassi lí tutto e andassi subito da lui' (p. 958).
17. Levi's words to Grassano, 1981, p. 4-5.
18. Tesio, 'Ritratti critici di contemporanei', *Belfagor*, 1979, p. 672.
19. Levi's words to Philip Roth, 'Salvarsi dall'inferno come Robinson', *La Stampa*, 26 November 1986. Levi is not alone in this observation: Aleksandr Solzhenitsyn also writes of the immense satisfaction to be gained from performing manual work to the very best of your ability even whilst imprisoned in *One Day in the Life of Ivan Denisovich*, 1991, in particular pp. 79-93; and Bruno Bettelheim, in *The Informed Heart: The Human Condition in Mass Society*, 1970, writes that even in the concentration camp it was important to work well 'in order to feel like a man' (p. 187).
20. Levi's words to Philip Roth, 'Salvarsi dall'inferno come Robinson'.
21. Levi's words spoken at a conference at Teatro Carignano, Turin, 19 November 1976, transcribed in Poli and Calcagno, 1992, p. 97.
22. Levi's response to an anonymous question at a talk given at the Leo Club, Cuneo, 1975, transcribed in Poli and Calcagno, 1992, p. 195.

6
Lilít e altri racconti, *L'altrui mestiere*, *Racconti e saggi:* Una certa curiosità per i vortici'

This chapter will examine *Lilít e altri racconti* (1981), *L'altrui mestiere* (1985), and *Racconti e saggi* (1986) together, firstly because all three are collections of Levi's various stories, essays and articles published, for the most part, in *La Stampa*, and secondly because the composition and publication of the items which constitute these collections also overlap considerably. The writings which make up *Lilít e altri racconti* were first published between 1975 and 1981, the essays contained in *L'altrui mestiere* first appeared between 1976 and 1985, and the collection of Levi's articles and essays for *Racconti e saggi* were published in *La Stampa* over the largest period of time, between 1960 and 1986.

Lilít e altri racconti is divided into three sections, entitled 'Passato prossimo', 'Futuro anteriore' and 'Presente indicativo'. The first section, 'Passato prossimo', contains new Auschwitz stories based around experiences of the concentration camps and their aftermath and is therefore most closely connected to both *Se questo è un uomo* and *La tregua*. The provocative title of 'Passato prossimo' indicates both the continued proximity of Auschwitz itself and of Levi's memories of the concentration camp; here this near past remains explicitly close rather than distant or concluded. Yet in spite of comparisons with Levi's earlier texts, the content of 'Passato prossimo' does not bear much resemblance to that of Levi's other concentration camp writings: the nearness implied by the title of the section is countered by the distance of time passed, meaning that Levi's urge to bear witness has passed, for the moment, leaving him able to focus on the recounting of the more unusual episodes of the *Lager*. This is no longer a grave documentation of the horrors of the concentration camp experience and system, but is instead a collection of stories narrating bizarre and anomalous events. The stories here have therefore changed considerably in both content and tone:

> A distanza di circa trent'anni, mi era sembrato che il patrimonio di ricordi del Lager non fosse stato ancora tutto speso in *Se questo è un uomo* e in *La tregua* e che valesse la pena di tornarci sopra.

Naturalmente il punto di vista è cambiato: non provavo piú l'urgenza della testimonianza e della liberazione interiore. Mi pareva di aver detto tutto sulla situazione sociologica del Lager, sul suo orrore essenziale, sul suo aspetto di specchio distorto del nostro mondo odierno, sulle sue regole. Provavo invece il desiderio, abbastanza sereno, di rivedere e ristudiare da vicino alcune figure di quel tempo, vittime, superstiti e oppressori, che mi erano rimaste nitide nella memoria, individuali sullo sfondo grigio, collettivo, impersonale dei "sommersi".[1]

(At a distance of about thirty years, it seemed to me that my resources of *Lager* memories had not yet all been spent in *Se questo è un uomo* and *La tregua* and that it was worthwhile returning to them. The point of view has naturally changed: I no longer felt the urgency of testimony and internal liberation. I thought I had said everything possible about the sociological situation of the *Lager*, about its essential horror, about its aspect as a distorted mirror of today's world, about its rules. On the other hand I felt quite a calm desire to review and re-examine from close quarters some of the people from that time, victims, survivors and oppressors, who had remained clear in my memory, individuals against the grey, collective, impersonal background of the "drowned".)

The 'Passato prossimo' section of *Lilít* therefore testifies to the unique cases of survival during the war, to the more unusual occurrences in camp life, to its exceptional moments of reprieve,[2] its more bizarre episodes like the public bathing of Vladek or Levi's receipt of a letter from home, itself 'una falla, una lacuna dell'universo nero' (a breach, a lacuna in the black universe) (*L*, II, p. 27). It assumes, on the readers' part, a familiarity with *Se questo è un uomo* which forms the 'immediate intertextual background'[3] to the stories recounted here. Some of the 'Passato prossimo' tales elaborate upon people mentioned in *Se questo è un uomo* and *La tregua* and therefore build specifically upon these works: 'Il ritorno di Lorenzo' developing Levi's earlier depiction of Lorenzo Perrone who secured extra rations of food for Levi in Auschwitz; 'Il ritorno di Cesare' detailing the final part of Cesare's journey home, excluded from *La tregua* and other writings 'perchè Cesare me lo aveva vietato' (because Cesare had forbidden me to) (*L*, II, p. 54). In other cases, the stories here have their thematical basis in the issues rather than the people of *Se questo è un uomo*: the inhumane treatment and bestialization of prisoners as demonstrated by the public washing of Vladek in 'Il cantore e il veterano' and by Levi's acceptance of the inevitability of the beating he receives from his *kapo* described in 'Il giocoliere' as 'poco di piú insomma che una comunicazione non verbale' (little more, then, than an act of non-verbal communication) (*L*, II, p. 16); and the implicit return in 'Un discepolo' to the themes of the 'Al di qua del bene e del male' chapter of Levi's first work in its explanations of how 'per cavarsela, bisognava darsi da fare, organizzare cibo illegale, scansare il lavoro, trovare amici influenti, nascondersi, nascondere il proprio pensiero, rubare, mentire; che chi non faceva cosí moriva presto' (in order to get by you needed to keep busy, organise illegal food, dodge work, find influential friends, hide, hide your own thoughts, steal, lie; whoever failed to do this died quickly) (*L*, II, p. 26).

Other aspects of 'Passato prossimo' have altered entirely from their counterparts in *Se questo è un uomo*. The depiction of the prisoners featured here, for example, has changed dramatically as Levi describes the rare instances of solidarity and friendship which arose in this alienating world. Thus emphasis is placed upon the 'buona azione' (good action) (*L*, II, p. 17) of Eddy the vice-Kapo in 'Il giocoliere' who does not denounce Levi for attempting to write a letter home; upon Otto's remarkable storage of Ezra's soup for him whilst Ezra fasted in 'Il cantore e il veterano', and, in 'Il ritorno di Lorenzo', upon Lorenzo's exceptional assistance to many of the prisoners in the camps, including Levi and Alberto. With a stronger emphasis on the rare instances of good actions within the *Lager*, those who appear here are frequently more human and less bestial than those in *Se questo è un uomo*. Some prisoners, like Rappoport, Wolf, and Cesare succeed in asserting their humanity through rebellion: Rappoport through his cry that 'se all'altro mondo incontrerò Hitler, gli sputerò in faccia con pieno diritto [...] perché non mi ha avuto!' (if I meet Hitler in the next world, I'll spit in his face with every right [...] because he has not had me!) (*L*, II, p. 11); Wolf who, in non-compliance with the rules and against all probability, manages to acquire and play a violin, and Cesare's insistence that his repatriation be in a manner of his own choosing. Others prove their humanity through their refusal to behave like the animals they are treated as: both Levi and Lorenzo through their help to others (Levi's training of the Hungarian prisoner in 'Un discepolo', his help to the gypsy in 'Lo zingaro' with the composition of his letter, and Lorenzo's feeding of many prisoners besides just Levi and Alberto in 'Il ritorno di Lorenzo'); Wolf's refusal to scratch himself like a dog ('Il nostro sigillo'), and Joel and Avrom's protestations at their deportation in wagons to the camps ('La storia di Avrom' and 'Stanco di finzioni'). The people contained in 'Passato prossimo' are therefore no longer 'the anonymous, faceless, voiceless mass of the shipwrecked, but the few, the different, the ones in whom (if only for a moment) I had recognized the will and capacity to react, and hence a rudiment of virtue'[4] for these are men, if only briefly, fleetingly reprieved from their bestial state.

The large number of people who appear in 'Passato prossimo', as well as the nature of the episodes narrated, suggests that Levi is still bearing witness here, not this time to his own, or even a collective story, but to other prisoners' stories and lives, those who did not survive to recount their own testimony. Indeed in the first story of *Lilít*, Rappoport announces to Levi and Valerio that, 'nel caso deprecabile che uno di voi mi sopravviva, potrete raccontare [la mia storia]' (in the disgraceful event that one of you should outlive me, you can tell [my story]) and Levi, as author, comments at the end of this piece that 'ho ragione di ritenere che Rappoport non sia sopravvissuto; perciò stimo doveroso eseguire del mio meglio l'incarico che mi è stato affidato' (I have reason to believe that Rappoport did not survive; therefore I consider it only right to carry out the duty entrusted to me to the best of my ability) (*L*, II, p. 12). In the 'Passato prossimo' section of *Lilít* Levi's own experiences are on the sidelines as the centre of interest is focussed almost entirely on others. This is no longer the multiple testimony of *Se questo è un uomo* in which Levi's personal story can appear as part of the collective, but rather the relating of others' unique tales in which Levi's presence as narrative persona is negligible and, at times, non-existent. Of the stories contained in 'Passato prossimo', 'Capaneo', 'Il nostro sigillo', 'Il cantore e il veterano', 'La storia di Avrom', 'Stanco di finzioni', 'Il ritorno di Cesare', 'Il ritorno di Lorenzo' and 'Il re dei Giudei' are all Auschwitz-related stories featuring in a primary role someone other than Levi himself.

Whilst 'Passato prossimo' carries patent echoes of the Holocaust in its revisiting of Levi's camp memories, the resonances of *Se questo è un uomo* contained in the second section of *Lilít*, 'Futuro anteriore', are more subtle, bearing stronger comparisons with both the *Storie naturali* and *Vizio di forma* collections. A number of themes common to Levi's earlier science fiction writing persist in 'Futuro anteriore'. Issues of imprisonment, as portrayed in 'Angelica farfalla' and 'La bella addormentata nel frigo', continue their presence here: the beast entrapped in the ancient temple in 'La bestia nel tempio', who will be killed and eaten if he ever manages to escape; the eventual capture of the human being in 'I costruttori di ponti'; and the poem's attempts at escape from the imprisonment of the page in 'La fuggitiva'. The inhumane treatment of human beings in *Storie naturali*'s 'Il sesto giorno' and *Vizio di forma*'s two 'Recuenco' stories is mirrored here in 'I gladiatori' where the unemployed and those convicted of crimes are forced to fight automobiles in a mass circus; in 'I costruttori di ponti' where a human being is imprisoned as a pet, and in 'Tantalio' where Fassio is the victim of scientific experimentation. The hybrids of 'Quaestio de centauris' as well as the loss of humanity are here present in 'Disfilassi', dedicated to a futuristic portrayal of a world dominated by partly-human hybrids at a point in time in which mankind has been genetically invaded by other species: 'la ferrea barriera fra specie e specie era andata infranta, ed ancora non si sapeva se per il bene o per il male' (the iron barrier between species and species had been shattered, and no-one knew yet whether it was for the better or for the worse) (*L*, II, p. 97). As was often the case with *Storie naturali* and *Vizio di forma*, apparently innocuous stories are here often coupled with an air of quiet menace: the deceptive appearance and hidden strength of 'Una stella tranquilla'; the threat of imminent death offered in a painless version at a price in 'A tempo debito'; the gradual threat of human extinction in 'Disfilassi'; the human source of blood for the bloodsuckers in 'Le sorelle della palude', and the suddenly tragic effects of the previously beneficial tantalum paint in 'Tantalio'. The permanent threat of danger, imprisonment and inhumane treatment at the hands of others are all thematic continuities from *Storie naturali* and *Vizio di forma*, but these, in turn, lead back more directly to the issues initially raised in *Se questo è un uomo*. The continuation of these themes here is therefore inextricably linked to Levi's original portrayal of his concentration camp experiences.

The third section of *Lilít*, 'Presente indicativo', contains tales with a mainly contemporary setting, yet if these are to be stories 'indicative' or definitive of the present, as the title would suggest, then the picture Levi paints is one of imprisonment, prejudice, and a lack of comprehension. The tale of the two Englishmen taken hostage and imprisoned by the Siriono people in 'Gli stregoni' is echoed by that of the two German soldiers kept hostage in 'Ospiti', and by the imprisoned soul of Miss MacLeish's mother in 'L'anima e gli ingegneri'. 'Decodificazione' and 'Fine settimana' contain parallel themes of prejudice and anti-Semitism, the former in the form of pro-Nazi graffiti, the latter in the form of Levi and Silvio's overnight detention in a hostel, prior to deportation. 'La sfida della molecola' contains another chemistry story in which the quest for comprehension is uppermost, if fruitless in a world in which there is a prevalence 'della confusione sull'ordine, e della morte indecente sulla vita' (of confusion over order, and of indecent death over life) (*L*, II, p. 167). In this particular story, not only does the search for understanding mirror that of Levi's in the concentration camp, but the parallels Levi draws between science and the outside world are particularly significant:

> La "molecula" unica, degradata ma gigantesca, che nasce-muore fra le tue mani è un messaggio e un simbolo osceno: simbolo delle altre brutture senza ritorno né rimedio che oscurano il nostro avvenire, del prevalere della confusione sull'ordine, e della morte indecente sulla vita. (*L*, II, p. 167)

> (The single "molecule", broken but enormous, which is born and dies in your hands, is a message and an obscene symbol: symbol of the other awful, irreversible and incurable things which darken our future, symbol of the prevalence of confusion over order, and of indecent death over life.)

Levi's portrayal here, then, is of a world in which confusion and disorder equate with death, order and clarity with life. Moreover, the notion of death here is of a *morte indecente* which epitomises the deaths of the concentration camps, a *bruttura* which darkens Levi's own life. All three sections of *Lilít e altri racconti* therefore provide a perpetuation of the Holocaust themes as the *passato prossimo* of the *Lager* is incumbent upon the entire collection. 'Passato prossimo' physically revisits the concentration camps, 'Futuro anteriore' depicts a concerning image of a future dependant on today's wrongs, and 'Presente indicativo' exhibits a number of contemporary evils, ending, in the final tale, and reminiscent of the concluding lines of *La tregua*, with only the 'Breve sogno' of respite.

This period of respite reappears in *L'altrui mestiere*, which differentiates itself from *Lilít* by its almost total lack of direct reference to the concentration camp. Of the fifty-one articles contained here, ten have an autobiographical element in them, but none focusses directly on Levi's experiences in Auschwitz. Belpoliti believes this was a deliberate choice, writing that in *L'altrui mestiere* 'restano esclusi articoli o interventi legati al tema del Lager, della deportazione e le rievocazioni di eventi della seconda guerra mondiale o dello sterminio ebraico. Ne risulta un libro privo di ombre o punti oscuri'[5] (articles or interventions linked to the themes of the *Lager*, deportation and the remembrance of events of the Second World War or of the extermination of the Jews are excluded. What results is a book without shadows or dark areas). Instead the articles here cover a wide range of topics embracing Levi's family home, going back to school, his first adventures with a microscope, an encounter with a snake and his work on a word processor, to name but a few examples. Only five of the articles here contain any explicit reference to Auschwitz: in 'Ex chimico', Levi writes of his profession as chemist that 'durante la mia prigionia ad Auschwitz mi ha salvato la vita' (saved my life during my imprisonment in Auschwitz) (*AM*, II, p. 641); 'La lingua dei chimici II' features 'un vecchio compagno di prigionia' (an old prison mate) (*AM*, II, p. 746); 'Il teschio e l'orchidea' refers to 'il mio ingresso in Lager' (my entrance into the *Lager*) (*AM*, II, p. 823); 'Il linguaggio degli odori' mentions 'quando ho rivisitato Auschwitz dopo quasi quarant'anni' (when I revisited Auschwitz after almost forty years) (*AM*, II, p. 840); and, perhaps most significantly, 'Eclissi dei profeti', the last in the collection, describes the *Lager* again as a 'feroce osservatorio sociologico' (ferocious sociological observatory) (*AM*, II, p. 854). This depiction of the concentration camps as a sociological observatory is reminiscent of Levi's earlier sentence in *Se questo è un uomo* that 'vorremmo far considerare come il Lager sia stato, anche e notevolmente, una gigantesca esperienza biologica e sociale' (we would like you to consider that the *Lager* was also, notably, a gigantic biological and social experiment) (*SQ*, I, p. 83). This perception of the camp system is particularly significant because Levi continues to portray the world here as though it forms part of an experiment in need of analysis. That Levi is truly in the role of observer here is often made clear by his use of verbs: in 'Segni sulla pietra', (*AM*, II, p. 685-8), to provide just one example, verbs of observation, 'si vede', 'si osserva che', 'si nota che', and 'ad un esame piú attento si nota che...' appear six times in total. In the *premessa* to *L'altrui mestiere* Levi writes that 'mi sono divertito *a guardare il mondo* sotto luci inconsuete, invertendo per cosí dire la strumentazione: a rivisitare le cose della tecnica con l'occhio del letterato, e le lettere con l'occhio del tecnico' (I enjoyed *looking at the world* in an unusual light, inverting, as it were, the instruments: revisiting the world of technology from the viewpoint of a man of letters, and the world of letters from the viewpoint of the technologist) (*AM*, II, p. 631, my italics). *L'altrui mestiere* is the result of Levi's time spent 'a guardare il mondo', recording what he sees, observing and bearing witness, in a sense, to certain aspects of this world. Thus Levi's remarks and observations on animals in articles such as 'Romanzi dettati dai grilli', 'Lo scoiattolo', 'Il salto della pulce', 'Le farfalle', 'Gli scarabei', 'Il mondo invisibile', 'Le piú liete creature del mondo' and 'Paura dei ragni' are 'visto dal nostro osservatorio umano' (seen from our human observatory) (*AM*, II, p. 757), exactly as though Levi is observing the animal world through the microscope given to him by his father in 'Il mondo invisibile'. Microscope imagery as well as a microscopic approach to detail recurs frequently throughout the animal articles in particular, connecting the role of observer with that of scientist. In 'Il salto della pulce' Levi writes that 'l'aspetto che la pulce presenta sotto il microscopio è talmente insolito da apparire diabolico' (the appearance of a flea under the microscope is so strange that it appears diabolic) (*AM*, II, p. 727); in 'Le farfalle' that admiration turns to horror and disgust 'quando esaminiamo al microscopio il capo di una farfalla' (when we examine a butterfly's head under the microscope) (*AM*, II, p. 752); there are various experiments with the microscope described in 'Il mondo invisibile', and his detailed examination of *I promessi sposi* in 'Il pugno di Renzo', is similarly microscopic in approach as Levi refuses to accept the validity of Manzoni's description of Renzo's gestures.

Levi's approach to writing in this collection is varied, however, and often unpredictable. 'La lingua dei chimici I' and 'II' are not written from the scientific angle implied by their titles, for in these items Levi is in the role of linguist, examining the names of chemical elements and compounds. Equally unanticipated are 'L'ispettore Silhouette', 'Le parole fossili' and 'Leggere la vita' which are written in the style of detective stories, tracing the unknown origins and solving the mysteries of language. 'Segni sulla pietra' is structured from an archaeological-historical angle; 'La luna e noi' and 'Ex chimico' from a literary rather than a scientific point of view, and 'Notizie dal cielo' from a humanist standpoint. Levi is indeed reviewing 'le cose della tecnica con l'occhio del letterato, e le lettere con l'occhio del tecnico' then, as outlined in the preface. Regardless of the writer's variation of approach to his subject matter, what connects these articles is the observational aspect of each. Even the autobiographical stories here often have a scrutinizing, investigating angle to them: 'Tornare a scuola' is an observation on the act and means of learning a new language; 'Il fondaco del nonno' notes Levi's ancestors at work as well as their unique coded language incomprehensible to customers, and 'Lo scriba' contains Levi's comments and reflections on working with a word processor. The non-autobiographical items are similarly observational, recording Levi's scrutiny of literature, animals, nature, scientific developments, language, and writing. Levi's examination of the world around him in *L'altrui mestiere* is an intensely passionate and enthusiastic examination of areas of particular interest to Levi personally. The writings here are:

> "invasioni di campo", incursioni nei mestieri altrui, bracconaggi in distretti di caccia riservata; scorribande negli sterminati territori della zoologia, dell'astronomia, della linguistica: scienze che non ho mai studiato sistematicamente, e che appunto per questo esercitano su di me il fascino durevole degli amori non soddisfatti e non corrisposti, e stimolano le mie pulsioni di voyeur e di ficcanaso. (*AM*, II, p. 631)
>
> ("invasions of the field", incursions into other people's trades, poachings in the region of a hunting preserve; forays into the boundless territories of zoology, astronomy, linguistics: sciences which I have never studied systematically, and which, for precisely this reason, exercise over me the lasting fascination of unsatisfied and unrequited loves, and arouse my urges to be voyeuristic and a nosey parker.)

This 'fascino durevole' (lasting fascination) is clear throughout the collection: Levi's enthusiasm for language, revealed in 'Leggere la vita' as 'la gratuita curiosità' (gratuitous curiosity) as Levi outlines the joy of playing at 'a fare il filologo' (being a philologist) (*AM*, II, p. 683), whilst in 'Le parole fossili' the discovery of 'la presenza di una determinata parola in aree perifiche' (the presence of a particular word in peripheral areas) becomes something which 'per decenni mi sono tenuta in corpo' (I kept inside me for decades) (*AM*, II, p. 819). The number of articles dedicated to animals (nine in total) highlights Levi's interest here, as well as comments such as 'se potessi, [...] mi riempirei la casa di tutti gli animali possibili' (if I could, [...] I would fill my house with all the animals possible) and 'leggo con godimento e stupore sempre rinnovati molti libri vecchi e nuovi che parlano di animali' (I read with continually renewed enjoyment and amazement many books old and new which talk about animals) (*AM*, II, p. 690), whilst Levi's passion for literature is indicated by his reference to Aldous Huxley as 'una tentazione permanente' (a permanent temptation) (p. 8) and by the five items dedicated to literature here.

The very fact that Levi continues to write out of curiosity, in his own words, as a 'ficcanaso' (nosey parker), with a view to both gaining for himself and conveying to others some degree of comprehension of the world around him suggests that he is still writing from a position of wanting to understand an apparently confusing world. Exploring the world's *perché* forms a vital aspect of many of the articles here: thus in 'La luna e noi' Levi attempts to establish why the moon holds such a fascination for us and our motives for visiting it (*AM*, II, p. 649); in 'Tornare a scuola' understanding how we learn; in 'Perché si scrive?', the motives for writing; the reasons behind the evolution of various words and phrases in 'Leggere la vita', the two 'Lingua dei chimici' articles, and 'Le parole fossili'; why animals behave the way they do in 'Romanzi dettati dai grilli', why butterflies are considered beautiful in 'Le farfalle', and why we are afraid of spiders in 'Paura dei ragni'. Continuing his non-acceptance of the notion that 'Hier ist kein Warum – (qui non c'è perché)' (here there is no why) (*SQ*, I, p. 23), Levi goes in search of the answers he requires, commencing in this text numerous pursuits of understanding which, of themselves, provide a line of continuation between *L'altrui mestiere* and *Se questo è un uomo*. His words published in the preface to the English translation of *Lilít* are particularly relevant here: 'It seems to me obvious today that this attention of mine at that time [in the concentration camp], turned to the world and to the human beings around me, was not only a symptom but also an important factor of spiritual and physical salvation'.[6] Levi's attention to detail and his efforts to understand the concentration camp world have, in this collection, simply been transferred to a wider range of objects.

Levi's quest to understand the world around him in *L'altrui mestiere* is also extended to the desire to have others comprehend, to 'fare gli "altri" partecipi' (to render the others participant) (*SQ*, I, p. 5). To this end Levi writes that 'ho sempre pensato che si deve scrivere con ordine e chiarezza' (I have always thought that one should write with order and clarity) (*AM*, II, p. 766), and that 'non è vero che il disordine sia necessario per dipingere il disordine; non è vero che il caos della pagina scritta sia il miglior simbolo del caos' (it is not true that confusion is necessary in order to depict confusion; it is not true that the chaos of the written page is the best symbol of chaos) (*AM*, II, p. 680) since 'chi non viene capito da nessuno non trasmette nulla, grida nel deserto' (he who is understood by nobody transmits nothing, he is shouting in the desert) (*AM*, II, p. 678). Levi's desire for clarity precisely in order to restore or establish communication, and to transmit his message with no fear of incomprehension, is an ordering factor in this text. For just as in *Lilít* the prevalence of 'confusione sull'ordine' (confusion over order) (*L*, II, p. 167) signified death, here also 'ogni problema risolto è una vittoria' (every problem solved is a victory) (*AM*, II, p. 762) and 'la vita è regola, è ordine che prevale sul Caos' (life is rules, it is order which prevails over chaos) (*AM*, II, p. 798).

The ordering of his writing here, the order of words and subsequent comprehension which Levi brings about through his *scrivere chiaro*, reacts specifically against the linguistic confusion of the concentration camps where 'le differenze linguistiche erano sentite come una maledizione' (linguistic differences were felt to be a curse) (*AM*, II, p. 730). Yet it is not simply that Levi's desire to *scrivere chiaro* and his quest for understanding of the world around him have their origins in his experience of the concentration camps: even Levi's organisation of the articles in this collection place his own careers, rather than *mestieri altrui*, and his personal life experiences in predominant positions. The ordering of the articles here according to sequences of composition or publication is somewhat confused. The first twelve items, from 'La mia casa' to 'Dello scrivere oscuro', follow no particular chronological pattern, yet from 'Dello scrivere oscuro' onwards they are arranged here in consecutive order according to their previous publication, with the exceptions of 'Le parole fossili' and, notably, the concluding item, 'Eclissi dei profeti'.[7] Levi's organisation of these articles is what results in the unexpected, unspoken, and perhaps even unintentional emphasis which remains on his personal experiences. For a collction of writings about a wide range of interests, Levi himself is at the beginning ('La mia casa'), his full-time career is at the centre ('La lingua dei chimici II', precisely central in its positioning as the 26th item), fragmented details of his life are sporadically present throughout the collection ('La mia casa'; 'Tornare a scuola'; 'Trenta ore sul *Castoro sei*'; 'Il mondo invisibile'; 'Il segno del chimico'; 'Il teschio e l'orchidea'; 'Il fondaco del nonno'; 'Un lungo duello'; 'Il linguaggio degli odori'; 'Lo scriba' and 'Bisogno di paura'), and he concludes, most significantly and deliberately, with 'Eclissi dei profeti', an article in which he cites and discusses the continued relevance of a passage from *Se questo è un uomo*. Levi ends *L'altrui mestiere* with an article which examines contemporary unease as well as the fear and the threat of nuclear Holocaust. His demonstration of the enduring pertinence of his words on human nature in the concentration camps from *Se questo è un uomo*, ('Mi sembra che, salvo qualche cambiamento nelle unità di misura, queste osservazioni siano valide anche per il mondo in cui oggi noi europei viviamo, liberi dal bisogno ma non dalla paura' [It seems to me that, apart from some changes in the units of measurement, these observations are still valid for the world in which we Europeans live today, free from need but not from fear] [*AM*, II, p. 855]) suggest that the lessons learned from his experience of the concentration camp are as relevant and as necessary to convey now as ever, and that aspects of the concentration camp world are as applicable to contemporary topics as they are to Levi's previous writings. In *L'altrui mestiere* Levi's approach to writing often has its roots embedded in his experience of the *Lager*: he cites his previous writings on the Holocaust in order to demonstrate their continued present-day aptness and pertinence; he specifies his need for clear, concise language and comprehensibility as a reaction against the events portrayed in *Se questo è un uomo*, and his intense awareness of the minutiae of life, his querying, questioning and investigation of the world as well as his pursuit of understanding all stem from his time in the Buna-Monowitz satellite camp of Auschwitz.

The subject matter of the *Racconti e saggi* collection is as varied as that of *L'altrui mestiere*, dealing with an exploration of the animal world and animal behaviour in 'Nozze della formica' and 'Ranocchi sulla luna'; Levi's persistent fascination with potential future inventions in 'Il fabbricante di specchi'; further commentary on chemical elements and the role of science in 'Bionda ossigenata' and 'Covare il cobra'; language in '"Bella come una fiore"'; literature in 'Tradurre Kafka', 'La rima alla ricossa' and 'Caro Orazio'; a variety of topical issues in 'La luna e l'uomo', 'Lotta per la vita', 'Roulette dei batteri', 'Le lance diventino scudi', 'Il vino dei Borgia' and 'Il giocatore occulto'; and the concentration camps in 'Auschwitz, città tranquilla', 'Pipetta da guerra', 'Un "giallo" del Lager' and 'Il comandante di Auschwitz'.

Many of the items here, particularly the *saggi*, contain few thematic echoes of the Holocaust, but a number of the *racconti* of this collection have strong connections to Levi's earlier themes and works. Isabella's transformation and the growth of her wings in 'La grande mutazione' contain echoes of the enforced metamorphosis of humans into vultures in 'Angelica farfalla', whilst her treatment by her doctor as a fascinating specimen in which he soon loses interest is reminiscent of the guests' behaviour towards 'La bella addormentata nel frigo' in *Storie naturali*, both of which in turn reflect the parallel issues of the transformation of the concentration camp prisoners and their inhumane treatment in *Se questo è un uomo*. 'Il fabbricante di specchi' bears comparison with 'Il misuratore della bellezza' in its assessment of others' physical appearance by the standards of the observer, but is also particularly significant when considered in the light of a comment Levi made several years after the publication of this tale with reference to the concentration camps: 'il Lager era uno specchio della situazione esterna, però uno specchio deformante'[8] (the *Lager* was a mirror of the external situation, but a distorting mirror). The concept of a distorting mirror, precisely the invention designed by Timoteo, is thus connected, certainly subsequently, to the concentration camp world. The fact that some of the secret mirrors created by Timoteo specifically reflect an image of 'il mondo capovolto' (the world turned upside down) (*RS*, II, p. 895) which is identical to Levi's definition of the *Lager* as 'il mondo intorno a noi [che] appariva capovolto' (the world around us [which] appeared upside down) in 'Auschwitz, città tranquilla' (*RS*, II, p. 873), increases the association between the two representations. Likewise related to *Lager* themes is 'Scacco al tempo' which bears correlation with all Levi's previous depictions of his experience of time 'checkmated' and frozen in the concentration camp. The outlining in 'Scacco al tempo' of the subjectivity of time, particularly T.K's experience of imprisonment in which 'ha scontato trentacinque mesi di detenzione valutandoli in quattro giorni' (he has served thirty-five months of detention, evaluating them as four days) (*RS*, II, p. 915), can be compared with many of the passages in *Se questo è un uomo* which deal with perceptions of time, perhaps epecially with Levi's ironic comment that 'Quest'anno è passato presto' (This year has gone quickly) (*SQ*, I, p. 140). One of the *saggi*, 'Una bottiglia di sole', also bases its definitions of what it means to be human on a fundamental component of camp-time: 'mi pare, insomma, che il fabbricare recipienti sia indizio di due qualità che [...] sono squisitamente umane. La prima è la capacità del pensare al domani' (it seems to me, then, that making recipients is a sign of two qualities which [...] are typically human. The first of these is the capacity to think about tomorrow) (*RS*, II, p. 958), emphasising the degradation and inhumanity of those deprived of the ability to conceive of a future time. Clear thematic continuities of hatred, imprisonment and violence are evident in stories like 'Le due bandiere' where two races despise each other for no valid reason, in 'Il passa-muri' with the imprisonment of Memnone and in 'Forza maggiore''s menacing abuse of an innocent passer-by.[9] Human violence here is also placed in parallel with the unconscious emotional cruelty of Lidia in 'Meccano d'amore' or the natural violence of animals in 'Nozze della formica'. In the *Racconti e saggi* collection, however, all violence is continually juxtaposed with the violence of Auschwitz which is never allowed to recede into the background for long.

Throughout this collection Levi returns sporadically to dealing with the concentration camps, even ending his *premessa* with reference to them: 'Sono un uomo normale di buona memoria che è incappato in un vortice, che ne è uscito piú per fortuna che per virtú, e che da allora conserva una certa curiosità per i vortici, grandi e piccoli, metaforici e materiali' (I am a normal man with a good memory who fell into a maelstrom and got out of it more by luck than by virtue, and who, from that time onwards, has preserved a certain curiosity about maelstroms large and small, metaphorical and actual) (*RS*, II, p. 859). The Auschwitz stories here, like those in *Lilít*, often deal with more bizarre or unusual episodes: how Levi was saved by a pipette which infected him with scarlet fever ('Io fui salvato, nel modo piú imprevedibile, dall'affare delle pipette rubate, che mi avevano procurato una provvidenziale malattia proprio nel momento in cui, paradossalmente, non poter camminare era una fortuna' [I was saved, in the most unforeseeable manner, by the matter of the stolen pipettes, which had brought me a providential illness right at the moment in which, paradoxically, not being able to walk was a stroke of luck] [*RS*, II, p.889]); how a German chemist who worked at the Buna factory, described by Levi as 'un quasi-me, un altro me stesso ribaltato' (an almost-me, another, overturned version of myself) (*RS*, II, p. 873) was able to be contacted by Levi years later through mutual colleagues, and how the family of Gerhard Goldbaum, named in *Il sistema periodico*, were able to confirm his identity through a meeting with Levi. In spite of the fact that the majority of the events of the Auschwitz stories here take place physically outside the camp itself, this major maelstrom of Levi's life is never far, even from this essentially disparate collection.

The paragraph which opens 'Auschwitz, città tranquilla' holds the key to interpreting both *Racconti e saggi* and *L'altrui mestiere*:

> Può stupire che in Lager uno degli stati d'animo piú frequenti fosse la curiosità. Eppure eravamo, oltre che spaventati, umiliati e disperati, anche curiosi: affamati di pane e anche di capire. Il mondo intorno a noi appariva capovolto, dunque qualcuno doveva averlo capovolto, e perciò essere un capovolto lui stesso. (*RS*, II, p. 873)

> (It can amaze people to learn that one of the most frequent states of mind in the *Lager* was curiosity. Yet we were, as well as frightened, humiliated and desperate, also curious: starving for bread and also for understanding. The world around us appeared upside down, therefore someone must have turned it upside down, and therefore be an upside down person himself.)

The link between these collections and Levi's concentration camp experiences is therefore curiosity, the curiosity that began in the camps and expanded after release to explore the wide variety of topics Levi covers here. The topics which feature in *Lilít*, *L'altrui mestiere*, and *Racconti e saggi* affirm not only Levi's interests but also his values post-Auschwitz. Thus his fascination with life in all its forms, human, animal and plant, stems from his own close encounter with death and from his year surrounded continually by death's presence; his avid interest in various forms of communication can be seen to have its origins in a time where the art of communication and the ability to communicate were lost; his scrutiny of science emanates from his education which was a factor in his very survival as well as from his exposure to what the horrors of science can be capable of, and his concern with the issues of frozen time originate from the moment when any conception of a possible future was unthinkable. The hunger for understanding which grew from Levi's original curiosity about the workings of the concentration camp, its rulers and its prisoners proceeds throughout *Lilít*, *L'altrui mestiere* and *Racconti e saggi*, providing a continuation of horror and wonder, but above all of curiosity and fascination with the world around him.

Notes

1. Levi's words spoken at an unspecified conference in America, April 1985, transcribed in

Poli and Calcagno, 1992, p. 289.
2. The English translation of *Lilít e altri racconti* (1985) was in fact published as *Moments of Reprieve*.
3. See Cicioni, 1995, p. 116.
4. Levi's preface to the English translation of *Lilít*, *Moments of Reprieve*, dated 6 June 1985, translated by Ruth Feldman (London: Michael Joseph, 1986), p. 10, also published in the original Italian as 'Prefazione a *Moments of Reprieve*' in the *Pagine sparse* section of *Opere II*, pp. 1314–6.
5. Belpoliti's 'Note ai testi: *L'altrui mestiere*', in *Opere II*, p. 1554.
6. *Moments of Reprieve*, p. 11.
7. The source for these details on the dates of the original publication of these articles is Belpoliti, 'Note ai testi: *L'altrui mestiere*', *Opere II*, p. 1557.
8. Levi's words to Ferdinando Camon, published in *Conversazione con Primo Levi*, 1991, p. 28.
9. The examination of 'Forza maggiore' has already been extensively carried out by Frederic D. Homer in *Primo Levi and the Politics of Survival* (Columbia and London: University of Missouri Press, 2001) where he writes that, 'In his short story "*Force Majeure*", Primo Levi compresses his experience of the Holocaust into a frightening confrontation between a citizen and a sailor'.

7
Se non ora, quando?: 'La dignità dell'uomo'

First published in 1982, Levi's decision to compose *Se non ora, quando?*, an historical novel recounting the journeys and adventures of a group of Jewish partisans during the Second World War was, in part, inspired by the controversy 'sul comportamento degli ebrei di fronte alla strage nazista: veramente si erano lasciati condurre al macello senza resistere? Se sí, perché? Se no, quanti, quando, dove, come avevano resistito?'[1] (over the behaviour of the Jews when faced with the Nazi massacre: had they really let themselves be taken to the slaughter without resisting? If so, why? If not, how many, when, where, how did they resist?). Some of the questions raised above are answered in the fictional context of Levi's text, which reaffirms instances of Jewish resistance during the war, after considerable research on Levi's part: 'Ho letto tanti libri sull'argomento. Poi ho tessuto insieme i fatti che ho trovato'[2] (I read so many books on the subject. Then I wove together the facts that I found); 'Per otto mesi ho studiato la lingua yiddish e ho frugato negli archivi, poi per un anno ho scritto'[3] (I studied Yiddish and searched the archives for eight months, then for a year I wrote). *Se non ora, quando?* documents a period of time in the lives of a group who are traditionally unrecognised by history; it is historical narrative as an 'act of representation'[4] of a certain community, with a background of accurate and true historical events providing the setting for a collection of fictitious characters and their adventures.[5] In *Se non ora, quando?* the historical factors of the Second World War and its aftermath place the events of the text in exactly the same time span as those of *Se questo è un uomo* and *La tregua*. Levi frequently employs identical, or very similar words to those of his earlier texts to describe the setting here: 'tutto è tornato nel caos' (everything has returned to chaos); 'una gran confusione, sul campo e anche nella testa della gente' (a great confusion, on the field and also in people's heads); 'il mondo si era capovolto' (the world had been overturned), and, closely echoing his words in *La tregua* that 'il mondo intorno a noi sembrava ritornato al Caos primigenio' (the world around us seemed to have returned to primeval Chaos) (*LT*, I, p. 226), 'la terra polacca [...] sembrava ritornata al Caos primigenio' (the Polish land [...] seemed to have returned to primeval Chaos) (*SNOQ*, II, pp. 217, 218, 331, 409). Located in the same historical timespan as Levi's first two works, and with an analogous geographical background to that of *La tregua*, some resonances are bound to occur between these texts. The partisans' adventures cross much of the same territory as Levi's journey home in *La tregua*, and both journeys end equally ambiguously: *La tregua* with the eventual culmination of Levi's journey home to Turin juxtaposed with his dream of remaining in the camps, and *Se non ora, quando?* with the juxtapositioning of the birth of a baby to two of the most innocent members of the group with the dropping of the first atom bomb. *Se non ora, quando?* therefore ends, like Levi's earlier text, with a similar note of enduring danger, for here, as in *La tregua*, 'sarà guerra sempre' (there will always be war) (*SNOQ*, II, p. 416), 'la guerra sarebbe durata sempre' (the war would last forever) (*SNOQ*, II, p. 284). Yet the experiences depicted here are so utterly antithetical, particularly to those of *Se questo è un uomo*, as to render thematic comparisons unlikely. What is most significant here is that Levi's experiences of the concentration camps, as portrayed in *Se questo è un uomo*, have often unexpectedly provided the framework in a number of ways for the depiction of the entirely different wartime experiences of *Se non ora, quando?* This chapter aims to outline and examine both the contrasts between the opposing portrayals of this historical period, and the similarities between the texts, paying particular attention to the echoes of Levi's concentration camp experience as they recur here even in the converse conditions and circumstances depicted in the later work.

The reference to time contained in the title of *Se non ora, quando?* is a motif which remains constant here since the measurement of time is continually present throughout the text. The precise historical setting of this work is established not only through the events but also through the chapter titles, each of which contains the name of at least one month, plus the year of the occurences. These chronological chapter headings specifically date the episodes of this text, precisely determining their timescale in the same way as the 'Storia di dieci giorni' chapter at the end of *Se questo è un uomo*. Although a number of the dates included in the timespan of *Se non ora, quando?* coincide with exceptionally significant moments in Levi's own life, Levi has, in this respect, successfully effaced much of his own story here. The events of February 1944, for example, which for Levi was the time of his deportation, here, in the chapter 'Gennaio-maggio 1944', bear no mark of the devastating incidents in Levi's own life. However, Levi's depiction of the end of the war is somewhat more reminiscent of episodes from his earlier work. The chapter 'Gennaio-febbraio 1945', which for Levi corresponds with the evacuation and eventual liberation of the Auschwitz concentration camp, refers to this time as 'una tregua' (a respite) (*SNOQ*, II, p. 436), specifically the same period in which *La tregua* commences. The partisan group's brief farewell to Edek 'attraverso i vetri' (through the windows) (*SNOQ*, II, p. 445) strongly recalls that between Levi and Alberto, 'venne finalmente Alberto, sfidando il divieto, a salutarmi dalla finestra' (Alberto finally came, defying the prohibition, to bid me farewell through the window) (*SQ*, I, p. 151), and Mendel's reaction to the end of the war, 'eppure io non sono contento' (yet I am not happy) (*SNOQ*, II, p. 441) bears comparison to that of Levi in *La tregua* where he writes that 'Così per noi anche l'ora della libertà suonò grave e chiusa, e ci riempì gli animi, ad un tempo, di gioia e di un doloroso senso di pudore [...] e di pena' (So for us even the hour of liberty rang out grave and muffled, and filled our souls with both joy and with a painful sense of shame [...] and of suffering) (*LT*, I, p. 206). Elements of the suffering of deportation have been eradicated from the month and year of their occurrence in Levi's life, then, but some aspects of his experience of the end of the war remain pertinent.

Levi's choice of dates as chapter headings throughout this work is indicative of the importance of the issue of time here. For many of the characters in this text, as for the prisoners in *Se questo è un uomo*, time is frozen, as 'sterile e stagnante' (*SQ*, I, p. 113) as the marshes, fields and woods they trudge through. The village Mendel comes from is utterly timeless, as 'Al mio paese, di orologi ce n'erano pochi. Ce n'era uno sul campanile, ma era fermo da non so quanti anni, forse fin dalla rivoluzione: io non l'ho mai visto camminare, e mio padre diceva che neanche lui. Non aveva orologio neppure il campanaro' (In my town there were few clocks. There was one on the bell tower, but it had stopped for I don't know how many years, perhaps since the revolution: I have never seen it turn, and my father said he hadn't either. Not even the bell-ringer had a watch) (*SNOQ*, II, p. 211) and when the bells employed to keep time break and the pistol formerly used to signal the time is confiscated, 'il paese è rimasto senza ore' (the town was left hourless) (*SNOQ*, II, p. 211) indefinitely. This inability to measure time is significant, not least because Mendel, as a watchmaker, is dependent upon the measurement of time for his livelihood. Mendel's profession is frequently reflected in his language as he uses watch imagery, on a variety of occasions, to assess or classify the other characters in the text:

> Quando un orologio è impolverato, è segno che è molto vecchio, oppure che la scatola non è stagna; allora bisogna smontarlo tutto e lavarlo pezzo per pezzo con benzina leggera. Leonid non era vecchio; dunque la sua scatola doveva avere delle fessure. Che genere di benzina ci sarebbe voluta per lavare gli ingranaggi di Leonid? (*SNOQ*, II, p. 235)

> (When a clock is dusty it is a sign that it is very old, or that the casing isn't airtight; then you need to take it all apart and wash it piece by piece with a light cleaning fluid. Leonid was not old; therefore his casing must have had some cracks. What kind of cleaning fluid would you need to wash Leonid's clockwork?)

Leonid gli ricordava certi altri orologi che gli avevano portati da riparare: forse avevano preso un urto, le spire della molla si erano accavallate, un po' ritardavano, un po' avanzavano follemente, e finivano tutti col guastarsi in modo irrimediabile. (*SNOQ*, II, p. 383)

(Leonid reminded him of some other clocks that had been brought to him for repair: perhaps they had taken a knock, the coils in the spring had piled up, they were running a bit slow, they were running a bit crazily ahead, and they all ended up being broken in an irreparable manner.)

Sembrava proprio che Edek rispondesse alle domande che Mendel poneva a se stesso, che gli leggesse nel fondo del cervello, nel letto segreto dove nascono i pensieri. Ma non è cosí strano, pensò Mendel; due buoni orologi segnano la stessa ora, anche se sono di marche diverse. (*SNOQ*, II, p. 427)

(It really seemed as though Edek were responding to the questions Mendel was posing himself, as if he were reading from the depths of his brain, from the secret bed where thoughts are born. But it is not that strange, thought Mendel: two good clocks tell the same time, even if they are of different makes.)

Mendel is fascinated by both watches and time at the same moment as time, for him, has stopped and become impossible to measure. Mendel describes himself as 'fuori del tempo e del luogo' (outside time and place) (*SNOQ*, II, p. 232) in much the same way as those depicted in *Se questo è un uomo* were 'dall'altra parte' (on the other side) (*SQ*, I, p. 13), 'fuori del mondo' (outside the world) (*SQ*, I, p. 17), and for whom 'la storia si era fermata' (history had stopped) (*SQ*, I, p. 113). A sense of existing in a timeless dimension, in a world in which time has stopped and frozen, is therefore as all-encompassing in this text as it was in *Se questo è un uomo*. The present is the only reasonable certainty these characters possess: as in *Se questo è un uomo*, 'il futuro [...] stava davanti grigio e inarticolato' (the future [...] faced us, grey and inarticolate) (*SQ*, I, p. 113). In *Se non ora, quando?*, as in *La tregua*, there is no concrete anticipation of the future, and the word 'futuro' does not appear here, perhaps appropriately since 'Il nostro tempo corre come corrono le lepri, veloce e a zig-zag. Chi fa un piano per il giorno dopo, e poi lo realizza, è bravo; chi fa piani per la settimana dopo è matto' (Our time runs like hares, quickly and in zig zags. Whoever makes plans for the next day, and manages to see them through, does well; whoever makes plans for next week is crazy) (*SNOQ*, II, p. 289). The future is rarely contemplated if not in a vague and distant way, and yet, again, it is the ultimate aim of the characters. The partisans are aware that after the war 'vorremmo andare in Italia, e di lí cercheremmo di passare in Palestina [...] a costruire il nostro stato' (we would like to go to Italy, and from there to try to pass into Palestine [...] to build our state) (*SNOQ*, II, p. 450) but the only conceivable certainty for their future is its desired geographical base. The partisans, 'senza domani' (without a tomorrow) (*SNOQ*, II, p. 332) like the prisoners, are therefore equally detached from space and time, unable to return to their destroyed homes, and in a state of limbo since 'i dispersi non sono né vivi né morti' (the dispersed are neither alive nor dead) (*SNOQ*, II, p. 216). Caught in this interstitial zone between life and death, a zone which functions outside the normal parameters of time, with no possible anticipation of the future and little continuity between past and present, the partisans here, like the prisoners of *Se questo è un uomo*, find their memories of their former lives growing distant:

> Gremito di memorie, e insieme pieno di dimenticanza: le sue [Mendel's] memorie, anche recenti, erano sbiadite, avevano contorni incerti, si accavallavano con sua fatica, come se qualcuno tracciasse disegni sulla lavagna e poi li cancellasse a mezzo e ne facesse dei nuovi sopra i vecchi. (*SNOQ*, II, p. 441)

> (Filled with memories and, at the same time, full of forgetfulness: Mendel's memories, even the recent ones, had faded, had uncertain outlines, accumulated under his efforts, as if someone were drawing pictures on the blackboard and then half erased them and drew new ones over the old.)

Life before the war is portrayed as belonging to 'mille anni prima' (a thousand years before) (*SNOQ*, II, p. 386, p. 483 and p. 484): these characters' previous lives are part of an ancient, unreachable past, which is equally unattainable in memory. The partisans here are separated from their past lives by the schism of war; not by the experience of the concentration camps as was the case for Levi, but by their own displacement and experiences of resistance. Although written thirty-five years after *Se questo è un uomo*, the characters of *Se non ora, quando?* have maintained an identical perception of time as the one revealed in Levi's first text, and his characters here display the same sense of timelessness as the prisoners of the concentration camp, the unaltered idea that 'a dare un colpo di spugna al passato e al futuro si impara assai presto' (one learns rather quickly to put the past and the future out of one's mind) (*SQ*, I, p. 30).

Like the issue of time, the themes of language and communication also maintain comparable roles here to those they played in *Se questo è un uomo*. The partisans, like the prisoners of the concentration camps, are obliged to communicate in a number of languages, Russian, Polish, Yiddish and, when necessary, German, yet in *Se non ora, quando?*, as in *La tregua*, multilingual communication poses few problems. Throughout *Se non ora, quando?* a shared language marks someone out as a potential ally: Line's ability to communicate in Hebrew with the Palestinian soldiers results in the partisans placing their trust in them, whilst Peiami from Uzbekistan is distrusted because 'aveva una bella voce di basso, educata e morbida, ma parlava il russo con incertezze ed errori, e con una lentezza irritante' (he had a beautiful low voice, refined and soft, but he spoke Russian falteringly and with errors, and irritatingly slowly) (*SNOQ*, II, p. 224). Yiddish is occasionally used divisively to communicate with a degree of secrecy (*SNOQ*, II, pp. 231, 272 and 459) or is employed as a measure of someone's Jewishness in the case of Francine who is not readily accepted as Jewish since 'non parlava jiddisch, non lo capiva, e raccontò che quando era a Parigi non sapeva neppure che lingua fosse' (she couldn't speak Yiddish, she couldn't understand it, and she told us that when she was in Paris she had never even heard of it) (*SNOQ*, II, p. 462), an episode which has clear parallels with Levi's own experience of Yiddish as portrayed within *La tregua*, 'voi non parlate yiddisch: dunque non siete ebrei' (you don't speak Yiddish, therefore you are not Jewish) (*LT*, I, p. 302). One of the few examples of linguistic differences serving as a dehumanizing force within this text occurs when the partisans arrive in Italy, almost totally unable to communicate in Italian. When Adele invites several members of the group for drinks at her house, their inability to talk fluently with the other guests makes Mendel in particular feel 'disorientato, [...] una pedina di un gioco gigantesco e crudele' (disorientated, [...] a pawn in a gigantic and cruel game) (*SNOQ*, II, p. 505), unable to explain himself, 'se parlassi la tua lingua potrei cercare di spiegarti' (if I spoke your language I could try to explain to you) (p. 505). This description of Mendel mirrors that of Levi in the camp laboratories, where Levi employs similar words to write that, 'se parlassi meglio tedesco, potrei provare a spiegare tutto questo a Frau Mayer' (if I spoke better German I could try to explain all of this to Frau Mayer) (*SQ*, I, p. 140). This loss of language, and the partisans' ensuing powerlessness to convey the reality of their experiences, is accompanied, as it was for the prisoners of the concentration camps, by a degree of dehumanisation from the perspective of others. The partisans become objects of historical interest in the eyes of their hosts, ('ciascuno di loro si trovò isolato, al centro di un cerchio di curiosi, e sottoposto a una grandine di domande melodiose ed incomprensibili. [...] Come le bestie al giardino zoologico' [each of them found themselves isolated, in the centre of a circle of curious people, and submitted to a hail of melodious and incomprehensible questions. [...] Like the beasts in the zoo) [*SNOQ*, II, p. 501]) and the objectification occurs precisely at the moment in which they are unable to communicate without the aid of a translator. This incident highlights a significant continuation of Levi's original depiction of the dehumanizing and alienating forces of language, which recurs even in a text in which the consequences of multilingual communication and the loss of man's dignity are rare.

The characters' feelings about religion and their attitudes towards God also bear the scars of Levi's wartime experiences. Just as Auschwitz was a confirmation for Levi of the non-existence of God, ('se non altro per il fatto che un Auschwitz è esistito, nessuno dovrebbe ai nostri giorni parlare di Provvidenza' [if only for the fact that an Auschwitz has existed, nobody in our time ought to speak of Providence] [*SQ*, I, p. 154], 'c'è Auschwitz, quindi non può esserci Dio' [there is Auschwitz, therefore there can be no God]),[6] in *Se non ora, quando?* Mendel is equally questioning of God. Mendel, with whom Levi identified strongly ('nel profondo, mi sono effettivamente identificato con Mendel' [deep down, I really identified with Mendel]),[7] shares many of his author's views on religion, but, unlike Levi, Mendel does turn to God frequently, without any certainty that his prayers are heard: 'i tedeschi li ha fatti Dio; e perché li ha fatti? O perché ha permesso che il Satàn li facesse? Per i nostri peccati?' (God made the Germans; and why did he make them? Or why did he permit Satan to make them? For our sins?) (*SNOQ*, II, p. 219); 'non sembrava che il Signore, fino allora, si fosse molto curato di salvare lui e i suoi' (it didn't seem as though the Lord, up to now, had cared very much about saving him and his people) (*SNOQ*, II, p. 234); 'E l'Eterno, benedetto Egli sia, perché se ne stava nascosto dietro le nuvole grige [...] invece di soccorrere il Suo popolo?' (And the Eternal, blessed be He, why was He hiding behind the grey clouds [...] instead of saving His people?) (*SNOQ*, II, p. 277); 'Il Signore nostro Dio, il Padrone del Mondo, aveva diviso le acque del Mar Rosso, e i carri erano stati travolti. Chi avrebbe diviso le acque davanti agli ebrei di Novoselki? Chi li avrebbe sfamati con le quaglie e la manna? Dal cielo nero non scendeva manna, ma neve spietata' (The Lord our God, Master of the world, had parted the waters of the Red Sea, and the carts had been overturned. Who would part the waters before the Jews of Novoselki? Who would feed them with quails and manna? No manna descended from the black sky, only ruthless snow) (*SNOQ*, II, p. 281). Whilst appearing to believe in the existence of God throughout much of the text, Mendel's lack of faith is clarified towards the end of the war: 'Che la guerra finisca, Signore a cui non credo. Se ci sei, fa' finire la guerra' (Let the war end, Lord in whom I do not believe. If you are there, put an end to this war) (*SNOQ*, II, p. 426); 'io non sono neppure un ebreo pio' (I am not even a pious Jew) (*SNOQ*, II, p. 433), and 'io non credo nel Signore' (I don't believe in the Lord) (*SNOQ*, II, p. 434). For both Levi and his character, Mendel, their experience of the war serves as confirmation of their religious doubts.

However, whilst the temporal, religious and linguistic elements of *Se non ora, quando?* have retained a connection with *Se questo è un uomo*, other factors have altered completely, providing a stark contrast to Levi's first text. The most immediate dissimilarity between the works lies in the juxtapositioning of the imprisonment of *Se questo è un uomo* with the total freedom of the partisans, 'la libertà del bosco' (the freedom of the forest) (*SNOQ*, II, p. 317), and the characters' independence of movement:

Erano allegri [...]: nell'avventura ogni giorno diversa della Partisanka, nella steppa gelata, nella neve e nel fango avevano trovato una libertà nuova, sconosciuta ai loro padri e ai loro nonni, un contatto con uomini amici e nemici, con la natura e con l'azione [...]. Erano allegri e feroci, come animali a cui si schiude la gabbia, come schiavi insorti a vendetta. (*SNOQ*, II, p. 331–2)

(They were happy [...]: in the ever-varying adventures of partisanship, in the frozen steppe, in the snow and in the mud they had found a new freedom, unknown to their parents and to their grandparents, a contact with friends and foes, with nature and with action [...] They were happy and wild, like animals let out of their cage, like insurgent slaves out for revenge.)

Although described here as 'allegri e feroci, come animali' (happy and wild, like animals), the degradation of the prisoners of the concentration camps in Levi's first text, emphasised through his use of animal metaphors, is absent from *Se non ora, quando?*. The partisans' dignity and non-bestiality is explicitly asserted, drawing attention to the contrast between this aspect of the two works:

- Questo è russo, - disse Gedale indicando Piotr; - tutti noi altri siamo ebrei, russi e polacchi. Ma come ci hai riconosciuti?
- Dagli occhi, - disse il sindaco. - C'erano ebrei anche qui fra noi, e avevano gli occhi come i vostri.
- Come sono i nostri occhi? - chiese Mendel.
- Inquieti. Come quelli delle bestie inseguite.
- Noi non siamo piú bestie inseguite, - disse Line. - Molti dei nostri sono morti combattendo. I nostri nemici sono i vostri, quelli che hanno distrutto le vostre case. (*SNOQ*, II, p. 387)

('This one is Russian', said Gedale, pointing to Piotr, 'all the rest of us are Jewish, either Russian or Polish. But how did you recognise us?' 'From the eyes', said the mayor. 'There were some Jews here with us too, and they had eyes like yours.' 'What are our eyes like?' asked Mendel. 'Restless. Like those of hunted beasts.' 'We are no longer hunted beasts', said Line. 'Many of our people have died in battle. Our enemies are your enemies, those who have destroyed your homes.')

The partisans reassert their humanity continually through their activity, their decisions and their battles for survival. Yet although living in deliberately opposite circumstances to those of *Se questo è un uomo*, certain aspects of Levi's depiction of the partisans' life of non-imprisonment are still comparable to those of the *Lager* prisoners: the partisans are similarly attempting to resist death at the hands of their adversaries, as well as to survive the harsh conditions of bitter winters and acute hunger and thirst. They live each day with the *misurarsi* ethic of both *Il sistema periodico* and *La chiave a stella*, testing and proving themselves to each other and individually, struggling against their human enemies and also contending with their environment and the elements. On an emotional and psychological level the partisans' experiences are closer to those of the ex-deportees of *La tregua*: they possess a similar sense of rootlessness to the ex-prisoners since they too are homeless, and brutally deprived of family, homeland, and possessions. The partisans, however, in spite of the months of deprivation, are in a position of strength in comparison to the ex-prisoners and are capable of fighting to preserve and protect their dignity: 'combattiamo per salvarci dai tedeschi, per vendicarci, per aprirci la strada; ma soprattutto […] per dignità' (we fight to save ourselves from the Germans, to avenge ourselves, to open up the road ahead of us; but above all […] for dignity) (*SNOQ*, II, p. 422). The battle for dignity runs in parallel with the search for identity; the seeking to re-establish a sense of self manifests itself in this work in a similar fashion to in *La tregua*, for, in Levi's words, 'questo è il libro di una ricerca d'identità […] una ricerca di se stessi da parte di questi dispersi'[8] (This is a book about a search for identity […] a search for the self on the part of those dispersed). The characters' quest for identity manifests itself for the most part through the character of Mendel, whose loss of identity is experienced, in his dreams, as the inability to remember his name and origins, 'non ricordava piú il suo nome, né dove era nato, nulla' (he could no longer remember his name, nor where he was born, nothing) (*SNOQ*, II, p. 402), and, when conscious, through a sense of disorientation, 'non so piú che cosa voglio né dove sono, e forse non so piú neppure chi sono io' (I don't know what I want any more, nor where I am, and perhaps I don't even know who I am anymore) (p. 405) which reaches its culmination as the war ends and he questions his place in the world:

> Dov'è la mia casa? È in nessun luogo. È nello zaino che mi porto dietro, è nel Heinkel abbattuto, è a Novoselki, è nel campo di Turov e in quello di Edek, è di là del mare, nel paese delle fiabe, dove scorre il latte e il miele. Uno entra in una casa e appende gli abiti e i ricordi; dove appendi i tuoi ricordi, Mendel, figlio di Nachman? (*SNOQ*, II, p. 441)

(Where is my home? It is nowhere. It is in the rucksack I carry behind me, it is in the dejected Heinkel, it is in Novoselki, it is in Turov's camp, and in Edek's, it is beyond the sea, in the land of fables, where milk and honey flow. You enter a house and you hang up your clothes and memories; where do you hang your memories, Mendel, son of Nachman?)

The solidarity within the group constitutes, for the duration of the war and its immediate aftermath, the boundaries of home and family, reinforcing a sense of dignity and providing another point of stark contrast with *Se questo è un uomo*. In both texts the role played by friendship is of vital importance,[9] but whereas comradeship was both rare and almost impossible to maintain in the concentration camp conditions, here it can and does flourish, serving to emphasise the partisans' status as *men*. Whilst in the *Lager* 'ognuno è disperatamente ferocemente solo' (everyone is desperately ferociously alone) (*SQ*, I, p. 84) and a prisoner would search for 'un contatto umano, e non trova che schiene voltate' (human contact and find nothing but turned backs) (*SQ*, I, p. 51), in this text the main core of the group collaborate with each other, work together and support each other with their various difficulties. Although it is still the case in *Se non ora, quando?* that 'ogni straniero è nemico' (every stranger is the enemy) (*SQ*, I, p. 5), friendships are able to grow and survive in the less harsh conditions of partisan life and are, in fact, vital for the success of the group. Mendel's double denial of his friendship with and responsibility for Leonid (*SNOQ*, II, p. 269 and 370-3) is regretted 'come un prurito intorno al cuore' (like an itch around the heart) (p. 269) leaving him feeling 'spregevole come un verme' (despicable as a worm) (p. 381), and intimate relationships between members of the group are encouraged when the balance in numbers between men and women becomes more even. The partisans' protectiveness of each other and the group as a whole is essential for their survival, and gestures of revenge against the common enemy occur frequently in order to demonstrate the group's solidarity. Leonid's destruction of the railway track, Ulybin's placing of landmines in his camp at the moment of evacuation, the killings of the officers in charge of the concentration camp they liberate, and the steps taken to avenge themselves against the murder of Ròkhele Nera are necessary both for the morale of the group as a whole and to reaffirm their self-respect. The partisans' dignity and humanity is therefore emphasized through direct action and revenge: the partisans' own killing is justified since 'noi uccidiamo solo i tedeschi, e neanche sempre. Non siamo come loro; uccidere non ci piace' (we only kill Germans, and even then, not always. We are not like them; we don't like killing) (*SNOQ*, II, p. 292); 'crediamo che fare la guerra sia una brutta cosa, ma che uccidere i nazisti sia la cosa piú giusta che si possa fare oggi sulla faccia della Terra' (we think that war is a horrible thing, but that killing Nazis is the most just thing one can do today on the face of the earth) (p. 390), and 'ammazzare i tedeschi è come quando il chirurgo fa un'operazione: tagliare un braccio è orribile, ma va fatto e si fa' (killing Germans is like when a surgeon performs an operation: cutting off an arm is horrible but it needs doing and gets done) (p. 426). Revenge killings are justifiable precisely because they reassert the partisans' dignity in the eyes of those who wish to destroy them, the German soldiers who 'pensano che un ebreo valga meno di un russo e un russo meno di un inglese, e che un tedesco valga piú di tutti' (think that a Jew is worth less than a Russian, a Russian less than an Englishman, and that a German is worth more than anyone) (*SNOQ*, II, p. 294), so that 'solo se io uccido un tedesco riuscirò a persuadere gli altri tedeschi che *io sono un uomo*' (only if I kill a German will I manage to persuade the other Germans that *I am a man*) (p. 295, my italics). The exacting of retribution is therefore necessary both to consolidate the group in the face of a common foe and to establish and confirm the partisans' status as *men*, as men free to live, to feel, to act, and to take responsibility for their actions.

It is action as an affirmation of dignity which is further highlighted by the freedom of choice which accompanies the partisans' way of life, envied by those encountered within the text whose experiences have not been the same:

- [...] ammiro te e i tuoi compagni, e vi invidio anche un poco.
- Ci invidi? Non siamo da invidiare. Non abbiamo avuto un cammino facile. Perché ci invidi?
- Perché la vostra scelta non vi è stata imposta. Perché avete inventato il vostro destino. (*SNOQ*, II, p. 466)

('I admire you and your companions, and I envy you a bit too.' 'You envy us? There is nothing to envy. We have not had an easy path. Why do you envy us?' 'Because your choice was not imposed upon you. Because you have invented your own destiny.')

This creation of their own destinies and the ability to make free decisions exists in this text in precise contrast to its opposite, to the imprisonment and enslavement of the concentration camp. Characters to have survived or escaped from concentration camps are thus especially outspoken when issues regarding the determination of their own lives are raised. Leonid, for example, an escapee from Smolensk *Lager*, quickly resents decisions being made for him, feeling an urgent need to assert this element of his independence. In the course of the second chapter, Leonid's reactions develop from a slight resistance to Mendel's decisions, 'non che rifiutasse le proposte di Mendel, o che si ribellasse alle sue decisioni, ma esercitava un sottile attrito passivo contro ogni spinta attiva' (not that he was refusing Mendel's propositions, or that he was rebelling against his decisions, but he exercised a light, passive friction against every active pressure) (*SNOQ*, II, p. 234), to outright rebellion:

- [...] Ormai abbiamo preso una decisione, non è vero?
- Quale decisione?- domandò Leonid ostile.
- Di raggiungere la banda, no?
- È una decisione che hai preso tu. Non mi hai chiesto niente.

- Non c'era bisogno di chiedere. Sono giorni che se ne parla, e tu sei sempre stato zitto.
- E adesso non sto piú zitto. Se vuoi andare con la banda, ci vai da solo. Io di guerra ne ho abbastanza. (*SNOQ*, II, p. 241)

('We have made a decision today, right?' 'What decision?' asked Leonid, with hostility. 'To join the group, haven't we?' 'It's a decision that you have made. You never asked me.' 'There was no need to ask. We have been talking about it for days and you have always been silent.' 'And now I'm not being silent any longer. If you want to go with the group, go by yourself. I've had enough of war.')

Similarly, after being liberated by the partisan group, the remaining ten prisoners at the Chmielnik *Lager* insist upon their independence almost instantly as Goldner announces that 'ognuno di noi farà la sua scelta' (each of us will make his own choice) (*SNOQ*, II, p. 401) over whether to join the partisans or not. The freedom of movement and of decision-making is therefore vital precisely because of its disparity with the alternative option history offers the partisans, that of imprisonment, slavery and death.

Freedom of work is likewise contrasted with the constant possibility of the slave labour of the concentration camps. In *Se non ora, quando?*, as in *La chiave a stella*, useful, positive work continues to be a vital factor in maintaining human dignity. Thus it is precisely at the moments when this activity is halted and enforced idleness prevails that the group feel most alienated and depressed: 'L'intero mese di marzo passò in una inazione quasi totale, che si rivelò nociva per tutti' (The entire month of March passed in almost total inaction, which was harmful for everyone) (*SNOQ*, II, p. 318), 'Gedale sopportava male la clausura. A lui, e non solo a lui, quel modo di vivere sembrava vuoto, umiliante e ridicolo' (Gedale bore enclosure badly. To him, and not only to him, that way of living appeared empty, humiliating and ridiculous) (p. 447). The partisans' dignity is maintained by way of their work and their resistance: the degradation of man through futile work in *Se questo è un uomo* is largely turned on its head in *Se non ora, quando?* for this is the very antithesis of slave labour, a group of men actively fighting for their own survival, against the possibilities of imprisonment or death. The differences between these two existences, the life of resistance and the life of incarceration, are further illustrated through the comparisons made between the emotional state of the two groups of people, prisoners and partisans, within *Se non ora, quando?*. The 'vergogna di non essere morti' (shame of not being dead) (*SNOQ*, II, p. 463) felt by the prisoners, and exemplified here by Francine as a survivor of Auschwitz, is contrasted against the partisans' incomprehension of such feelings and their pride in their own actions and survival. The feelings invoked by the degradation and terror suffered by the prisoners cannot be shared by the partisans precisely because of the opposite circumstances of their existence and the freedom of their experiences.

The exceptionally noteworthy aspect of these questions of dignity in *Se non ora, quando?* is the fact that the pride and self-respect of these characters is founded precisely upon the humanising elements denied the prisoners of the concentration camps. The loss of identity, of homeland, and of a sense of continuity with the past, common to both the prisoners and the partisans, can, in this text, be recompensed with a notion of dignity built upon resistance, action, revenge, friendship, freedom of choice and an independent life, all impossible for the prisoners of the concentration camps, as explicitly outlined by Levi in *Se questo è un uomo*. In *Se non ora, quando?* Levi is therefore rewriting the concept of dignity precisely on the basis of and as a reaction against his concentration camp experience.

Even in the aspects of *Se non ora, quando?* which seem to depict the opposite, counter-experience to Levi's own, the influence of the *Lager* is therefore still in evidence. In spite of Levi's efforts to distance himself more in *Se non ora, quando?* than in his previous works through the narration of a Second World War tale which superficially excludes his own experience and is, in many ways, the antithetical experience to his own, this is not the anti-*Lager* novel it has often been assumed to be. This authorial distancing is a purposeful self-effacement from the narrative which is also accompanied by the thematic distancing, as Levi deals explicitly with his own experiences as little as possible, and yet Levi's time in the concentration camps is not erased to the degree that it appears. Auschwitz functions as a permanent background to the events of *Se non ora, quando?*: it hovers continually, firstly as the potential fate of the partisans and then later as the horrifying alternative they managed to escape. Other concentration camps are also permanently present, referred to as the haunting near-past of some of the characters who have physically escaped them, and as the location for one of the episodes of the text, the liberation of the *Lager* in 'Luglio-agosto 1944'. Yet the concentration camps are not just present physically in the text in this way; Levi's experience of them also contributes considerably to the creation of this text. His very ability to comprehend the temporal aspects of war: the distancing of former lives and memories; the feeling that time has stopped; a sense of detachment from the rest of the world and an uncertain future, and to describe the ambivalent emotional experience of war, the dehumanising power of language, issues of displacement and deprivation, the necessity of regaining a sense of self and of independence, and the construction of a sense of dignity all stem from Levi's time either during or immediately after Auschwitz. As is so often the case in Levi's writing, even when the subject matter departs radically from the topic of the concentration camps, the echoes of the Holocaust continue to recur.

Notes

1. Levi's words, spoken at the Rockefeller Foundation conference, Bellagio, 29 November–2 December 1982, transcribed in Poli and Calcagno, 1992, p. 253.
2. Levi's comments to Roberto Vacca, 'Un western dalla Russia a Milano', *Il Giorno*, 18 May 1982, (also in Poli and Calcagno, 1992, p. 257).
3. Levi's words spoken to Piero Bianucci, 'Sí, anche la mia cultura può essere considerata yiddish', *La Stampa*, 6 September 1982, (also in Poli and Calcagno, 1992, p. 266).
4. This definition is taken from Robert Holton, *Jarring Witnesses: Modern Fiction and the Representation of History*, 1994, p. 250.
5. In Levi's own words, in *Se non ora, quando?* 'quasi tutte le cose che racconto sono successe davvero […] Invece i personaggi sono inventati'. (Roberto Vacca, 'Un western dalla Russia a Milano', *Il Giorno*, 18 May 1982, also in Poli and Calcagno, 1992, p. 257).
6. Levi's words to Camon, 1991, p. 72.
7. Levi's words to Rosellina Balbi, 'Mendel, il consolatore', *la Repubblica*, 14 April 1982, also published in Belpoliti, 1997a, pp.129-35.
8. Levi's words at his reception speech for the Premio Campiello for *SNOQ*, transcribed in Poli and Calcagno, 1992, p. 261.
9. For writings on the issue of friendship in Levi's works see Pietro Frassica, 'Primo Levi: Eroe, antieroe o alter ego?' in Ioli, ed., 1995 and the section entitled 'Amicizia' in Robert Gordon, 'Etica', published in Belpoliti, ed., 1997b, pp. 315-30.

8
Ad ora incerta and *Altre poesie*: 'Dopo Auschwitz non si può piú fare poesie se non su Auschwitz'

Levi's poetry covers the widest period of composition of any of his collections, beginning with 'Crecenzago' in February 1943 and ending with 'Almanacco' in January 1987. Some of Levi's earliest poems were first published as *L'osteria di Brema* in 1975 prior to their inclusion in *Ad ora incerta* in 1984, whilst the *Altre poesie* were published posthumously in the earlier edition of *Opere II: Racconti e poesie* in 1988. For the publication of each collection of Levi's poetry, the poems are organised chronologically according to composition rather than according to their original date of publication either in *L'osteria di Brema* or in *La Stampa*. After 'Crescenzago' in *Ad ora incerta* there are fifteen poems written between 1945 and 1946; there are three written in the decade between 1949 and 1959; four in the 1960s; one in 1970; one in 1973; two in 1974, and thirty-five between 1978 and 1984. The *Altre poesie* number eighteen and are the very last of Levi's poems, composed between September 1982 and January 1987.

Of the earliest poems, those written in 1945 and 1946, immediately after Levi's return from the concentration camp and composed at the same time as *Se questo è un uomo*, a significant number deal directly with Auschwitz: 'Buna'; '25 febbraio 1944'; 'Shemà'; 'Alzarsi' and 'Il tramonto di Fossoli'. Some, like 'Buna', are set, wholly or in part, in the *Lager* and are written in the present tense as if its author were still within the confines of the camp itself: 'Fuma la Buna dai mille camini,/ Un giorno come ogni giorno ci aspetta' (Buna smokes with its thousand chimneys,/ A day like every other awaits us); others, like '25 febbraio 1944', are written retrospectively: 'Vorrei poter dire la forza/ Con cui desiderammo allora,/ Noi già sommersi,/ Di potere ancora una volta insieme/ Camminare liberi sotto il sole' (I would like to be able to express the strength/ With which we yearned then,/ We the already drowned,/ To be able once more/ To walk together free in the sun). 'Alzarsi', the epigraph to *La tregua*, is written in the first-person plural, and clearly continues the multiple testimony perspective of *Se questo è un uomo* ('Ora abbiamo ritrovato la casa,/ Il nostro ventre è sazio,/ Abbiamo finito di raccontare' [Now we have found our homes again,/ Our stomachs are full,/ We have finished telling our tale]), whilst 'Il tramonto di Fossoli' and the beginning of '25 febbraio 1944' retain the first-person singular required, even in *Se questo è un uomo*, for the narration of Levi's own experiences.

In this first period of Levi's poetry writing which coincides so closely with the composition of *Se questo è un uomo*, there exist not just echoes of the Holocaust, but an actual appropriation of phrasing from the testimonial work.[1] Examining the poems in the order in which they are arranged, the depiction of the *compagno* in 'Buna' is strongly echoed in Levi's description of the *sommersi* of the concentration camp (*SQ*, I, p. 86), and a couple of lines are closely echoed by sentences from *Se questo è un uomo*: 'Un giorno come ogni giorno ci aspetta' (A day like every other awaits us) is repeated in 'incomincia un giorno come ogni giorno' (begins a day like every other) (*SQ*, I, p. 57), and 'È nato un altro giorno di dolore' (Another day of pain is born) mirrors the closing words of the 'Le nostre notti' chapter of *Se questo è un uomo*, 'Allora mi si riaprono le piaghe dei piedi, e incomincia una nuova giornata' (Then the sores on my feet reopen, and a new day begins) (*SQ*, I, p. 58). The singing of 'Cantare' coupled with the line 'E i mesi passano piuttosto rapidi,/ Ma davanti ne abbiamo tanti!' (And the months pass rather quickly,/ But we have so many of them ahead of us!) appears to reflect the singing of the girls in the Buna laboratory: 'Queste ragazze cantano, come cantano tutte le ragazze di tutti i laboratori del mondo' (These girls sing, as all the girls in all the laboratories in the world sing) and their words, overheard by Levi, that 'non sembra vero, quest'anno è passato cosí presto!' (it doesn't seem real, this year has passed so quickly!) (*SQ*, I, p. 139). The statement, also in 'Cantare', that 'Cosa cattiva ci parve uccidere;/ Morire, una cosa lontana' (Killing seemed to us a terrible thing:/ Dying, something in the far distance) has its parallel in Levi's description of himself prior to deportation: 'uccidere e morire mi parevano cose estranee e letterarie' (killing and dying were alien and literary things) (*SQ*, I, p. 139). Much of 'Cantare' therefore has a strong relationship with the 'Die drei Leute vom Labor' chapter of *Se questo è un uomo*. Similarly, a number of lines in 'Il canto del corvo' match phrases from *Se questo è un uomo*: 'Sono venuto di molto lontano/ Per portare mala novella' (I have come from very far away/ To bring bad tidings) echoes 'Nessuno deve uscire di qui, che potrebbe portare al mondo, insieme col segno impresso nella carne, *la mala novella* di quanto, ad Auschwitz, è bastato animo all'uomo di fare dell'uomo' (No one must leave here who could carry to the world, together with the sign impressed on his skin, *the bad tidings* of what man intended to do to man in Auschwitz) (*SQ*, I, p. 49, my italics), and 'Per portarti la nuova trista/ Che ti tolga la gioia del sonno' (To bring you the bad news/ May it take the joy from your sleep) reproduces 'un nucleo doloroso si condensa, e ci punge, e cresce fino a varcare le soglie della coscienza, e *ci toglie la gioia del sonno*' (a painful nucleus condenses, and pierces us, and grows until it crosses the threshold of consciousness, and takes the joy from our sleep) (*SQ*, I, p. 64, my italics). 'Alzarsi' contains the most instances of what Dällenbach terms *autocitation*, most of which occurs with the chapter of *Se questo è un uomo* entitled 'Le nostre notti' and occasionally with the dream recounted in the conclusion to *La tregua*. The opening lines of 'Alzarsi', 'Sognavamo nelle notti feroci/ Sogni densi e violenti/ Sognati con anima e corpo:/ Tornare; mangiare; raccontare' (We used to dream during the ferocious nights/ Dreams dense and violent/ Dreamt with body and soul:/ Of returning; eating; telling our story) are paraphrased on a number of occasions towards the end of 'Le nostre notti' chapter: 'il dolore di tutti i giorni si traduce nei nostri sogni cosí costantemente, nella scena sempre ripetuta della narrazione fatta e non ascoltata' (the pain of each and every day is constantly translated into our dreams in this way, in the continually repeated scene of a story told and not listened to) (*SQ*, I, p. 54), 'Sognano di mangiare: anche questo è un sogno collettivo' (They dream of eating: even this is a collective dream) (*SQ*, I, p. 55), and 'Cosí si trascinano le nostre notti. Il sogno di Tantalo e il sogno del racconto si inseriscono in un tessuto di immagini piú indistinte: la sofferenza del giorno, composta di fame, percosse, freddo, fatica, paura e promiscuità, si volge di notte in incubi informi di inaudita violenza, quali nella vita libera occorrono solo nelle notti di febbre' (Our nights drag on in this way. The dream of Tantalus and the dream of telling our story become part of a fabric of more indistinct images: the day's suffering, composed of hunger, blows, cold, exhaustion, fear and promiscuity, turns at night into shapeless nightmares of unheard-of violence, which in free life only occur during feverish nights) (*SQ*, I, p. 56). Following on from these lines, 'Finché suonava breve e sommesso/ Il comando dell'alba:/ "Wstawać"' (Until, briefly and subdued, sounded/ The dawn command:/ "Wstawać") reduplicates 'Pochissimi attendono dormendo lo Wstawać [...] La guardia notturna lo sa, ed è per questo che non lo pronunzia con tono di comando, ma con voce *piana e sommessa*' (Very few await the *Wstawać* in a state of slumber [...] The night guard knows it, and for this reason does not utter it in a tone of command, but in a *soft and subdued* voice) (*SQ*, I, p. 57, my italics) and is more precisely replicated by the later definition in *La tregua* of the wake-up call as 'una sola parola, non imperiosa, anzi *breve e sommessa*' (a single word, not imperious, but *brief and subdued*) (*LT*, I, p. 395, my italics). The next line, 'E si spezzava in petto il cuore' (And our hearts broke) is summarised less succinctly by the narrative: 'La parola straniera cade come una pietra sul fondo di tutti gli animi. "Alzarsi": l'illusoria barriera delle coperte calde, l'esile corazza del sonno, la pur tormentosa evasione notturna, cadono a pezzi intorno a noi, e ci ritroviamo desti senza remissione, esposti all'offesa, atrocemente nudi e vulnerabili' (The foreign word falls like a stone to the bottom of every soul. "Get up": the illusory barrier of the warm blankets, the thin armour of sleep, the nightly escape even though torturous, drops to pieces around us, and we find ourselves mercilessly awake, exposed to the offence, atrociously naked and vulnerable) (*SQ*, I, p. 57). The final lines of the poem, 'È tempo. Presto udremo ancora/ Il comando straniero:/ "Wstawać"' (It is time. Soon we shall hear again/ The foreign command:/ "Wstawać") are reiterated in the concluding lines of *La tregua*: 'È il comando dell'alba in Auschwitz, una parola straniera, temuta e attesa: alzarsi, "Wstawać"' (It is the dawn command in Auschwitz, a foreign word, feared and expected: get up, "Wstawać") (*LT*, I, p. 395).

At times, then, there is a direct borrowing of phrasing between Levi's poetry and his prose and at other times merely a paraphrastic echo. That the poems written contiguously to *Se questo è un uomo* would employ identical phrases to the testimony itself, is perhaps to be expected to a certain extent. It does raise the question, however, of whether this really constitutes a *rewriting* of *Se questo è un uomo* if in fact the works are being written simultaneously. Since one of the Auschwitz poems, 'Shemà', even appears as epigraph to *Se questo è un uomo*, the earliest of these poems ought perhaps to be considered complementary to the testimony in spite of the fact that they were not published until much later. The relationship between the poem entitled 'Il tramonto di Fossoli' and the section of the 'Il viaggio' chapter of *Se questo è un uomo* which deals precisely with Levi's departure from the Fossoli detention camp highlights the contributing and completing nature of the association between Levi's poetry and his prose. The fact that, in the case of 'Alzarsi', the conclusion of *La tregua* is built upon Levi's earlier phrasing of his poem complicates the issue of the intertextuality at play here. The relationship between Levi's poetry and his narrative would appear to be two-directional: it is not the case that Levi's experience of the concentration camps as portrayed in *Se questo è un uomo* is reworded in his poetry as the narrative does not precede the poetry, nor the poetry precede the narrative; rather that the writing of both the poetry and the testimony reflect upon each other precisely because of the overlapping of their composition and subject matter.

The relationship between Levi's poetry and his testimony to the concentration camps does not end with the earliest poems written at the same time as *Se questo è un uomo* as even some of Levi's later poems closely echo the wording of parts of this first narrative. The affirmation in 'Partigia' (1981) that 'ognuno è nemico di ognuno' (everyone is the enemy of everyone else) reproduces Levi's statement in the preface to *Se questo è un uomo* that 'ogni straniero è nemico' (every stranger is an enemy) (*SQ*, I, p. 5) and later in the text that 'tutti ci sono nemici o rivali' (all of them are either our enemies or our rivals) (*SQ*, I, p. 36). The lines in 'Canto dei morti invano' (1985) which declare that 'Siamo invincibili perché siamo i vinti./ Invulnerabili perché già spenti' (We are invincible because we are the defeated ones./ Invulnerable because already lifeless) echo the end of the 'L'ultimo' chapter of *Se questo è un uomo*: 'Possono venire i russi: non troveranno che noi domati, noi *spenti*'

(The Russians can come: they will only find us, broken and *lifeless*) (*SQ*, I, p. 146, my italics) and 'Perché, anche noi siamo rotti, *vinti*' (Because we too are broken, *defeated*) (p. 146, my italics). There are also a number of instances in which Levi's poetry has been affected and guided by earlier writing other than the testimony of *Se questo è un uomo*. Two of the poems written in 1984, 'Scacchi' and 'Scacchi II' were preceded by 'Gli scacchisti irritabili' (later in *L'altrui mestiere*), and they bear strong comparisons: the following lines from 'Scacchi II', 'Rifare i tratti che hai mossi all'inizio?/ Via, le hai pure accettate,/ Queste regole,/ Quando ti sei seduto alla scacchiera./ Il pezzo che hai toccato è un pezzo mosso' (Remake the moves you made at the beginning?/ Come on, you accepted these rules,/ When you sat down at the chessboard./ If you touch a piece you have to move it) result from a similar analysis of chess in 'Gli scacchisti irritabili': 'il pezzo che è stato toccato deve essere mosso, e non è ammesso rifare un tratto di cui si è pentiti' (the piece which has been touched must be moved, and it is not permitted to remake a move you regret) (*AM*. II, p. 763). 'Partigia', written during the composition of *Se non ora, quando?*, echoes, in its concluding line, 'La nostra guerra non è mai finita' (Our war is never over), the words attributed to Mordo Nahum in *La tregua* almost two decades earlier: 'Guerra è sempre' (War is always) (*LT*, I, p. 242). The poem entitled 'Il disgelo' (1985) bears the same name as the opening chapter of *La tregua*, and lines from the concluding verse of 'Il disgelo', 'Il morso/ Del gelo ha lasciato il suo segno/ Su carne, mente, fango e legno' (The bite/ Of the frost has left its mark/ On flesh, mind, mud and wood) allude to those written in the earlier chapter, that 'i segni dell'offesa sarebbero rimasti in noi per sempre, e nei ricordi di chi vi ha assistito, e nei luoghi ove avvenne, e nei racconti che ne avremmo fatti' (the signs of the offence would remain in us forever, and in the memories of those who witnessed it, and in the places where it took place, and in the tales we would tell of it) (*LT*, I, p. 206).

The later poems are therefore periodically influenced by the preceding prose. Equally significant is the fact that, alongside this orderly and chronological association between the prose which antecedes the subsequent poems, on occasion Levi's poetry has also affected the phrasing of some of his later narrative. The afore-mentioned examples with regard to the impact of 'Alzarsi' on the conclusion of *La tregua* is just the tip of the iceberg as Levi's use of self-quotation of and self-reference to his poetry also occurs in relation to some of his other writings. The most obvious example is in the reappearance of Lilít in the eponymous chapter of the collection *Lilít e altri racconti*, published sixteen years after the composition of the poem of the same title. In the poem (1965) Levi writes that Lilít 'Fruscia improvvisa contro le finestre/ Dove dormono i bimbi appena nati./ Li cerca, e cerca di farli morire' (Rustles suddenly against the windows/ Where newborn babies sleep./ She looks for them and tries to make them die) whilst in the narrative, 'fruscia contro i vetri delle case dove ci sono dei bambini appena nati e cerca di soffocarli' (she rustles against the windows of houses where there are newborn babies and tries to suffocate them) (*L*, II, p. 21); the poem states that 'Ma di lei non sono nati/ Che spiriti senza corpo né pace' (But there is nothing born of her/ But bodiless spirits without peace), and the short story that 'partorisce diavoli [...] spiritelli maligni, senza corpo (she gives birth to devils [...] evil goblins, without a body) (*L*, II, p. 22). Somewhat less patent echoes resound through some of Levi's other works, where the titles do not already suggest a connection with an earlier poem. The final line of the third verse of 'Cantare' (1946), 'Non martiri, non infami, non santi' (not martyrs, not infamous, not saints) is reproduced in 'Cromo' in *Il sistema periodico* as: 'scrivendo mi sentivo ridiventare uomo, uno come tutti, né martire né infame né santo' (writing, I felt myself rebecome a man, the same as everyone else, neither a martyr nor infamous nor a saint) (*SP*, I, p. 871). Of the large number of poems written concurrently with *I sommersi e i salvati*, 'Il superstite' (1984) contains an identical phrasing of Levi's reaction to one particular incident: in the poem Levi writes, with certainty, that 'Non ho soppiantato nessuno,/ Non ho usurpato il pane di nessuno,/ Nessuno è morto in vece mia. Nessuno' (I haven't supplanted anyone,/ I haven't seized anyone's bread,/ No one has died in my place. No one) compared to the more qualified version in the later narrative that 'non hai soppiantato nessuno [...] non hai rubato il pane a nessuno; tuttavia non lo puoi escludere. È solo la supposizione, anzi, l'ombra di un sospetto' (you haven't supplanted anyone [...] you haven't stolen anyone's bread; yet you cannot exclude it. It is only the supposition, indeed the shadow of a suspicion) (*SS*, II, p. 1054); whilst the response of Alex Zink in 'A giudizio': '- Usavi lana buona?/ - Lana fuor del comune, o giusto giudice./ Lana sciolta od in trecce,/ Lana di cui avevo il monopolio./ Lana nera e castana, fulva e bionda;/ Più spesso grigia o bianca./ - Da quali greggi?/ - Non so. Non m'interessava' ("Did you use good wool?"/ "Above average wool, o fair judge./ Loose or plaited wool,/ Wool over which I had the monopoly."/ "From which flocks?"/ "I don't know. I was not interested") (1985) is a prime example for Levi's remarks in the preface to *I sommersi e i salvati* that:

> Nessuno riuscirà mai a stabilire con precisione quanti, nell'apparato nazista, *non potessero non sapere* delle spaventose atrocità che venivano commesse; quanti sapessero qualcosa, ma fossero in grado di fingere d'ignorare; quanti ancora avessero avuto la possibilità di sapere tutto, ma abbiano scelto la via piú prudente di tenere occhi ed orecchi (e soprattutto la bocca) ben chiusi. (*SS*, II, p. 1000)

(No one will ever manage to establish precisely how many in the Nazi apparatus *couldn't not know* about the frightening atrocities which were being committed; how many knew something but were able to pretend not to know; how many more had the chance to know everything but chose the more prudent route of keeping their eyes and ears (and especially their mouths) well closed.)

Between Levi's narrative and his poetry there therefore exists a very unique form of intertextuality and a very original form of rewriting. The rewriting of lines from his poetry into his prose, and, vice versa, of parts of the narrative into the poetry, as well as the thematic rewriting of issues back and forth between the two genres places an entirely new angle on Genette's theories on hypertextuality. What is present in Levi's *oeuvre* is not simply an affiliation which links 'un texte B (que j'appellerai *hypertexte*) à un text antérieur A (que j'appellerai, bien sûr, *hypotexte*)'[2] (a text B [which I will call *hypertext*] to a text A [which I will naturally call *hypotext*]) but a two-way hypertextual relationship with both the poetry collections and *Se questo è un uomo* serving simultaneously as hypotext and hypertext to each other.

The rewriting and recurrence of themes from *Se questo è un uomo* is also not limited to the poems which deal with explicitly similar issues. Very few of Levi's later poems after the end of the 1940s deal directly with the Holocaust,[3] yet there are a significant number of disguised returns to concentration camp themes as many of the later poems which appear to deal with other topics remain, as with Levi's prose, thematically connected to his writing of the *Lager*. Of the wide range of topics covered by Levi's poetry: the animal world ('Schiera bruna', 'Aracne', 'Vecchia talpa', 'Un topo', 'La chiocciola', 'L'elefante', 'La mosca' and 'Il dromedario'); the natural world ('Cuore di legno', 'Agave', 'Meleagrina'); science ('Nel principio', 'Le stelle nere', 'Sidereus nuncius'); historical figures ('Plinio', 'La bambina di Pompei', 'Huayna Capac', Galileo in 'Sidereus nuncius', 'Sansone', 'Delila'); daily life ('Via cigna', 'Cuore di legno', 'Aeroporto', 'Agosto'); writing ('L'opera', 'Un mestiere'), and countless others, many continuities with concentration camp themes remain present. Of the various motifs connected to Levi's portrayal of his experience of Auschwitz, a number recur with a degree of frequency and are worth listing here. A sensation of being under threat, usually the threat of death, first written as 'mi sento minacciato, insidiato, ad ogni istante sono pronto a contrarmi in uno spasimo di difesa' (I feel threatened, beseiged, I am ready at any moment to draw myself into a spasm of defence) (*SQ*, I, p. 32), reappears here in various contexts: in 'Agenda' there is the physical risk to humanity of 'una cometa che ci piomba incontro' (a comet bearing down upon us) and of the research of the white-coated young students who 'Disegnano un lunghissimo canale/ Per convogliarvi un fascio di protoni/ Veloci quasi quanto viaggia la luce:/ Se riusciranno, il mondo esploderà' (Are designing a very long canal/ To carry a beam of protons/ Almost as fast as the speed of light:/ If they manage it, the world will explode); there is the menace of the final lines of 'Attesa', 'davanti alle nostre porte,/ Il percuotere di passi ferrati' (Outside our doors,/ The beating of hobnailed steps); and the portent of the destruction of the planet in 'Almanacco'. The idea of death, Levi's own in 'Carichi pendenti', that of the 'Agave' who declares the blooming of its flower to be 'il nostro modo di gridare che/ Morrò domani' (our way of shouting that/ I will die tomorrow), and that of 'L'elefante' for whom 'quando si cade, non c'è salvezza' (when we fall, there is no salvation) also recurs.

The notion of life being pointless revealed in 'Le stelle nere', 'E tutti noi seme umano viviamo e moriamo per nulla' (And all of us human seed live and die for nothing) alongside the repetition of 'assurdo' (absurd) in 'L'elefante' is linked to Levi's experience of life as valueless and without aim in Auschwitz:

> La persuasione che la vita ha uno scopo è radicata in ogni fibra di uomo, è una proprietà della sostanza umana. Gli uomini liberi dànno a questo scopo molti nomi, e sulla sua natura molto pensano e discutono: ma per noi la questione è piú semplice.
>
> Oggi e qui, il nostro scopo è di arrivare a primavera. Di altro, ora, non ci curiamo. Dietro a questa meta non c'è ora, altra meta. (SQ, I, p. 66)

(The belief that life has an aim is deep-rooted in every fibre of man, it belongs to the human essence. Free men give many names to this aim, and they think about and discuss its nature a lot: but for us the issue is more simple.

Here and now, our aim is to arrive at spring. For now we do not care about anything else. There is no other goal, now, behind this one.)

The pointlessness of life is experienced particularly acutely by the animals in Levi's poetry, many of whom suffer at the hands of mankind. The degradation and misery of the animals here belong mostly to those enslaved: the elephant who recounts that 'L'indiano astuto mi ha allettato e domato,/ L'egizio m'ha impastoiato e venduto,/ Il fenicio m'ha ricoperto di armi/ E m'ha imposto una torre sulla groppa' (The astute Indian enticed and tamed me,/ The Egyptian fettered and sold me,/ the Phoenician wrapped me in arms/ And imposed a tower on my back) ('L'elefante'); 'Pio' who comments that 'm'inchino al giogo, pensi quanto contento' (I bow under the yoke, just think how happy I am); the draught horse in 'Lunedì' who 'Non può neppure guardarsi a lato./ La sua vita è camminare' (Cannot even look to the side./ Its life is walking), and, to an extent, even the camel of 'Il dromedario', 'Sì, sono un servo, ma il deserto è mio:/ Non c'è servo che non abbia il suo regno./ Il mio regno è la desolazione;/ Non ha confini' (Yes, I am a servant, but the desert is mine:/ There is no servant without kingdom./ My kingdom is desolation:/ It knows no bounds). The humiliation of these creatures reflects the degradation of the prisoners of the concentration camps, and alludes to Levi's statement that 'Piú giú di cosí non si può andare: condizione umana piú misera non c'è, e non è pensabile' (One cannot sink lower than this: there is no human condition more miserable than this, it is inconceivable) (*SQ*, I, p. 20). The loneliness of the concentration camps where 'ognuno è disperatamente ferocemente solo' (everyone is desperately ferociously alone) (*SQ*, I, p. 84) continues with reference to the animal world in the poetry too, yet it is mostly in evidence with regard to the free animal characters who have actively selected a life of solitude. Thus in 'Lunedì' Levi remarks that 'Non è triste un uomo?/ Se vive a lungo in solitudine' (Is a man not sad?/ If he lives for a long time in solitude); the 'Vecchia talpa' chooses to live alone, 'In altri tempi seguivo le femmine,/ E quando ne sentivo una grattare/ Mi scavavo la via verso di lei:/ Ora non più; se capita, cambio strada' (Once I used to follow the females,/ And when I heard one scratching/ I would dig my way towards her:/ Not any longer; if it happens, I change my route); 'La chiocciola' is able to 'sigillarsi silenziosamente/ Dietro il suo velo di calcare candido/ Negando il mondo e negandosi al mondo' (seal itself silently/ Behind its veil of white limestone/ Denying the world and denying itself to the world), and 'La mosca' delights in stating that 'Qui sono sola' (Here I am alone).

The fear in *Se questo è un uomo* of telling of the events of the concentration camps and being neither heard nor understood ('il dolore di tutti i giorni si traduce nei nostri sogni cosí costantemente, nella scena sempre ripetuta della narrazione fatta e non ascoltata' [the pain of every day is translated into our dreams constantly in this way, in the continually repeated scene of a story told and not heard] [*SQ*, I, p. 54]) is conveyed in Levi's poetry through 'Shemà', 'Voci', 'Il canto del corvo' and 'Huayna Capac' ('Non è un portento, non è un presagio nefasto./ Non ti voglio ascoltare' [It is not a portent, it is not a bad omen./ I do not want to listen to you]). Similarly, the theme of others' incomprehension, and of being unable to convey your message, expressed in *Se questo è un uomo* as the need for a new language with which to articulate the prisoners' suffering (*SQ*, I, p. 119-20) and in sentences such as 'se parleremo, non ci ascolteranno, e se ci ascoltassero, non ci capirebbero' (if we speak they won't listen to us, and if they listened they would not understand us) (*SQ*, I, p. 20), is continued here. In 'Le pratiche inevase' Levi writes that 'dovevo dire qualcosa a qualcuno,/ Ma non so più che cosa e a chi: l'ho scordato./ [...] avevo in animo un libro/ Meraviglioso [...] Non ho avuto tempo per svolgerla. È peccato,/ Sarebbe stata un'opera fondamentale' (I had something to say to someone,/ But I no longer know what I had to say, nor to whom: I've forgotten./ [...] I had a book in mind/ Marvellous [...] I haven't had time to develop it. It's a shame,/ It would have been a fundamental work); in 'Voci' he writes of 'Voci che dicono e non si fanno intendere:/ Cori e cimbali per contrabbandare/ Un senso nel messaggio che non ha senso' (Voices which talk and do not make themselves understood:/ Choirs and cymbals to smuggle/ A sense into the message which has no sense), and in 'Agave' the plant states that 'Sono muta. Parlo solo il mio linguaggio di pianta,/ Difficile a capire per te uomo./ [...] È il nostro modo di gridare che/ Morrò domani. Mi hai capito adesso?' (I am mute. I can only speak my plant language,/ Difficult for man to understand./ [...] It is our way of shouting that/ I will die tomorrow. Have you understood me now?).

What connects many of the poems here is therefore the pervasion of pain and suffering, of loneliness, degradation, and an inability or failure to communicate, aptly expressed in 'La bambina di Pompei as 'poiché l'angoscia di ciascuno è la nostra' (since everyone's anguish is our own). Regardless of the subject of Levi's poems, whether they be human, animal or plantlife, many of them suffer: the 'agonia senza fine' (unending agony) of 'La bambina di Pompei'; the tree whose roots are run over by the tram and which is urinated on by passing dogs in 'Cuore di legno'; Empedocles' suffering in 'Autobiografia' ('Ho sofferto la frusta/ E caldi e geli e la disperazione del giogo' [I have suffered the whip/ And heat and frost and the desperation of the yoke]); the bridge which 'non ha pace mai' (never has peace) in 'Un ponte'; the elephant taken to new climates who finds its existence and its manner of death absurd in 'L'elefante'; the futility of human life in 'Le stelle nere'; thirst in 'Fuga' ('Acqua niente per lui/ Che solo d'acqua aveva bisogno' [No water for he/ Who only had need of water]), and the profound unhappiness in 'Pio'.

Further anguish is caused by one of the most extensive and pervalent topics throughout Levi's poetry which is, again, time. On only one occasion, however, does time appear here as frozen, in the closing metaphor of 'Il canto del corvo II' ('Come si trova fermo un orologio' [As a clock stops]), since the concept of time is here very much in motion. The predominant impression given is that time is too short: 'nel poco tempo che resta' (in the short time remaining) and 'Non ho avuto tempo per svolgerla' (I haven't had time to develop it) ('Le pratiche inevase'); that time is passing too quickly: 'Muovi, che il tuo tempo è scarso;/ Non senti ticchettare l'orologio?' (Move, you are short of time:/ Can't you hear the ticking of the clock?) ('Scacchi II'), and 'Che non devo perdere tempo,/ Bla bla, che il tempo stringe,/ E che il tempo perduto non ritorna,/ E che il tempo è denaro,/ E che chi ha tempo non aspetti tempo' (That I mustn't lose time,/ Blah blah, that time is pressing,/ And that time lost never returns,/ And that time is money,/ And make hay while the sun shines) ('Un topo'); that time is never appreciated or cherished: 'Sono i ladri del tempo,/ Fluidi e viscidi come le mignatte:/ Bevono il tuo tempo e lo sputano via/ Come si butterebbe un'immondezza' (They are the thieves of time,/ fluid and slimy like leeches:/ They drink your time and spit it out/ Like you would throw away garbage) ('Ladri'), and that time itself is merciless: 'Lo stesso tempo che ci partorisce e travolge' (The same time which bears us and knocks us down) ('Nel principio') and 'Ora che il tempo urge da presso' (Now that time presses us with force) ('Agli amici'). This movement of time, as is clear from the above quotations, does not suggest an improvement on the perception of time as frozen; the continuing negativity of time itself, particularly its insufficiency and its tendency to rush us towards the termination of our lives, is simply a speeding up of the conception of time as tortuous and torturing in the concentration camp. The divergent portrayal of free time, of non-prisoner time, is depicted as the precise opposite of camp time in which 'Quando si aspetta, il tempo cammina liscio senza che si debba intervenire per cacciarlo avanti, mentre invece quando si lavora ogni minuto ci percorre faticosamente e deve venire laboriosamente espulso' (When you wait, time passes smoothly without you having to intervene to drive it on, yet while you work every minute passes through you arduously and must be laboriously expelled) (*SQ*, I, p. 100). If camp time is unbearably slow, then time as it appears from a position of liberation is insufferably fast. In both cases, however, the only prospect of a near future is death: 'Conchiuso il tempo in cui i giorni si inseguivano vivaci, preziosi e irreparabili, il futuro ci stava davanti grigio e inarticolato, come una barriera invincibile' (Concluded the time in which vivacious, precious and irreparable days would follow each other, the future faced us, grey and inarticulate, like an invincible barrier) (*SQ*, I, p. 113), against the often implicit lack of a future in 'Le pratiche inevase', 'Attesa', 'Il canto del corvo II', 'Agave' and 'Almanacco' and for the creatures in 'Vecchia talpa' and 'L'elefante'.

All of the themes examined here are the continuation of issues from *Se questo è un uomo*, portrayed in the poetry in varying contexts. The composition of Levi's poetry over such a large period of time demonstates, perhaps more clearly than an analysis of his narrative, his persistent focus, even over time, on what are, in essence, concentration camp themes. The arrangement of the poems chronologically in these collections highlights the fact that after the initial 'Auschwitz poems', many identical themes dominate Levi's poetry even four decades later. Levi's poems are both interspersed and concurrent with his prose writing and Cesare Segre's statement that 'le poesie contengono la quintessenza dell'opera' (the poems contain the quintessence of his work) is true.[4] The poems fit around both the composition and the themes of Levi's other works as they 'isolano, sviluppano, de- e ri-contestualizzano immagini e motivi delle scritture in prosa'[5] (isolate, develop, de- and re-contextualise images and motives of the prose writings). The poems are consonant with and temporally frame Levi's other texts, and yet they still, like the texts themselves, revolve around the event which began Levi's writing career, the Holocaust. Particularly revealing is Levi's response in an interview in 1984, with reference to the immediate post-war period of Levi's poetry writing:

[G.N]- *Eppure Adorno aveva detto che "dopo Auschwitz non si può più fare poesia".*

[P.L] - La mia esperienza è stata opposta. Allora mi sembrò che la poesia fosse piú idonea della prosa per esprimere quello che mi pesava dentro. [...] In quegli anni, semmai, avrei riformulato le parole di Adorno: dopo Auschwitz non si può piú fare poesia se non su Auschwitz.[6]

([G.N] – "Yet Adorno said that 'after Auschwitz one can no longer write poetry'".
[P.L] – "My experience has been the opposite. It seemed to me then that poetry was more suitable than prose to express what was weighing inside me. [...] In those years, in any case, I would have reformulated Adorno's words: after Auschwitz one can no longer write poetry if it is not about Auschwitz.)

These words are applicable not just to the early years of Levi's poetry writing, but to its entire duration. The perpetual recurrence of Auschwitz themes in his poetry, combined with the unique intertextual and hypertextual relationship that exists between Levi's poetry and his prose, but especially between his poetry and *Se questo è un uomo*, makes *Ad ora incerta* and *Altre poesie* some of the strongest examples of cases in which Levi rewrites his Holocaust experiences, proving, in fact, that 'dopo Auschwitz non si può piú fare poesia se non su Auschwitz' (after Auschwitz one can no longer write poetry if it is not about Auschwitz).

Notes

1. Some, but not all of the following examples have been noted in Italo Rosato's research, in particular the chapter entitled 'Poesia', in Belpoliti ed., 1997b, pp. 413-425.
2. Gérard Genette, 1982, p. 11.
3. The most notable exceptions are 'Per Adolf Eichmann (July 1960) and 'Il superstite' (February 1984), the first five lines of which feature in English, as the epigraph to I *sommersi e i salvati* (quotation from S. T. Coleridge's *The Rime of the Ancient Mariner*).
4. Cesare Segre's 'Introduzione' to the first edition of *Opere II: Racconti e poesie*, 1988, p. xxiii.
5. Italo Rosato, 'Primo Levi: sondaggi intertestuali', *Autografo*, vol 6, June 1989, pp. 31-43, p. 32.
6. Giulio Nascimbeni, 'Levi: l'ora incerta della poesia', *Corriere della Sera,* 28 October 1984, also in Belpoliti, ed., 1997a, pp. 136-41, p. 137.

9
I sommersi e i salvati: 'Alla ricerca permanente di una giustificazione'

I sommersi e i salvati marks a return in Levi's writing, forty years after the first publication of *Se questo è un uomo*, to a direct, undisguised commentary on the concentration camps. After the international success of the second edition of *Se questo è un uomo* in 1958, open discussion of the Holocaust on Levi's part was, on the whole, confined to the many interviews he granted and the conferences he attended and spoke at, with the notable exception of the 'Passato prossimo' section of his *Lilít e altri racconti* collection.[1] The subject matter of *I sommersi e i salvati* therefore constitutes a cyclical return in Levi's writing to the issues of his first work of testimony, a perhaps unexpected return after Levi's remark in 1963 that 'quello che dovevo dire l'ho detto tutto'[2] (I have said everything I had to say). Levi's comments in a television interview in February 1985, whilst he was still composing *I sommersi e i salvati*, shed light upon his reasons for the regression to his original subject matter: when asked whether 'se questo è un uomo è una domanda tuttora valida?' (is it still valid to question 'if this is a man'?) Levi replied that 'Temo di sí, perché l'umanità è minacciata nel suo complesso per i motivi ben noti; e anche ogni singolo. Ognuno di noi, oggi, in un modo non cosí diverso dal passato, deve lottare per restare uomo'[3] (I am afraid so, because humanity as a whole, as well as every single individual, is threatened for well-known reasons. Every one of us, these days, in a manner not entirely dissimilar to in the past, must battle to remain human). This pervasive perception of humanity continuing to exist under threat, and still battling to retain the very essence of its humanity therefore influences Levi's return to the topic of the *Lager*, the embodiment of the biggest threat *dal passato* to humanity. Levi began writing *I sommersi e i salvati* as early as 1979[4] as a response to the rising trend of Holocaust denial. In Levi's article 'Ma noi c'eravamo', written as a reaction against the remarks of the French revisionist historian, Robert Faurisson, several issues to be later expanded in *I sommersi e i salvati* are already addressed, in particular the workings of memory and guilt.[5] Yet there were also personal motives for Levi's return to the camps:

Io sento passare gli anni, anche i miei. E col passare degli anni mi è parso di cogliere una deriva nel modo in cui vengono intese queste memorie. Incontro ancora i giovani nelle scuole: c'è in loro una partecipazione emotiva, anche violenta: non storica. Quando entro in un'aula colgo un lampo di stupore nel vedere l'autore del libro che hanno letto e che è ancora vivo, parla italiano, non latino e neppure greco. A me interessava far vedere che queste cose appartengono a un passato vicino, non solo geograficamente.[6]

(I feel the years passing, even my own. And with the passing of the years I have seemed to grasp a drift in the way in which these memories [of the concentration camps] are understood. I still meet young people in schools: in them there is an emotional involvement in the events, even a violent one, but no sense of an historical participation. When I walk into a classroom I sense a flash of amazement in seeing the author of a book they have read, and one who is still alive and speaks Italian, not Latin or Greek. I was interested in showing that these things are close in time, as well as geographically.)

Noto spesso anche nelle lettere che ricevo – e ne ricevo molte – commozione, anche partecipazione, ma come se si trattasse di un evento che non ci riguarda piú, che non appartiene all'Europa, non al nostro secolo [...]. In piú abbiamo assistito a dei tentativi di negare, addirittura, l'Olocausto [...]. Poi mi è venuto in mente che valeva la pena, siccome si intensificava questa sensazione di dissolvimento, di *fading away*, di annebbiamento di quei fatti; ho pensato che era il momento di radunarli, o di scrivere altri saggi [...]. Mi è sembrato quindi opportuno radunare otto o nove saggi su alcuni aspetti non trattati, o trattati secondo me in modo distorto.[7]

(I often note in the letters I receive as well – and I receive a lot of them – emotion, participation too, but not as if it were an event which has nothing more to do with us, which does not belong to Europe, or to our century [...]. Moreover we have witnessed attempts to actually deny the Holocaust [...]. Then it came to my mind that it was worthwhile, since this sensation of dispersion, of fading away, of clouding over of those facts was intensifying, I thought that it was time to gather them together, or to write other essays [...]. I therefore thought it was the right time to gather together eight or nine essays on some aspects not dealt with, or dealt with in my opinion in a distorted fashion.)

A me è sembrato opportuno tornare, dopo quarant'anni, su questo tema, a scopo di antidoto, a scopo, appunto, di mettere in allarme, di mettere all'erta i lettori, e soprattutto i lettori giovani, affinché si rendano conto che occorre predisporre delle linee di difesa personale, di ciascuno, di difesa psicologica, tali da evitare l'instaurarsi di nuovi regimi, simili a quelli che io ho descritto.[8]

(It seemed to me to be the right time to return to this topic after forty years as an antidote, in order to warn and alert the readers, especially the young readers, so that they would be aware of the need to prepare lines of personal and psychological defence in advance, for everyone, such as will avoid the beginning of new regimes similar to those I have described.)

Levi writes with a sense of *un passato vicino*, echoing the 'Passato prossimo' of *Lilít*, in an effort to convey to others the very nearness of his memories and experiences, and to serve as a warning to a new generation of the horrors of which man is capable. One sentence in the preface to *I sommersi e i salvati* contains a declaration of intentions which is particularly revealing of Levi's motives for returning to the topic of the concentration camps when contrasted with that of the preface to *Se questo è un uomo*: 'questo libro intende contribuire a chiarire alcuni aspetti del fenomeno Lager che ancora appaiono oscuri' (this book intends to contribute to the clarification of some aspects of the *Lager* phenomenon which still seem obscure) (SS, II, p. 1004) against the previous statement that 'questo mio libro, in fatto di particolari atroci, non aggiunge nulla a quanto è ormai noto ai lettori di tutto il mondo sull'inquietante argomento dei campi di distruzione' (this book of mine, with regard to individual atrocities, adds nothing to what is already known to readers from all over the world about the disturbing topic of the camps of destruction) (SQ, I, p. 5). It would appear that in the period between the publication of *Se questo è un uomo* and *I sommersi e i salvati*, details about the concentration camps originally felt to be 'ormai noto ai lettori di tutto il mondo', were, years later, perceived as obscure and in need of elaboration and clarification precisely in order to bring about a greater understanding and to shed further light on the effects of these particular atrocities.

With its subject matter patently unchanged in many respects from that of *Se questo è un uomo*, *I sommersi e i salvati* functions as metatext to all of Levi's writings and interviews about the Holocaust, elucidating and expanding on many aspects of his concentration camp experiences in far greater detail than previously.[9] It does not form a commentary or a critique of *Se questo è un uomo* itself, however: Levi neither mentions nor alludes to his first work until the third chapter of this text (SS, II, p. 1048), and then only with reference to one particular person, casually named in the earlier text, whose role is of relevance here. Little, if any, of Levi's personal experience is added here, beyond that recounted already in *Se questo è un uomo* and the

'Passato prossimo' section of *Lilít e altri racconti*. Levi's approach to writing of the concentration camps has altered entirely here from the relating of strictly first-hand experiences in *Se questo è un uomo* to the construction of *I sommersi e i salvati* around analysis and commentary on the basis of Levi's accumulated knowledge. His study here is not limited to Buna Monowitz, nor even to Auschwitz, but embraces the wider Holocaust experience beyond that of Levi's personal suffering.

Published in 1986, *I sommersi e i salvati* was given the title Levi originally intended for *Se questo è un uomo*, the title he eventually gave to the central chapter of his first testimony.[10] The naming of *I sommersi e i salvati* indicates a paratextual relationship with the first work and signals this text's place as an extension of the chapter of *Se questo è un uomo* of the same title.[11] It is to this chapter of *Se questo è un uomo* that we can turn for another insight as to why Levi chose to return to this subject forty years after his original testimony, for here Levi wrote of the concentration camps and the state of his and his fellow prisoners' existence that:

> ci si potrà forse domandare se proprio metta conto, e se sia bene, che di questa eccezionale condizione umana rimanga qualche memoria.
> A questa domanda ci sentiamo di rispondere affermativamente. Noi siamo infatti persuasi che nessuna umana esperienza sia vuota di senso e indegna di analisi, e che anzi valori fondamentali, anche se non sempre positivi, si possano trarre da questo particolare mondo di cui narriamo. (*SQ*, I, p. 83)
>
> (we will perhaps ask ourselves if it is really worthwhile or good to retain any memory of this exceptional human condition.
> To this question we feel we have to reply in the affirmative. We are in fact convinced that no human experience is without meaning or unworthy of analysis, and that, moreover, fundamental values, even if they are not always positive, can be deduced from this particular world of which we narrate.)

I sommersi e i salvati expands precisely upon these earlier statements, investigating the experience of the *Lager* on the basis that it is indeed worth remembering and deserving of analysis, that it is a subject worth returning to directly even after four decades, specifically 'affinché il ricordo duri' (so that the memory lasts) (*SS*, II, p. 1004). As with the chapter of the same title, Levi's focus in this text is not so much on his own experience as on the interpretation, clarification and examination of aspects of the camp system. *I sommersi e i salvati* sets out to answer many of the questions raised by and after *Se questo è un uomo*; it is, like its precursor, writing to 'fare gli "altri" partecipi' (to render the 'others' participants) of aspects of the concentration camp experience (*SQ*, I, p. 5), but here the emphasis is on analysis rather than testimony. As Levi states in the *Prefazione*, *I sommersi e i salvati*:

> Vorrebbe rispondere alla domanda piú urgente, alla domanda che angoscia tutti coloro che hanno avuto occasione di leggere i nostri racconti: quanto del mondo concentrazionario è morto e non ritornerà piú, come la schiavitù ed il codice dei duelli? quanto è tornato o sta tornando? che cosa può fare ognuno di noi, perché in questo mondo gravido di minacce, almeno questa minaccia venga vanificata? (*SS*, II, p. 1004-5)

> (Would like to respond to the most urgent question, to the question which distresses all those who have had occasion to read our accounts: how much of the concentration camp world has died and will never return, like slavery and the code of duelling? How much has returned or is in the process of returning? What can each of us do so that in this world full of threats, at least this threat is frustrated?)

The status of this work as a response to the questions cited above renders this only barely an independent text in its own right, functioning less brilliantly without prior knowledge of *Se questo è un uomo*. As a work of reflection and explanation, the reader is required to return to Levi's first work in order to gain a greater understanding of *I sommersi e i salvati*: in order to comprehend Levi's personal experiences of the *Lager* in detail, and to grasp the very basis upon which this work is founded, the reading of *Se questo è un uomo* is compulsory. A number of phrases from *Se questo è un uomo* reverberate here: the reader, for example, is invited to share in Levi's assessment of guilt, 'vorrei invitare chiunque osi tentare un giudizio' (I would like to invite whoever dares to attempt a judgement) (*SS*, II, p. 1036) in much the same way as he invited the reader to weigh the significance of right and wrong in the chapter entitled 'Al di qua del bene e del male' of *Se questo è un uomo*, 'vorremmo ora invitare il lettore a riflettere' (we would now like to invite the reader to reflect) (*SQ*, I, p. 82). However, whilst the first person plural of *vorremmo* has here altered to the singular *vorrei* this is not an indication of a modification in authorial voice in this text. Levi is still writing in many instances here from a collective standpoint, as a continuation of the implied multiple authorship of *Se questo è un uomo*. The collective *noi* of *I sommersi e i salvati* does nonetheless alternate between different groups of people with whom Levi identifies, recalling the ever-varying *noi* of *Il sistema periodico*. Here Levi fluctuates between *noi* survivors, 'siamo stati capaci, noi reduci, di comprendere e di far comprendere la nostra esperienza?' (have we been able, we survivors, to understand and to make our experience understood?) (*SS*, II, p. 1017); *noi* prisoners, 'nessuno di noi sarebbe tornato' (none of us would return) (p. 1071); a more general, unspecified *noi* as human beings, 'i ricordi che giacciono in noi non sono incisi sulla pietra' (the memories which lie within us are not carved in stone) (p. 1006), and 'noi italiani' (we Italians) (p. 1068). The collective viewpoint here has been expanded beyond the limits of the *noi*-prisoners of *Se questo è un uomo*, to include a wider range of people, both during and post-Auschwitz. It is a multiple identification with various narrating groups which perhaps has its roots in the very experience of the concentration camps since it so forcefully echoes Levi's words to describe the collective *noi* of the prisoners, how 'il 'noi' perdeva i suoi confini [...] non si distingueva una frontiera ma molte e confuse, forse innumerevoli' (the 'we' lost its borders [...] you could not distinguish one boundary but many, confused, perhaps innumerable ones) (*SS*, II, p. 1018).

This multiple narrative voice is also accompanied by a pluralisation of temporal perspectives. Levi switches frequently between a post-Auschwitz time zone and a during-Auschwitz commentary: he begins post-Auschwitz with 'La memoria dell'offesa' necessitating a retrospective narrative, before returning to elaborate on his experiences in the second chapter which analyses 'La zona grigia'; the third chapter, 'La vergogna' is partly post-Auschwitz in its depiction of the emotional aftermath, and partly set within the camp in its explanation and justification of the emotions dealt with; 'Comunicare' plunges us back into the depths of the camp's linguistic confusion, just as 'Violenza inutile' and 'L'intellettuale ad Auschwitz' re-submerge the reader in the story of the destruction of the prisoners' humanity and culture; and the final two chapters, 'Stereotipi' and 'Lettere di tedeschi' are a post-Auschwitz response to common assumptions about the camps and specific correspondence to Levi himself. There is a necessary fluidity of time here, then, between the during and the after, between the exigency to return to the camps in order to extract further examples and to explain things more clearly, which now coincides with the distance and hindsight imposed by time lapsed, a distance which can provide clarity on certain issues, and a clearer impression of the wider picture. As a consequence, Levi continues to write in this interstitial part-prisoner, part-survivor mode, with a unique perspective on both experiences. The wider picture provided here also helps to shed significant light on various aspects of Levi's other texts: the elaboration on his feelings at the time of liberation (*SS*, II, p. 1045) clarifies much of the opening chapters of *La tregua*; the tale of Rumkowski (*SS*, II, p. 1037-44) places a new angle on the story of the same person as told in *Lilít*, and Levi's discussions on the value of work, 'L'ambizione del "lavoro ben fatto" è talmente radicata da spingere a "far bene" anche lavori nemici, nocivi ai tuoi e alla tua parte, tanto che occorre uno sforzo consapevole per farli invece "male"' (the ambition of "work well done" is so deep-rooted as to compel us to "do well" even inimical jobs, harmful to your family and friends and to yourself, so much so that it requires a conscious effort to do them "badly"') (*SS*, II, p.

1087) and 'una dignità poteva essere trovata nel lavoro manuale, anche nel piú faticoso, ed era possibile adattarvisi, magari ravvisandovi una rozza ascesi, o, a seconda di temperamenti, un "misurarsi" conradiano, una ricognizione dei propri confini' (some dignity could be found in the manual work, even in the most exhausting, and it was possible to adjust to it, perhaps recognising a rough ascesis in it, or, according to temperament, a Conradian "measuring", a recognition of one's limits) (p. 1097) are particularly relevant to *La chiave a stella*. By this point in his literary career Levi is therefore rewriting more than just his experience of the Holocaust, more than simply *Se questo è un uomo*; *I sommersi e i salvati* in fact builds on a number of *Lager*-related aspects, themes and even character portrayals of Levi's other previous works.

One of the most noticeable alterations between *I sommersi e i salvati* and Levi's other texts is in the tone of writing. Whilst in Levi's first text there are few instances of outright judgement or condemnation, *I sommersi e i salvati* establishes itself from the outset as an act of revenge, asserting his survival to those who tried to destroy him, acting as 'un atto di guerra contro il fascismo' (an act of war against fascism) (SS, II, p. 1003) since 'l'intera storia del breve "Reich Millennario" può essere riletta come guerra contro la memoria' (the entire history of the brief "Millenary Reich" can be reread as a war against memory) (SS, II, p. 1013). Whereas in Levi's first testimony the reader is placed in the role of judge ('i giudici siete voi' [you are the judges] [Appendix to SQ, I, p. 175]), in *I sommersi e i salvati* Levi himself passes judgement frequently, both on individuals such as Hoss and Eichmann (SS, II, pp. 1010-11), and on events, referring, for example, to 'il massimo crimine nella storia dell'umanità' (the greatest crime in the history of humanity) (p. 999); 'la mancata diffusione della verità sui Lager costituisce una delle maggiori colpe collettive del popolo tedesco' (the non-circulation of the truth about the *Lager* constitutes one of the greatest collective offences of the German people) (p. 1000); 'la colpa vera, collettiva, generale, di quasi tutti i tedeschi di allora, è stata quella di non aver avuto il coraggio di parlare' (the real, collective, general offence of nearly all Germans at that time was that of not having had the courage to speak out) (p. 1136), and perhaps most significantly in the concluding lines of the text:

> Sia ben chiaro che responsabili, in grado maggiore o minore, erano tutti, ma dev'essere altrettanto chiaro che dietro la loro responsabilità sta quella della grande maggioranza dei tedeschi, che hanno accettato all'inizio, per pigrizia mentale, per calcolo miope, per stupidità, per orgoglio nazionale, le "belle parole" del caporale Hitler, lo hanno seguito finché la fortuna e la mancanza di scrupoli lo hanno favorito, sono stati travolti dalla sua rovina, funestati da lutti, miseria e rimorsi, e riabilitati pochi anni dopo per uno spregiudicato gioco politico. (SS, II, p. 1153)

(Let it be clear that, to a greater or lesser extent, all were responsible, but it must be equally clear that behind their responsibility lies that of the great majority of Germans, who accepted from the start, through intellectual laziness, through short-sighted reckoning, through stupidity, and through national pride, corporal Hitler's fine words, they followed him for as long as fortune and a lack of scruples favoured him, they were overwhelmed by his ruin, devastated by mourning, poverty and remorse, and rehabilitated a few years later for an unscrupulous political game.)

Levi's words of judgement in this text are frequently linked to his greater desire to understand the possible reasons, motives and justifications behind the concentration camps, for 'la vendetta non mi interessava [...] A me spettava capire, capirli' (I was not interested in revenge [...] It was up to me to understand, to understand them) (*SS*, II, p. 1125). Throughout this work Levi is, in his own words, 'alla ricerca permanente di una giustificazione' (in permanent search of a justification) (*SS*, II, p. 1055) for the *Lager* itself; he is still attempting to understand what cannot truly be comprehended. Whereas in the camps incomprehension dominates, ('qui non c'è perché' [here there is no why] [*SQ*, I, p. 23]; 'la nostra sagezza era il "non cercar di capire"' [our wisdom lay in "not trying to understand"] [*SQ*, I, p. 112]; 'cercar di capire, là, sul posto, era uno sforzo inutile' [trying to understand, there, on the spot, was a pointless effort] [*SS*, II, p. 1103]), in *I sommersi e i salvati* answers can be at least sought for some of the many questions remaining, even if 'non è detto che ogni svolta segua da un solo perché [...] i perché possono essere molti, confusi fra loro, o inconoscibili, se non addirittura inesistenti' (no-one said that every turning follows on from one reason [...] the reasons can be many, confused among themselves, or unknown, if not actually non-existent) (*SS*, II, p. 1110). The indecipherable world of the concentration camps, Levi's original source of incomprehension, remains his inspiration for writing this text. Here, however, Levi does not limit himself to an attempt to comprehend the events surrounding himself and the other prisoners, for he is searching to explore not simply the concentration camps themselves but also the reasons, logic, and psychology behind them. *I sommersi e i salvati* is an analysis of the wider picture: of why the guilty alter their memories of the motives behind their actions ('La memoria dell'offesa'); of the moral ambiguity of prisoner cooperation with the system ('La zona grigia'), and of the effects and rationale behind violence ('Violenza inutile'). Yet *I sommersi e i salvati* is also a reaction against the very indecipherability of Levi's experience of the concentration camps; it is an attempt to impose a degree of understanding on events which could not be understood either then or now: 'quanto è avvenuto non si può comprendere, anzi, *non si deve* comprendere, perché comprendere è quasi giustificare. [...] Non possiamo capirlo; ma possiamo e dobbiamo capire di dove nasce, e stare in guardia. Se comprendere è impossibile, conoscere è necessario, perché ciò che è accaduto può ritornare' (what happened cannot be understood, moreover, *ought not to be* understood, because to understand is almost to justify. [...] We cannot understand it; but we can and must understand where it comes from and be on our guard. If understanding is impossible, knowledge is necessary, because what has happened could return) (Appendix to *SQ*, I, p. 197, written in 1976). There is a tension in *I sommersi e i salvati*, between the strong urge to comprehend certain aspects of the *Lager* experience, and the disinclination to understand entirely since this understanding would, in effect, be tantamount to an unacceptable justification of the events.[12] The apparent paradox underlying this pursuit of justification and comprehension which, if found, would be rejected, leads to the inference that the act of searching is more important than that of discovering, that the process is of greater consequence than the culmination of the search itself, and that the *ricerca permanente* remains more important for Levi than any *giustificazione* could ever be. The quest for understanding is therefore necessarily limited: it is restricted to an awareness and a comprehension of certain motives behind these events but not an identification with them. Knowledge is the key weapon here for whilst the 'sonno della ragione' (sleep of reason) (*LT*, I, p. 362) led to the concentration camps and to the abuse of science in both the *Storie naturali* and *Vizio di forma*, knowledge was the key to win the battle against Matter in *Il sistema periodico* ('non ci si deve arrendere alla materia incomprensibile [...] la natura è immensa e complessa, ma non è impermeabile all'intelligenza' [one must not surrender to incomprehensible matter [...] nature is immense and complex, but it is not impermeable to intelligence] [*SP*, I, p. 804]) and it continues to be vital here: the knowledge of history to prevent its recurrence, 'conoscere è necessario, perché ciò che è accaduto può ritornare' (knowledge is necessary, because what happened could return) (Appendix to *SQ*, I, p. 198).

Knowledge and understanding in their various forms (linguistic, scientific, historical) are recurrent themes throughout much of Levi's work, as indicated by the notion of 'salvazione del capire' which Levi selected as a key thread to his design at the beginning of *La ricerca delle radici*. The choice of Darwin's *The Origin of Species* as one of the texts which contributes to this *salvazione del capire* is important as it is again Levi's comments on Darwin which are the most significant here. Levi's description of Darwin in *La ricerca delle radici*, where he writes that 'dal groviglio estrae l'ordine' (he extracts order from confusion) (*RR*, II, p. 1383), is echoed here in Levi's statement that 'senza una profonda semplificazione, il mondo intorno a noi sarebbe un groviglio infinito e indefinito' (without a profound simplification, the world around us would be an infinite and indefinite confusion) (*SS*, II, p. 1017). Levi is likewise attempting to extract a sense of order through his elaboration and extension of his original portrayal of the chaos which was the concentration camps. It is a perpetuation of Levi's motif of creating order from the chaos of language and events, a continuation of his desire to *scrivere chiaro* as it appeared in *L'altrui mestiere*, and it is, still, the same urge to impose clarity (clarity = order = comprehension) upon the tumultuous, confused and dis-ordered events of the concentration camps. Levi is writing to make sense of his experiences, and the act of re-writing serves not only as a re-evaluation but also as a mental re-ordering of the memory of his experiences: 'nel recente *I sommersi e i salvati*, ravviso semmai un grande bisogno di riordinare, di rimettere in ordine un mondo caotico, di spiegare a me stesso e agli altri'[13] (in the recent *I sommersi e i salvati* I perceive a great need to reorder, to re-put in order a chaotic world, to explain to myself and to others). Levi, for whom 'l'essenziale sia capire e far capire'[14] (the essential thing is to understand and to make understood) is here undertaking, again, precisely this, to explain to others something of his experiences in order to bring about a higher level of understanding.

I sommersi e i salvati therefore has a moral purpose, for just as bearing witness in *Se questo è un uomo* is a moral act, so does Levi's commitment to share his experiences and to impart a sense of comprehension of these experiences to others stem from an ethical conviction, a belief in the potential of knowledge and understanding to prevent such atrocities from recurring. The strength of his message is increased through its repetition twice in the course of *I sommersi e i salvati*: 'perché ciò che è stato possibile perpetrare ieri potrà essere nuovamente tentato domani' (because what it was possible to commit yesterday could be newly attempted tomorrow) (*SS*, II, p. 1031) and 'è avvenuto, quindi può accadere di nuovo: questo è il nocciolo di quanto abbiamo da dire' (it happened, therefore it can happen again: this is the heart of what we have to say) (*SS*, II, p. 1150). Levi's message of warning provides a higher significance for *I sommersi e i salvati* beyond that of bearing witness and imparting a degree of comprehension about his experiences to others. Levi is writing again about the concentration camps here not to alter or to add to his original testimony but to re-state, re-clarify, expand and extend his message. Thus *I sommersi e i salvati* exists almost as a kind of appendix to *Se questo è un uomo*, the two texts forming part of a macrotext which needs to be read in its entirety as each text illuminates and explicates the other. Levi's earlier battle for survival in the *Lager* itself became, through the act of writing both *Se questo è un uomo* and *I sommersi e i salvati*, a battle to remember and to counter oblivion, which runs parallel to the struggle in both texts to have others comprehend the nature of the offence committed against mankind by mankind, in the attempt to avoid any possibility of history repeating itself. For this to happen, knowledge and a degree of understanding of the concentration camps is essential. Levi, who commented that 'da 40 anni sono in giro per capire i tedeschi'[15] (for forty years I have been going around trying to understand the Germans) discovered over the forty years spanning his first testimony and the composition of *I sommersi e i salvati* that 'qualcosa che non si può capire costituisce un vuoto doloroso, una puntura, uno stimolo permanente che chiede di essere soddisfatto' (something which cannot be understood constitutes a painful void, a sharp pain, a permanent stimulus asking to be satisfied) (*SS*, II, p. 1130). It is the same *stimolo permanente* which drives him in his quest to understand the camp system, to comprehend 'l'evento che [...] ha segnato la [...] esistenza intiera' (the event which [...] marked my [...] entire existence) (*SS*, II, p. 1109) since 'capire come abbia potuto succedere è per me uno scopo della vita'[16] (understanding how it can have happened is the aim of my life). By the end of *I sommersi e i salvati*, however, Levi is no closer to being liberated from this aim of his life: no justification is possible and nor, consequentially, is any true degree of comprehension. 'Guerra è sempre' (war is always), still, whether this be a war to survive or a battle to remember, to keep the memory of Auschwitz alive, to understand, and to prevent its recurrence at any future date. Levi is one of the *salvati* but his life remains here partly *sommerso* by the weight of his responsibility to convey his message.

Notes

1. Although *Ad ora incerta*, published in 1984, contained a number of poems which deal directly with Levi's experiences in Auschwitz, this marked the publication of previous work, composed in the period between 1943 and 1949, rather than a return to writing of the camps.
2. Levi's words to Pier Maria Paoletti, 'Sono un chimico, scrittore per caso', *Il Giorno*, 7 August 1963, also in Belpoliti 1997a, pp. 101-5 (p. 104).
3. Levi's words from his interview with Lucia Borgia, 'Rifarsi una vita', broadcast on Rai 3, 3 February 1985, transcribed in Poli and Calcagno, 1992, p. 333.
4. According to Belpoliti, 1998, p. 161, and Bianchini, 2000, p. 172.
5. *Corriere della Sera*, 3 January 1979, also in *Pagine sparse*, *Opere I*, pp. 1251-2. These issues are also touched upon in Levi's foreword of March 1985 to the second edition of the memoirs of SS Kommandant Rudolf Höss (Höss, *Death Dealer: The Memoirs of the SS Kommandant at Auschwitz*, 1992), published in Italian in the *Pagine sparse*, *II*, 1276-83.
6. Levi's words to Giorgio Calcagno, 'Primo Levi: capire non è perdonare', *La Stampa*, 26 July 1986, also in Belpoliti, 1997a, pp. 142-6, p. 143.
7. Levi's words to Milvia Spadi, in a radio interview for *Westdeutscher Rundfunk*, September 1986, transcribed in *La Terra vista dalla Luna*, I, February 1995, and published as 'Capire e far capire' in Belpoliti, 1997a, pp. 242-59, p. 243-4.
8. Levi's words from his speech given in reception of the Premio Testimone del Tempo for *SS*, published in Colombo, Arturo, 'Primo Levi: A Acqui quella sera', *Nuova Antologia*, vol. 558, July-September 1987, p. 211.
9. For more on metatexts and metatextuality see Gérard Genette, 1982, p. 10, in which he

writes that: '*métatextualité*, est la relation, on dit plus couramment de "commentaire", qui unit un texte à un autre texte dont il parle, sans nécessairement le citer (le convoquer), voire, à la limite, sans le nommer'.

10. 'I sommersi e i salvati' is a central chapter in *SQ* both physically and in significance, ninth of the seventeen chapters, with eight on either side, later reflected by the identical centrality of the 'Cerio' chapter of *SP*, with ten chapters on either side. (See chapter four)
11. For more on paratextuality see Genette, 1982, p. 9.
12. Similarly resigned to the impossibility of comprehension is Elie Wiesel where he writes that 'I didn't understand, though I wanted to. Ask any survivor and you will hear the same thing: above all, we tried to understand […]. Perhaps there was nothing to understand'. (*All Rivers Run to the Sea*, 1996, p. 79).
13. Levi's words to Roberto Caro, 'La fatica di vivere', *L'Espresso*, 26 April 1987.
14. His words to Milvia Spadi, *int cit*, in Belpoliti, 1997a, p. 248.
15. Levi's words to Giorgio Calcagno, *int cit, La Stampa,* 26th July 1986.
16. *Ibid.*

Conclusion

The works of Primo Levi serve a dual purpose. In addition to bearing witness to the significance of the events of *Se questo è un uomo* as the thematic foundation to Levi's writing, his works also testify to their author's own survival:

> The memoirist documents nothing more persuasively than his own existence after the Holocaust. The survivor's literature thus becomes testimony not so much to the deaths at Auschwitz but to his life after Auschwitz. A survivor's writing after the Holocaust is proof that he has defeated the 'final solution'; it is indisputable evidence that he now exists, a notion that no survivor ever takes for granted.[1]

In Levi's case, writing is an endless provision of the evidence of his continued existence: it is not merely his first testimony to the *Lager* which proves his survival, but each of his subsequent texts as well through their connections to the first. Alvin Rosenfeld writes of how, for Holocaust survivors, writing itself succeeds as 'an effective counterforce to nihilism, not so much as an answer to death as an answer to barbarism, a last-ditch means of approximating and preserving the human in the face of a viciousness poised to destroy it'.[2] For Levi, so much of whose writing deals, in particular, with the effects and the aftermath of the loss of human dignity, it is certainly true that writing functions as a means of reasserting and preserving the human, precisely through his descriptions of the act of its dismantling, the warnings contained within his works, and his application of the destruction of mankind's humanity to society as a whole, not simply that of the concentration camp world.

The fact that almost forty years after the first publication of *Se questo è un uomo*, Levi should still be writing directly about the topic which occupied this first text, is of critical importance. It is not merely that the publication of *I sommersi e i salvati* indicates a return to explicit discussion of the *Lager* but rather, as this study has shown, that so many of the themes that occupy Levi's writing never truly departed from the concentration camps from the outset. The recurrent issues present throughout Levi's *oeuvre* of abuse and degradation, of imprisonment, of a heightened consciousness of the importance of language and communication, of a sense of timelessness and of detachment from both past and future, of the importance of free, positive work, and of the quest for knowledge and understanding of both our past and present, to name but a few, are all direct continuations of topics originally encountered in Levi's first testimony. It is not simply that Holocaust themes are repeated throughout Levi's writing, however, for the resonances of *Se questo è un uomo* which recur throughout the body of Levi's work are not mere reduplications of identical themes. Many of the instances of a perpetuation of issues originally arising in *Se questo è un uomo* are also thematic extensions which have been expanded beyond the confines of the concentration camp world, altered and applied to diverse environments and conditions in the subsequent texts. Elements of *Se questo è un uomo* re-emerge in various contexts, guises and circumstances throughout the body of Levi's work, in what is, on occasion, a patent manner, and at other times a more covert fashion. Yet the reverberations of these issues, amplified and developed throughout Levi's subject matter, invariably stem from Levi's first, crucial text. It is the prevalence of these topics over the course of the four decades of Levi's literary career which is most revealing, for it indicates that, for Levi, certain elements of his experience of Auschwitz remain applicable to a wide range of situations and continue to influence not only the way he writes, but also his choice of subject matter.

It is the re-emergence of themes from *Se questo è un uomo* over the course of Levi's later texts which constitutes the rewriting of the title of this book. The rematerialization in successive works of topics from *Se questo è un uomo*, accompanied by Levi's elaboration upon and expansion of these topics in order to increase and broaden their relevance in different contexts, ultimately results in the rewriting of these issues. This act of rewriting in its various forms is critical for our understanding of Levi's works; for whilst each of Levi's texts can stand individually, separate and independent from the others, it is also true that they each gain far greater meaning when considered in the light of *Se questo è un uomo*, particularly under an identification and examination of the specific issues from *Se questo è un uomo* which are rewritten in each of the subsequent texts. To comprehend the essence and the full implications of Levi's work it is therefore essential to be familiar not only with *Se questo è un uomo* but with its influence on the rest of Levi's writing and with the ways in which Levi's ensuing texts revisit and rewrite aspects of his first work.

The two main concentration camp writings in the body of Levi's work, *Se questo è un uomo* and *I sommersi e i salvati*, which are also, chronologically, his first and last works, provide a frame around the rest of Levi's writing, all of which has to be considered within the context of this framework. This element to Levi's writing is important: not only is Auschwitz, as the surrounding structure, essential to gaining a deeper understanding of the recurring themes of Levi's works, but Auschwitz also functions as the structural frame, as the foundation upon which and within which Levi's texts are built. There are a number of implications for our understanding of Levi's works to be gained from this analysis of the role of *Se questo è un uomo*. Not only does this study emphasise the central significance of Auschwitz in both Levi's life and his writing, and the necessity of understanding this influence on his *oeuvre*, but the consideration of Levi's entire literary output as a continuous exercise in rewriting his experiences would suggest that the process of distancing himself from this past is never fully completed.

The exceptional relationship which exists between Levi's portrayal of his concentration camp experiences and his later works has been demonstrated as being a firmly intertextual one. Whilst parts of *Lilìt e altri racconti* and *I sommersi e i salvati* are metatextual in their commentary and elaboration on sections of *Se questo è un uomo*, the aspects of all of Levi's other works examined here are hypertextual in their rewriting of the first work, as well as functioning within the parameters of a wider sister-textual relationship, as defined by Jefferson. That *Se questo è un uomo* should function as the thematic and frequently the linguistic foundation for Levi's subsequent writing definitively places this first work of testimony in the role of hypotext and sister-text to Levi's other works. Yet perhaps, as the term sister-text suggests an intertextual relationship of equality which does not exist between these works, the unique position of *Se questo è un uomo* with regard to the works which follow is deserving of a new term reflecting the true extent of its function, that of mother-text to the later writings, the text from which all else originates.[3] Having established a role of such fundamental importance for *Se questo è un uomo*, the shadow of the concentration camp can no more be erased from Levi's writing than it was from his life: each of Levi's works operates on a number of levels as a supplement or appendix to certain elements of *Se questo è un uomo* as Levi, over the course of his literary career, rewrites his hypotext and rewrites the Holocaust.

Notes

[1.] James Young, *Writing and Rewriting the Holocaust: Narrative and the Consequences of Interpretation*, 1990, p. 37.

[2.] Alvin Rosenfeld, *A Double Dying: Reflections on Holocaust Literature*, 1980, p. 13.

[3.] Interesting parallels exist between Levi's works and the works of another Holocaust survivor, Elie Wiesel, whose first testimony, *Night*, similarly resonates throughout his later fictional writing. In Wiesel's own words: 'In truth, I think I have never spoken about the Holocaust except in one book, *Night* – the very first – where I tried to tell a tale directly, as though face to face with the experience. All my subsequent books are built around it.' It is precisely this 'building around' the Holocaust which is so significant in both Wiesel's and Levi's corpus of writing. (Elie Wiesel's words in 'Richard L. Rubenstein and Elie Wiesel: An Exchange', in John K. Roth and Michael Berenbaum, eds., *Holocaust: Religious and Philosophical Implications*, 1989, pp. 349-373, p. 362.)

Bibliography

Levi's collected works

Opere I: Se questo è un uomo; La tregua; Storie naturali; Vizio di forma; Il sistema periodico; La chiave a stella; Pagine sparse, Marco Belpoliti, ed. (Turin: Einaudi, 1997)
Opere II: Lilít e altri racconti; Se non ora, quando?; Ad ora incerta; Altre poesie; L'altrui mestiere; Racconti e saggi; I sommersi e i salvati; Pagine sparse; La ricerca delle radici, Marco Belpoliti, ed. (Turin: Einaudi, 1997)

(Vol I contains the most comprehensive bibliography of Levi's published interviews and conversations, *Bibliografia delle conversazioni e delle interviste con Primo Levi apparse su quotidiani e periodici*, pp. cxvii–cxxvi. The *Pagine sparse* of both volumes contain Levi's previously uncollected articles and short stories.)

Opere I: Se questo è un uomo; La tregua; Il sistema periodico; I sommersi e i salvati (Turin: Einaudi, 1987)
Opere II: La chiave a stella; Se non ora, quando?; Ad ora incerta (Turin: Einaudi, 1988)
Opere III: Storie naturali; Vizio di forma; Lilít e altri racconti; L'altrui mestiere; Racconti e saggi (Turin: Einaudi, 1990). With introductory essays by Cesare Cases, Cesare Segre and Pier Vincenzo Mengaldo
I racconti: Storie naturali, Vizio di forma, Lilít e altri racconti, Ernesto Ferrero, ed., (Turin: Einaudi, 1996)
L'ultimo natale di guerra, Marco Belpoliti, ed. (Turin: Einaudi, 2000)

Levi's published works

Se questo è un uomo (Turin: De Silva, 1947)
Se questo è un uomo, 2nd edn. (Turin: Einaudi, 1958)
La tregua (Turin: Einaudi, 1963)
Storie naturali (Turin: Einaudi, 1966)
Vizio di forma (Turin: Einaudi, 1971)
Il sistema periodico (Turin: Einaudi, 1975)
L'osteria di Brema (Milan: Scheiwiller, 1975)
La chiave a stella (Turin: Einaudi, 1978)
La ricerca delle radici (Turin: Einaudi, 1981)

Lilít e altri racconti (Turin: Einaudi, 1981)
Se non ora, quando? (Turin: Einaudi, 1982)
Ad ora incerta (Milan: Garzanti, 1984)
L'altrui mestiere (Turin: Einaudi, 1985)
Racconti e saggi (Turin: Editrice La Stampa, 1986)
I sommersi e i salvati (Turin: Einaudi, 1986)

Secondary sources

Adelsberger, Lucie, *Auschwitz: A Doctor's Story*, trans. by Susan Ray (London and New York: BCA, 1997)
Allen, Graham, *Intertextuality* (London: Routledge, 2000)
Améry, Jean, *At the Mind's Limits: Contemplations by a Survivor on Auschwitz and its Realities*, trans. by Sidney Rosenfeld and Stella P. Rosenfeld (London: Granta, repr. 1977 and 1999)
Amsallem, Daniela, 'Conversazione con Daniela Amsallem', 15 July 1980, in Belpoliti, ed., 1997b, 55–73
Anissimov, Myriam, *Primo Levi: Tragedy of an Optimist*, trans. by Steve Cox (London: Aurum, 1998)
Balbi, Rosellina, 'Mendel, il consolatore', *la Repubblica*, 14 April 1982, 20–21, also in Belpoliti, ed., 1997a, 129–35
Beccaria, Gian Luigi, 'L' "altrui mestiere" di Primo Levi', in Cavaglion, ed., 1993a, 130–6
Belpoliti, Marco, ed., (1997a) *Primo Levi: Conversazioni e interviste 1963-1987* (Turin: Einaudi, 1997)
Belpoliti, Marco, ed., (1997b) *Primo Levi* (Milan: Marcos y Marcos, 1997)
Belpoliti, Marco, 'Animali', in Belpoliti, ed., 1997b, 157–209
Belpoliti, Marco, *Primo Levi* (Milan: Bruno Mondadori, 1998)
Bertinetto, Gabriel, 'La fanta-violenza di Primo Levi', *l'Unità*, 13 January 1978
Benchouiha, Lucie, 'The Perversion of a Fairy Tale: Primo Levi's 'La bella addormentata nel frigo'', *Modern Language Review*, April 2005, 356–366.
Bettelheim, Bruno, *The Informed Heart: The Human Condition in Mass Society* (London: Paladin, repr. 1970)
Bianchini, Edoardo, *Invito alla lettura di Primo Levi* (Milan: Mursia, 2000)
Bianucci, Piero, 'Sí, anche la mia cultura può essere considerata yiddish', *La stampa*, 6 September 1982
Biasin, Gian Paolo, 'Till My Ghastly Tale is Told: Levi's Moral Discourse from *Se questo è un uomo* to *I sommersi e i salvati*', in Tarrow, ed., 1990, 127–141
Bitton-Jackson, Livia, *I Have Lived A Thousand Years: Growing Up in the Holocaust* (London: Simon & Schuster, 1999)
Bluhn, H. O., 'How did they survive?', *American Journal of Psychotherapy*, 2, 1948
Borowski, Tadeusz, *This Way for the Gas, Ladies and Gentlemen*, trans. by Barbara Vedder (London: Penguin, 1967)

Borri, G., *Le divine impurità: Primo Levi tra scienza e letteratura* (Rimini: Luisé Editore, 1992)
Borri, Giancarlo, 'Primo Levi tra scienza e letteratura', in Ioli, ed., 1995, 207-15
Brambilla, Rosa, and Giuseppe Cacciatore, eds., *Primo Levi: La dignità dell'uomo* (Assisi: Cittadella, 1995)
Brand, Peter, and Lino Pertile, eds., *The Cambridge History of Italian Literature* (Cambridge: Cambridge University Press, 1996)
Bravo, Anna, and Daniele Jalla, eds., *La vita offesa: Storia e memoria dei Lager nazisti nei racconti di duecento sopravvissuti* (Milan: FrancoAngeli, 1988)
Bravo, Anna, and Daniele Jalla, *La memorialistica della deportazione in Italia* (Turin: Centro Stampa del Consiglio Regionale, 1990)
Bravo, Anna, 'Una memoria per tutti', in Ioli, ed., 1995, 33-39
Buzzati, Dino, *Sessanta racconti* (Verona: Arnoldo Mondadori, 1958)
Buzzolan, Ugo, 'Primo Levi: Come scongelare la bella ragazza dopo cent'anni', *La stampa*, 13 January 1978
Calcagno, Giorgio, 'Ancora un Lager per Primo Levi', *Il nostro tempo*, 18 April 1971
Calcagno, Giorgio, 'Primo Levi: capire non è perdonare', *La stampa*, 26 July 1986, also in Belpoliti, ed., 1997a, 142-6
Camon, Ferdinando, *Conversazione con Primo Levi* (Milan: Garzanti, 1991)
Cannon, JoAnn, 'Chemistry and Writing in *The Periodic Table*', in Tarrow, ed., 1990, 99-111
Cannon, JoAnn, 'Canon-Formation and Reception in Contemporary Italy: The Case of Primo Levi', *Italica*, 69, Spring 1992, 30-44
Cases, Cesare, 'L'ordine delle cose e l'ordine delle parole', Introduction to *Opere I*, also in Ferrero, ed., 1997, 5-33
Cavaglion, Alberto, 'Il termitaio', *L'Asino d'oro*, 4, 1991, 117-21, also in Ferrero, ed., 1997, 76-90
Cavaglion, Alberto, ed., (1993a) *Primo Levi: Il presente del passato*. Consiglio regionale del Piemonte-Aned (Milan: FrancoAngeli, 1993)
Cavaglion, Alberto, 'Argon e la cultura ebraica piemontese (con l'abbozzo del racconto)', in Cavaglion, ed., 1993a, 169-196
Cavaglion, Alberto, *Primo Levi e Se questo è un uomo* (Turin: Loescher, 1993)
Cavaglion, Alberto, ed., *Primo Levi per l'Aned: l'Aned per Primo Levi* (Milan: FrancoAngeli, 1997)
Cereja, Federico, 'La testimonianza di Primo Levi come documento di storia', in Cavaglion, 1993a, 95-104
Cicioni, Mirna, *Primo Levi: Bridges of Knowledge* (Oxford: Berg, 1995)
Cohen, Elie, H., *Human Behaviour in the Concentration Camps*, trans. by M. H. Braaksma (London: Jonathan Cape, 1954)
Colombo, Arturo, 'Primo Levi: A Acqui quella sera', *Nuova Antologia*, 558, July-September 1987
Dällenbach, Lucien, 'Intertexte et autotexte', *Poétique*, 27, 1976, pp. 282-96
Dante Alighieri, *Divina commedia* (Rome: Tascabili Economici Newton, 1993)
Debenedetti, Antonio, 'Vincitore il romanzo', *Corriere della sera*, 4 July 1979
De Caro, Roberto, 'Il necessario e il superfluo: Primo Levi e l'economia nella narrazione',

Piemonte vivo, 1 January 1987, 53–57. Reprinted as 'La fatica di scrivere', *L'Espresso*, 26 April 1987, 30–33, also in Belpoliti, ed., 1997a, 195–205

De Luca, Vania, *Tra Giobbe e i buchi neri: Le radici ebraiche dell'opera di Primo Levi* (Naples: Istituto Grafico, 1991)

De Rienzo, Giorgio and Ernesto Gagliano, 'La ragione non può andare in vacanza', *Stampa sera*, 13 May 1975, also in Belpoliti, ed., 1997a, 115–7

De Rienzo, Giorgio, 'In un alambicco quanta poesia', *Famiglia Cristiana*, 29, 20 July 1975, 40–43

Dini, Massimo, and Stefano Jesurum, *Primo Levi: Le opere e i giorni* (Milan: Rizzoli, 1992)

Emmett, Lucie, "'L'uomo salvato dal suo mestiere': Aspects of *Se questo è un uomo* Revisited in Primo Levi's *Il sistema periodico*', *Italian Studies*, 56, 2001, 115–28

Fadini, Edoardo, 'Primo Levi si sente scrittore "dimezzato"', *l'Unità*, 4 January 1966, also in Belpoliti, ed., 1997a, 106–9

Felman, Shoshana, and Dori Laub, eds., *Testimony: Crises of Witnessing in Literature, Psychoanalysis and History* (New York: Routledge, 1992)

Ferrero, Ernesto, ed., *Primo Levi e Tullio Regge: Dialogo* (Milan: Einaudi, 1984)

Ferrero, Ernesto, 'Introduzione' to Primo Levi, *I racconti: Storie naturali, Vizio di forma, Lilít e altri racconti* (Turin: Einaudi, 1996)

Ferrero, Ernesto, ed., *Primo Levi: Un'antologia della critica* (Turin: Einaudi, 1997)

Ferrero, Ernesto, 'La fortuna critica', in *Primo Levi: Un'antologia della critica*, pp. 303–384

Folena, Gianfranco, ed., *Tre narratori: Calvino, Primo Levi, Parise* (Padova: Liviana Editrice, 1989)

Frassica, Pietro, ed., *Primo Levi as Witness*. Proceedings of a Symposium held at Princeton University, April 30-May 2 1989 (Fiesole: Casalini, 1990)

Frassica, Pietro, 'Primo Levi: Eroe, antieroe o alter ego?', in Ioli, ed., 1995, 25–32

Galante Garrone, Alessandro, 'Il grido di Primo Levi', *Nuova Antologia*, 558, July-September 1987

Genette, Gérard, *Palimpsestes: La littérature au second degré* (Paris: Éditions du Seuil, 1982)

Giacomoni, Silvia, 'Il mago Merlino e l'uomo fabbro', *la Repubblica*, 24 January 1979, also in Belpoliti, ed., 1997a, 118–22

Giglioli, Daniele, 'Narratore', in Belpoliti, ed., 1997b, 397–408

Gordon, Robert, S. C., 'Per mia fortuna…: Irony and Ethics in Primo Levi's Writing', *Modern Language Review*, 1997, 337–347

Gordon, Robert, S. C., 'Etica', in Belpoliti, ed., 1997b, 315–330

Gordon, Robert, S. C., *Primo Levi's Ordinary Virtues: From Testimony to Ethics* (Oxford: Oxford University Press, 2001)

Gramigna, Giuliano, 'Il lavoro come un amore', *Corriere della sera*, 24 December 1978

Grassano, Giuseppe, *Primo Levi* (Florence: La Nuova Italia, 1981)

Grassano, Giuseppe, 'La "musa stupefatta": Note sui racconti fantascientifici', in Ioli, ed., 1995, 164-89, and also in Ferrero, 1997, 117–147

Greer, Germaine, 'Interview with Primo Levi', *The Literary Review*, November 1985, also published as 'Colloquio con Primo Levi', trans. by Erminio Corti, in Belpoliti, ed., 1997a, 65–78

Gusdorf, Georges, 'Conditions and Limits of Autobiography', in James Olney, ed., 1980

Holton, Robert, *Jarring Witnesses: Modern Fiction and the Representation of History* (Hertfordshire: Harvester and Wheatsheaf, 1994)

Homer, Frederic D., *Primo Levi and the Politics of Survival* (Columbia and London: University of Missouri Press, 2001)

Honderich, Ted, ed., *The Oxford Companion to Philosophy* (Oxford: Oxford University Press, 1995)

Höss, Rudolf, *Death Dealer: The Memoirs of the SS Kommandant at Auschwitz*, ed. by Steven Paskuly, trans. by Andrew Pollinger (New York: Da Capo, 1996)

Ioli, Giovanna, ed., *Primo Levi: Memoria e invenzione*. Atti del convegno Internazionale San Salvatore Monferrato 26-28 Settembre 1991 (San Salvatore Monferrato: Edizioni della Biennale, 1995)

Jefferson, Ann, 'Autobiography as intertext: Barthes, Sarraute, Robbe-Grillet', in Worton and Still, eds., 1990, 108–129

Kaplan, Chaim, A., *Scroll of Agony: The Warsaw Diary of Chaim A. Kaplan*, trans. and ed. by Abraham I. Katsh (Indiana: Indiana University Press, repr. 1999)

Kelly, Judith, *Primo Levi: Recording and Reconstruction in the Testimonial Literature* (Leicester: Troubador, 2000)

Klein, Ilona, ' "Official Science Often Lacks Humility": Humor, Science and Technology in Levi's *Storie naturali*', in Tarrow, ed., 1990, 112–126

Kristeva, Julia, *Desire in Language: A Semiotic Approach to Literature and Art*, ed. by Leon, S. Roudiez, trans. by Thomas Gora, Alice Jardine and Leon S Roudiez (New York: Columbia University Press, 1980)

Lamberti, Luca, 'Vizio di forma: ci salveranno i tecnici', *l'Adige*, 11 May 1971, also in Belpoliti, ed., 1997a, 110–4

Langer, Lawrence, L., *The Holocaust and the Literary Imagination* (Yale: Yale University Press, 1975)

La Torre, Armando, 'La fantascienza 'umana' di Primo Levi-Malabaila', *l'Unità*, 19 October 1966

La Torre, Armando, *Letteratura e comunicazione* (Rome: Bulzoni, 1971)

Lejeune, Philippe, *On Autobiography*, ed. by Paul John Eakin, trans. by Katherine Leary (Minneapolis: Minneapolis University Press, 1989)

Lengyel, Olga, *Five Chimneys* (London: Hamilton & Co., 1959)

Lo Presti, Virgilio, 'Tornare, mangiare, raccontare', *Lotta Continua*, 18 June 1979, also in Belpoliti, ed., 1997a, 48–57

Manacorda, Giuliano, *Storia della letteratura italiana contemporanea (1940–1965)* (Rome: Editori Riuniti, 1967)

Manzini, Giorgio, 'Elogio del libero lavoro', *Paese sera*, 11 December 1978, 3

Marcus, Laura, *Auto/biographical Discourses: Criticism, Theory, Practice* (Manchester: Manchester University Press, 1994)

Mattioda, Enrico, *L'ordine del mondo: Saggio su Primo Levi* (Naples: Liguori, 1998)

Mauro, Walter, 'Primo Levi: La sorte dell'uomo, dalla testimonianza dei Lager nazisti al futuro della civiltà tecnologica nella satira fantascientifica', in *Letteratura italiana: Novecento. I contemporanei*, ed. by Gianni Grana, (Milan: Marzorati, 1979), 6898–6901

May, Charles, E., ed., *The New Short Story Theories* (Ohio: Ohio University Press, 1994)

Mengaldo, Pier Vincenzo, 'Ricordando con lucidità gli orrori dei Lager', *La Nuova Venezia*, 12 June 1986, also in Belpoliti, ed., 1997b, 140–3

Mengaldo, Pier Vincenzo, 'Lingua e scrittura in Levi', Introduction to *Opere III*, also in Ferrero, ed., 1997, 169–242

Milano, Paolo, 'La guerra quella di sempre', *l'Espresso*, 21 April 1963

Milano, Paolo, 'Il tecnico e la sua anima', *l'Espresso*, 21 January 1979

Misch, Georg, *A History of Autobiography in Antiquity*, trans. by E. W. Dickens (London: Routledge and Kegan Paul, 1950)

Momigliano Levi, Paolo, and Rosanna Gorris, eds., *Primo Levi: Testimone e scrittore di storia* (Florence: La Giuntina, 1999)

Mondo, Lorenzo, 'Un operaio così', *La stampa*, 8 December 1978

Mondo, Lorenzo, 'Primo Levi e Dante', in Ioli, ed., 1995, 224–9

Mondo, Lorenzo, 'Lo spavento dei giusti', *La stampa*, 4 July 1986

Muecke, D. C., *The Critical Idiom: Irony and the Ironic* (London: Methuen, 1982)

Nascimbeni, Giulio, 'Levi: l'ora incerta della poesia', *Corriere della sera*, 28 October 1984, 3, also in Belpoliti, ed., 1997a, 136–41

Neiger, Ada, ed., *Primo Levi: Il mestiere di raccontare, il dovere di ricordare* (Pesaro, Metauro, 1998)

Nystedt, Jane, *Le opere di Primo Levi viste al computer: Osservazioni Stilolinguistiche* (Stockholm: Almqvist & Wiksell International, 1993)

Olney, James, ed., *Autobiography: Essays Theoretical and Critical* (Princeton: Princeton University Press, 1980)

Ozick, Cynthia, 'Il messaggio d'addio', in Ferrero, ed., 1997, 148–162

Paoletti, Pier Maria, 'Sono un chimico, scrittore per caso', *Il Giorno*, 7 August 1963, also in Belpoliti, ed., 1997a, 101–5

Pappalettera, Vincenzo, *Tu passerai per il camino: Vita e morte a Mauthausen* (Milan: Mursia, 1965)

Pappalettera, Vincenzo, ed., *Nei lager c'ero anch'io*, 4th edn (Milan: Mursia, 1973)

Papuzzi, Alberto, 'L'alpinismo? È la libertà di sbagliare', *Rivista della montagna*, 61, March 1984, also in Belpoliti, ed., 1997a, 27–32

Pascal, Roy, *Design and Truth in Autobiography* (London: Routledge and Kegan Paul, 1960)

Petrucciani, Mario, 'Tra algebra e metafora: La scienza nella cultura letteraria italiana 1945–1975', *Letteratura e scienza nella storia della cultura italiana* (Palermo: Manfredi, 1978) 273–330

Petrucciani, Mario, *Scienza e letteratura nel secondo Novecento: La ricerca letteraria in Italia tra algebra e metafora* (Milan: Mursia, 1978)

Piattelli Palmarini, M., 'Quando il romanzo 'parla' la scienza', *Corriere della sera*, 17 August 1979

Pierantoni, Ruggero, 'Il sistema Aperiodico', in Cavaglion, ed., 1993a, 165–8

Poli, Gabriella, 'L'alfabeto della chimica', *La stampa*, 6 December 1976

Poli, Gabriella, and Giorgio Calcagno, eds., *Echi di una voce perduta: Incontri, interviste e conversazioni con Primo Levi* (Milan: Mursia, 1992)

Poli, Francesco, 'Tino Faussone, la storia di un operaio specializzato', *Quotidiano dei Lavoratori*, 28 February 1979

Porro, Mario, 'Scienza', in Belpoliti, ed., 1997b, 434–75

Prosperi, Carlo, 'La gioia liberatrice del raccontare: Una lettura de *La tregua* di Primo Levi', in Ioli, ed., 1995, 85–101

Raboni, G., 'Riesce a creare suspense col montaggio di una gru', *Tuttolibri*, 23 December 1978, also in Belpoliti, ed., 1997b, 128–9

Rago, Michele, 'Tra ragni, pipstrelli e mestieri', *l'Unità*, 22 March 1985

Riatsch, C., and V. Gorgé, 'Né sistema né periodico: appunti per la lettura di *Il sistema periodico* di Primo Levi', *Esperienze letterarie*, 4, 1991, 65–81

Risk, Mirna, 'Razionalità e coscienza etica di Primo Levi', *Italian Studies*, 34, 1979, 122–131

Robertson, Jenny, *Don't Go To Uncle's Wedding: Voices From the Warsaw Ghetto* (London: Azure, 2000)

Rosato, Italo, 'Primo Levi: Sondaggi intertestuali', *Autografo*, 6, June 1989, 31–43

Rosato, Italo, 'Poesia', in Belpoliti ed., 1997b, pp. 413–425

Rosenfeld, Alvin, H., *A Double Dying: Reflections on Holocaust Literature* (Indiana: Indiana University Press, 1980)

Rosenthal, Raymond, 'Translating Primo Levi', in Frassica, ed., 1990, 76–85

Roth, John K. and Michael Berenbaum, eds., *Holocaust: Religious and Philosophical Implications* (New York: Paragon House, 1989)

Roth, Philip, 'A Man Saved by his Skills', *The New York Times Book Review*, 12 October 1986. Reprinted as 'L'uomo salvato dal suo mestiere', *La stampa*, 26 and 27 November 1986, also in Belpoliti, ed., 1997a, 84–94

Roth, Philip, 'Salvarsi dall'inferno come Robinson', *La stampa*, 26 November 1986

Rubenstein, Richard L.,and Elie Wiesel, 'An Exchange', in Roth and Berenbaum, 1989, pp. 349–373

Rudolf, Anthony, 'Primo Levi in London', *London Magazine*, 26, October 1986 (interview of April 1986), also published as 'Conversazione con Anthony Rudolf', trans. by Erminio Corti, in Belpoliti, ed., 1997b, 102–10

Rudolf, Anthony, *At An Uncertain Hour: Primo Levi's War Against Oblivion* (London: Menard, 1990)

Sachs, Dalya, M., 'The Language of Judgment: Primo Levi's *Se questo è un uomo*', *Modern Language Notes*, 110, September 1995, 755–784

Santagostino, Giuseppina, 'Destituzione e ossessione biologica nell'immaginario di Primo Levi', *Letteratura italiana contemporanea*, 12, January-April 1991, 127–45

Santagostino, Giuseppina, 'Nuove prospettive nell'interpretazione della narrativa fantascientifica di Primo Levi', *Narrativa*, 3, January 1993, 8–30

Santagostino, Giuseppina, 'Primo Levi e le facce nascoste del tempo', in Ioli, ed., 1995, 190–206

Scarpa, Domenico, 'Chiaro/oscuro', in Belpoliti, ed., 1997b, 230–253

Schehr, Lawrence, R., 'Primo Levi's Strenuous Clarity', *Italica*, 66, Winter 1989, 429–443

Schwarz, Catherine, ed., *The Chambers Dictionary* (Edinburgh: Chambers Harrap, 1993)

Scurani, Alessandro, 'Primo Levi', *Scrittori italiani* (Milan: Edizioni "Letture", 1983) also

published as 'Le tre anime di Primo Levi', *Letture*, 38, 1983
Segre, Cesare, 'Lettura di *Se questo è un uomo*', *Il Novecento: La ricerca letteraria* (Turin: Einaudi, 1996) 493–507, also in Ferrero, ed., 1997, 55–75
Segre, Cesare, 'Introduzione', *Opere II*, also as 'I romanzi e le poesie' in Ferrero, ed., 1997, 91–116
Segre, Cesare, 'Gli scritti d'invenzione di Primo Levi', in Cavaglion, ed., 1993a, 121–9
Shaw, Valerie, *The Short Story: A Critical Introduction* (New York: Longman, 1983)
Sodi, Risa, 'An interview with Primo Levi', *Partisan Review*, 54, 1987, also in Belpoliti, ed., 1997a, trans. by Erminio Corti, 223–41
Sofsky, Wolfgang, *The Order of Terror: The Concentration Camp*, trans. by William Templer (Princeton: Princeton Univeristy Press, 1997)
Solzhenitsyn, Aleksandr, *One Day in the Life of Ivan Denisovich*, trans. by H. T. Willetts (London: Harvill, 1996)
Spadi, Milvia, 'Capire e far capire', *La Terra vista dalla Luna*, 1, 1 February 1995 (interview of September 1986), also in Belpoliti, ed., 1997a, 242–59
Spadi, Milvia, *Le parole di un uomo: Incontro con Primo Levi* (Rome: De Renzo, 1997)
Spriano, Paolo, 'L'avventura di Primo Levi', *l'Unità*, 14 July 1963
Stajano, Corrado, 'Il lavoro e la sua qualità', *Il Messaggero*, 11 December 1978
Sturrock, John, *The Language of Autobiography: Studies in the First Person Singular* (Cambridge: Cambridge University Press, 1993)
Tarrow, Susan, ed., *Reason and Light: Essays on Primo Levi* (Cornell: Cornell University Press, 1990)
Tedeschi, Giuliana, *C'è un punto della terra... Una donna nel Lager di Birkenau* (Florence: La Giuntina, 1988)
Tesio, Giovanni, 'Ritratti critici di contemporanei: Primo Levi', *Belfagor*, 34, 1979, 657–676
Tesio, Giovanni, 'Credo che il mio destino profondo sia la spaccatura', *Nuovasocietà*, 208, 16 January 1981, also in Belpoliti, ed., 1997a, 185–7
Tesio, Giovanni, *Piemonte letterario dell'otto-novecento da Giovanni Faldella a Primo Levi* (Rome: Bulzoni, 1991)
Tesio, Giovanni, 'Primo Levi tra ordine e caos', *Studi Piemontesi*, 16, 1987, also in Ferrero, ed., 1997, 40–50
Toscani, Claudio, 'Incontro con Primo Levi', *Il Ragguaglio Librario*, no. 3, 1972
Toscani, Claudio, *Come leggere Se questo è un uomo di Primo Levi* (Milan: Mursia, 1990)
Vacca, Roberto, 'Un western dalla Russia a Milano', *Il Giorno*, 18 May 1982
Valabrega, Paola, 'Il segreto del cerchio: La percezione del tempo nell'opera di Primo Levi', *La rassegna mensile di Israele*, 56, May-December 1989, 281–287
Valabrega, Paola, 'Mano/cervello', in Belpoliti, ed., 1997b, 380–92
Varchetta, Giuseppe, *Ascoltando Primo Levi: Organizzazione, narrazione, etica* (Milan: Angelo Guerini, 1991)
Verdenelli, Marcello, '*La chiave a stella* e la scrittura "in bolla d'aria"', in Ioli, ed., 1995, 121–46
Vigevani, Marco, 'Le parole, il ricordo, la speranza', *Bollettino della Comunità Israelitica di Milano*, 60, May 1984, also in Belpoliti, ed., 1997a, 213–22
Vincenti, Fiora, Roberto Guiducci and Mario Miccinesi, 'Il sinistro potere della scienza',

Uomini e libri, 112, January-February 1987, also in Belpoliti, ed., 1997a, 58–60

Vincenti, Fiora, *Invito alla lettura di Primo Levi* (Milan: Mursia, 1973, 7th edn., 1993.)

Wiesel, Elie, *Night*, trans. by Stella Rodway (London, Penguin, 1981)

Wiesel, Elie, *All Rivers Run to the Sea: Memoirs. Volume 1, 1928–1969* (London: HarperCollins, 1996)

Woolf, David, *An Aspect of Fiction: Its Logical Structure and Interpretation* (Ravenna: Longo Editore, 1978)

Woolf, Judith, *The Memory of the Offence: Primo Levi's* If This Is A Man (Leicester: Troubador, 1995)

Worton, Michael, and Judith Still, eds., *Intertextuality: Theories and Practices* (Manchester: Manchester University Press, 1990)

Young, James, E., *Writing and Rewriting the Holocaust: Narrative and the Consequences of Interpretation* (Indiana: Indiana University Press, 1988)